# PRISON.

# PRISON.

Interviews by Leonard J. Berry

Edited by Jamie Shalleck

A Subsistence Press Book

GROSSMAN PUBLISHERS

New York 1972

Copyright © 1972 by Subsistence Press

All rights reserved
First published in 1972 in a hardbound and paperbound edition by
Grossman Publishers, 625 Madison Avenue, New York, N.Y. 10022
Published simultaneously in Canada by
Fitzhenry and Whiteside, Ltd.
SBN 670-57796-0 (hardbound)
    670-57797-9 (paperbound)
Library of Congress Catalogue Card Number: 72-185019
Printed in U.S.A.

Designed by Samuel N. Antupit

This book is dedicated to the people, both keepers and kept, who contributed to it.

GUARD WATCHING PEOPLE ENTER AND LEAVE BUILDING DURING SIT-DOWN STRIKE,
COLORADO STATE PENITENTIARY, CANON CITY, 1971.

# CONTENTS

**LUNCH.**

**AFTERNOON.**

**DINNER.**

**EVENING.**

**NIGHT.**

## INTRODUCTION

More than 400,000 people are now doing time in American prisons; another 900,000 are detained in police and sheriffs' lockups and community halfway houses, or are on probation and parole. The entire American correctional system, if such a chaotic affair can be called a system, handles some two and a half million offenders annually at a cost to the taxpayer of more than a billion dollars. The cost in human terms is disastrous and almost unfathomable.

Although imprisonment is as old as human society, prison as we know it today is an American invention. Counseled by their Constitution against "cruel and unusual punishment," Pennsylvania Quakers in the late eighteenth century abolished the age-old practices of capital and corporal punishment and replaced them with hard labor. But the labor, done in public for state profit, smacked too much of slavery, which the Quakers opposed. Hard labor soon gave way to imprisonment as a more humane punishment, and this method took hold and spread.

America now has about four hundred institutions for adult felons; ninety-five per cent of the people in them are men, and the visible minorities—Blacks, Puerto Ricans, Chicanos—are incarcerated in numbers vastly disproportionate to their representation in free society.

Almost all convicts are poor: although crimes are committed by people in every economic sector, few lawbreakers who are rich and powerful ever go to prison in this country.

Assigned by Subsistence Press to do the interviews for this book, I visited representative prisons across the country. In each I sought to interview wardens, guards, doctors, chaplains, guidance counselors, and of course, inmates—as broad a cross section of the prison community as time and authorities would allow. Though prison employees frequently complained that their side of the story was never told, they sometimes refused to be interviewed. In contrast, the inmates were most amenable. They all had plenty of time on their hands, and several told me they would do anything they could to help people understand what prison is all about.

The basic line of questioning was the same in all the interviews: describe in minute detail everything you do and everything that happens to you during a typical day. Within this structure everyone was able to say anything he wanted. The result was that almost every aspect of imprisonment was covered from many different points of view. Jamie Shalleck and I edited the 1,500 pages of raw transcript to construct in documentary fashion twenty-four hours in prison life.

The names of all the inmates have been changed at the request of prison authorities and inmates who feared reprisal if their real names were used. Two guards and one counselor asked to remain anonymous.

The book has been illustrated with press photographs, drawn from the U.P.I. files by Stan Friedman, and selected by Samuel Antupit, who designed this book.

Prisons do punish, they really do. At no time during my trip across America did I see or hear anything to refute this or the notion that our prisons are schools for crime. Instead I found loneliness, isolation from "normal" society, spiritual castration, wide-spread homosexuality, forced labor for little or no pay, ceaseless regimentation, not infrequent physical violence, insanity, deprivation.

Two of the inmates I saw at Indiana State Prison were black men of acute intelligence, who viewed their condition with bitter, yet gentle irony. One said he was unjustly convicted. The other, after a long, friendly conversation, turned to me as he was leaving a cramped, windowless room and said, "We are guilty. We are guilty. But so are you. This is your prison, and you are responsible for what it does to us."

Leonard J. Berry

## INSTITUTIONS AND CONTRIBUTORS

Arkansas State Penitentiary, Cummins Prison Farm, Grady, Arkansas
Opened: 1842
Security: Maximum
Planned Capacity: 800
Current Population: 1,200

Bealle, Inmate, 22, has done two years of a five-year sentence for armed robbery. He was here once before.

Michael Johnson Hawke, Field Major, 25, has spent seven years in corrections, but has been here only six months.

James Jesse Jones, Inmate, 26, violated parole and is serving an additional year beyond his original three-year sentence for robbery.

Clarence James Lee, Correctional Officer 1, is 22 years old.

Samuel Lexington, Inmate, 24, has served eight years of a fifteen-year sentence for armed robbery and car theft. He has also done time in Texas.

A. L. Lockhart, Superintendent, 31, has been here six months, has worked in corrections nine years.

Wayne E. Miflin, Inmate Trusty, 27, has served four and a half years of a five-year sentence for horse theft.

Robert Talbot, Inmate, 26, has done one month of a three-year sentence for armed robbery. This is his third time here.

Dewie E. Williams, Chaplain, is 51 years old.


Attica Correctional Facility, Attica, New York
Opened: 1931
Security: Maximum
Planned Capacity: 2,370
Current Population (after riot): 1,100


Matthew Baker, 25, convicted in 1969, served the first part of his sentence in Attica, is now in prison in the East, but will return to Attica to finish his prison term.

Anonymous Corrections Counselor, 34, holds a civil seryice position.

Herbert E. Perone, Inmate, 38, convicted of attempted extortion and conspiracy, serving a fifteen- to sixteen-year sentence and a five- to ten-year sentence concurrently.

Bedford Hills Women's Correctional Facility, Bedford Hills, New York
Opened: 1971
Security: Minimum
Planned Capacity: 450
Current Population: 308


Diane Laret, Inmate, 24, was sentenced to serve four years for criminal facilitation and possession of a dangerous weapon.

Elizabeth M. Lynch, Superintendent

Madeline Ray, Inmate

Michele Rivera, Inmate, 24, has been here nineteen months for robbery and attempted homicide and has served time before.

Bertha Waters, Inmate, 29, has served six years of a life sentence for first-degree murder.

Bucks County Department of Correction, Doylestown, Pennsylvania
Opened: 1894
Security: Maximum, Medium, Minimum
Planned Capacity: 50
Current Population: 177

Raymond Ward Burns, Inmate, 32, convicted on burglary charges, has spent a total of twelve years in prison here, Eastern State Penitentiary, Graterford, and Western State Penitentiary, all in Pennsylvania.

John D. Case, Superintendent

Presley Middleton, Captain of Operations and Security, is 31 years old.

Beatrice Smith, Matron

California Institution for Men, Chino, California
Opened: 1941
Security: Minimum, Medium, Maximum
Planned Capacity: 2,832
Current Population: 2,899

Donald E. Bailey, Surgeon 2, is 55 years old.

Michael Cooney, Chaplain, is 56 years old.

James M. Curtey, Inmate, 44, was convicted on bad-check charges and sentenced to serve six months to fourteen years. In addition, he is serving two and a half years' sentence for parole violation.

Joseph A. McCargar, Correctional Officer, 53, served in the Army before coming to C.I.M. in 1952.

Guff A. Rorex, Correctional Officer, 64, has spent seventeen years in corrections.

Comrade Simba, Inmate, 25, has served two and a half years of a six- to ten-year sentence for armed robbery.

Sancho Suarez, Inmate, 25, has received his release date and will have served three years and seven months of a six-month to five-year sentence for grand auto theft.

California State Prison at Folsom, Folsom, California
Opened: 1880
Security: Maximum
Planned Capacity: 2049
Current Population: 1500

Charles Amity, Inmate, 27, has served nine years of a life sentence for first-degree murder.

Douglas A. Borsin, 40, has done eight years of a six-month to fifteen-year sentence for second-degree burglary. He has also served time in Oklahoma, Nevada, and Ohio.

Walter E. Craven, Warden, is 44 years old.

Alexander M. Galbraith, Guidance Counselor

Archie Dale McDonald, Correctional Officer, 48, has spent his seven years in corrections at Folsom.

Garcia Perez, 42, has spent one year here, thirteen previously at San Quentin. He was charged with possession of narcotics while on parole.

Earl Straub, Correctional Officer, 51, has spent eight years at Folsom, was formerly a pilot in the Air Force.

California State Prison at San Quentin, San Quentin, California
Opened: 1852
Security: Maximum
Planned Capacity: 2,743
Current Population: 2,414

Harold W. Brown, Sergeant, Correctional Force, is 25 years old.

Rafael Hernandez, Inmate, 27, has served six years of a life sentence for robbery and murder.

Louis S. Nelson, Warden, 62, has spent thirty-one years in corrections; over twenty here at San Quentin.

Preston S. Smythe, Inmate, 42, has served thirty-one months of a five-year to life sentence for first-degree burglary.

George Russell Tolson, Congregational Chaplain, 56, has been chaplain at San Quentin for fifteen years.

Joey Williams, Inmate, 24, has served three years, eight months of a five-year to life sentence for armed robbery. He served two years on another charge in 1965–66.

District of Columbia Correctional Complex, Lorton, Virginia
Opened: 1916
Security: Maximum, Medium, Minimum
Planned Capacity: 1,700
Current Population: 2,271

John O. Boone, Superintendent of Adult Services

Charles Harman, Inmate, 39, has served seven years of a twenty-year to life sentence on first-degree murder charges. He has also done time in three other institutions.

George F. X. Lincoln, Inmate, 37, is sentenced to serve seven years for assaulting a police officer.

Lowell Miller, Inmate, 26, sentenced to serve two to six years and to pay a ten-thousand-dollar fine for possession and sale of marijuana.

Anonymous Correctional Officer, 44, has spent twenty-one years in corrections.

Phillip M. Perry, Inmate, 26, has done four years of a six- to eighteen-year sentence for bank robbery.

Joseph Sakalaukas, Sergeant, Correctional Force, 51, has spent ten years in corrections.

Clyde E. Settle, Sergeant, Correctional Force, is 25.

George L. White, Inmate, has served three and a half years of a five- to fifteen-year sentence for attempted bank robbery and assault with a dangerous weapon.

District of Columbia Jail, Washington, D.C.
Opened: 1876
Security: Maximum
Planned Capacity: 663
Current Population: 1,200

John A. Knight, Inmate, is awaiting trial for armed robbery while on parole. He has been in prison most of the time since 1946.

Anderson McGruder, Superintendent of Detention Services, has spent fourteen years in corrections, but has just taken this position.

Cecil Masterton, Inmate, 52, convicted of attempted robbery and assault, is here appealing his case. He has spent twenty years in prison to date on various charges.

District of Columbia Women's Detention Center
Opened: 1966
Security: Maximum
Planned Capacity: 80
Current Population: 105

Daisy La Belle, Inmate, 22, charged with soliciting.

Lucille McNeal, Captain, Correctional Force, 42 years old.

Jane Mason, Inmate, 35, here three months awaiting trial on charges of carrying a concealed weapon and live ammunition without a permit.

Federal Detention Headquarters (West Street Jail), New York, New York
Opened: 1929
Security: Maximum
Planned Capacity: 225
Current Population: 300

Anonymous Correctional Officer, 32, has been in corrections six months.

Anthony Corcione, Correctional Officer, 24, has worked here one year.

Chauncey O'Sullivan, Inmate, 25, is here appealing a ten-year sentence for bank robbery.

Gabriel Potter, Inmate, 32, is serving a three-year sentence for transporting a stolen motor vehicle.

Indiana State Prison, Michigan City, Indiana
Opened: 1859
Security: Maximum, Medium
Planned Capacity: 2,210
Current Population: 1,200

Daniel England, Correctional Officer 2, is 24, has spent about a year in corrections.

Earl Grady, Inmate, 31, has served six and a half years of a ten-year sentence for robbery.

William Simmons, Inmate, 31, has served four and a half years of a life sentence for first-degree murder.

Henry Walters, Inmate, 37, is serving a life sentence for second-degree murder and is currently appealing his sentence.

Manhattan House of Detention for Men, New York, New York
Opened: 1941
Security: Maximum
Planned Capacity: 932
Current Population: 1,400

Peter Bennett, Inmate, awaiting trial for grand auto theft and possession of narcotics.

Herman W. Green, Library Officer, 50, has spent seventeen years at The Tombs.

Edward Weinrauch, Assistant Deputy Warden, 51, has spent seventeen of his eighteen years in corrections here.

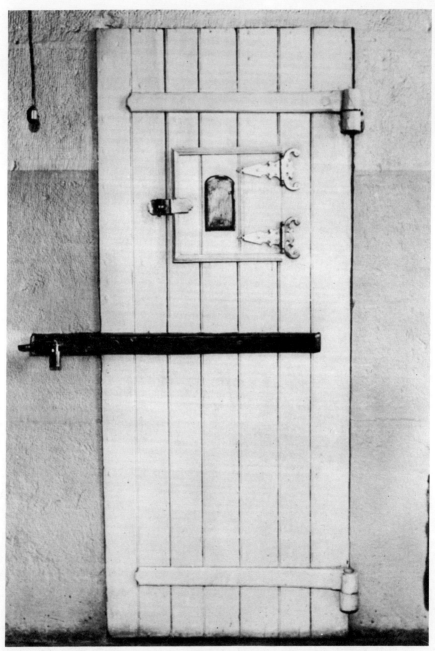

SOLITARY CONFINEMENT CELL, ILLINOIS STATE PENITENTIARY, JOLIET, 1948.

# MORNING.

CALIFORNIA STATE PRISON AT FOLSOM
DOUGLAS A. BORSIN, INMATE

All that wakes you up is yourself. No alarm clock. We're permitted watches, but no clocks yet. Usually get up about six, have a cup of coffee, a cigarette, and shave, get ready to go to work. They have tier-tenders, which bring water around periodically, both in the mornin and the evenin. There's no hot water in our building, though there are a few places in the institution that do have. Have a toilet in the cell and a cold water sink. Fluorescent lighting.

CALIFORNIA STATE PRISON AT SAN QUENTIN
JOEY WILLIAMS, INMATE

Well, I get up about six o'clock. And I get up and I wash up and sit back. I turn the radio on. I listen to the radio, fool around the cell, doin somethin, makin up my bed. It's about six-thirty when they open the door, and I go right out, get my hot water to shave. I have a bucket, a tumbler. I use either one of them, go fill it full of hot water, come back and shave so I won't have to wait around, you know. Like if you're ready when they call breakfast, I jus go run outta the cell, go to breakfast. Well sometimes I go out on the tiers. There're some guys on the tiers I know. They call me the alarm clock cause I wake em

1.

all up for breakfast, you know, get em all up for breakfast. A lotta guys don't hear the bell.

CALIFORNIA STATE PRISON AT SAN QUENTIN
RAFAEL HERNANDEZ, INMATE

There is a bell that gets us up for chow. It's usually about six o'clock. And then we got about a half hour, you know, before we go to chow. Wash up, get dressed, clean up the cell, make the bed, smoke or somethin.

CALIFORNIA STATE PRISON AT SAN QUENTIN
PRESTON S. SMYTHE, INMATE

I always get up at six o'clock. You don't have to. The bell first ringin is at six-thirty on weekdays. And go to chow seven. You can't shower, cause the showers aren't on that early in the mornin. If you shower, you shower the night before. And I generally shave the night before. It's convenient. Myself, like I say, I get up and get dressed and wash up, of course. Damn old cold water in the sinks isn't much fun. No hot water in the cell.

FEDERAL DETENTION HEADQUARTERS
CHAUNCEY O'SULLIVAN, INMATE

They give you razor blade—Brand X. You use it, take one stroke, and it's dull. So you have to use about two of em to get a shave. Well now they startin to use Magic Shave. Everybody's usin Magic Shave in here. It's like Nair for women's legs, for men's face. Magic Shave takes all the hair off, scrape it off your face. You wash your face with cold water. And on legs, fags use it.

INDIANA STATE PRISON
EARL GRADY, INMATE

Nothin's furnished, man. Only thing furnished is a haircut. But other'n that, man, all personal hygiene, you have to take care of it yourself. They furnish soap. That's about it. Furnish soap. Toothpaste and all that jazz, we have to furnish it. Sometimes they have these research projects comin in. They might bring in a shipment of toothpaste and pass it out to everybody—new product or inferior product, you know, use-it-at-your-own-risk thing. Institution furnishes nothin.

ARKANSAS STATE PENITENTIARY
SAMUEL LEXINGTON, INMATE GUARD

You get to wear whatever you can get. Some of em— now a lotta these guys got new clothes here. And a lot of em still wear old raggedy pants and shirts, pants fallin off em, raggedy and everythin, and some of em got shoes, some of em ain't got no shoes. They just'll wear whatever they can get. And they put your number—like on my pants and shirts I've got Y-nine, that's my laundry number. And on my shirt, I got my name. If anybody else wears that shirt but me, can get a disciplinary put on em and their good time take away. If I get ahold of somebody else's shirt, if I stamp their name out, put my name on the shirt, well, I get a disciplinary and lose all my good time and maybe get ranked. And there's more white clothes—inmate clothes—than there is khaki trusty clothes.

And the laundry is out of date. Prehistoric laundry. Everythin's out of repair. You got these ole, big washin machines over there. They wash the sheets one day, and like one bar, they'll wash their sheets one day, and the next day they'll wash the next bar of sheets, and next day they'll wash the next bar of sheets, and the next day. . . . And then they wash the clothes, they wash all the clothes, plus they wash the free man's clothes on this outdated laundry equipment.

They give you one razor blade a month. The state give you one razor blade to shave with. And if you don't buy one, your beard gets long, and then some of em—free man will walk up to you: "Hi. You missed a razor didn't ya?"

"I ain't got a razor blade. How am I gonna miss it?"

"Oh, you're gettin smart, huh? I'm gonna put insubordination charge on you."

"I'm not gettin smart, Captain. I jus don't have a blade to shave with."

"Well, find you one somewhere."

Well, for me that ain't got no money to buy one—what if you don't sell blood or get no medical, how're you gonna buy one? They don't look at it that way. They say get you a blade and shave. Okay.

They issue soap here, but they ration it. Ten bars a week. Ten bars a week for one hundred and thirty men. Ten bars of soap a week for one hundred and thirty men to bathe with, wash their clothes with—underwear, shorts and socks. And, um, they don't give you no kind of hair oil. You gotta buy your own hair oil. Everythin. You got to buy everythin here. The only things that they give you, they give you the clothes and the food. And that's it. They don't give you but one pair of socks a year. Can you believe that? One pair of socks a year. If you don't have no money and nobody to send you none from the free-world—like freeworld people bring some socks, you know, or send em in the mail—and you get hold of a dollar, you know, say, "Anybody wanna sell a pair of socks?"

3.

"Sure, I'll sell you a pair."

I've got two pair then, see. And the state don't give you but one pair of socks a year.

They give you one pair of work socks and when they get ragged and tore up, you throw em away and go without. You jus wear your shoes. Or wrap some rags aroun your feet, you know, to keep your feet warm. Or buy if you can get hold of some money.

ARKANSAS STATE PENITENTIARY
WAYNE E. MIFLIN, INMATE TRUSTY

And it's a lack of cleanliness and lack of clothin. If somebody told you on the outside that you'd get by with the same pair of pants all week, you'd say, "That's ridiculous. Nobody does that." Somebody coulda told me they don't have any socks, I'd say, "That's impossible. Socks are not that expensive." They can buy new trucks, new cars; they barely have socks for the inmates. And I worked in the clothin room when they had the—it was almost funny, cause they had twelve hundred inmates here at the time, and they had six hundred pair of socks—one sock apiece. Give em one for the left foot today, tomorrow give em one for the right foot.

You jus had to give em what you had. My wife sent me T-shirts, and they have my name and my number on em. Guess they do that when they come in the mail room—put your number on em, identification. Then when you send em to the laundry you get em back. She sends me gobs of T-shirts, and then every time I look aroun, I see somebody wearin one. All my underwear is on the other end of the hall.

The haircuttin, they degrade you jus by shavin your head—the barber's asleep all the time—rather'n have to give you a good hair cut.

ARKANSAS STATE PENITENTIARY
CLARENCE JAMES LEE, CORRECTIONAL OFFICER 1

I don't have a uniform. When I first came here, they told us that they'd furnish our uniforms, and you don't need to buy any uniforms. They furnish em. So I still waitin on it. So they never gotten any uniforms yet. So they back again sayin that they be here soon. So rather'n to buy one, throw it away, I'll wait and see if they are or not. And they passed word, you know, not to buy any uniforms, they will be in.

Some of em may want some boots, some boots or some item that we don't issue. The shorthairs are short of boots until they're assigned to a job, cause they may be wearin the boots and men in the field, workin all day, may not even have a pair, whereas he's in the building all day and he doesn't really need em anyway. We have enough boots really, but then I guess you'd say we wouldn't, cause they really don't come in that steady, but they do come in.

So he'll wear his freeworld shoes or he may wear some used boots, you know, jus to walk aroun inside here.

ARKANSAS STATE PENITENTIARY
ROBERT TALBOT, INMATE

Can't wear freeworld clothes. They let you keep your shoes. They cut a V in the heel in case you run off with em, you got that V on your footstep.

ARKANSAS STATE PENITENTIARY
A. L. LOCKHART, SUPERINTENDENT

He lied to you. We have shoes. Maybe on a particular job where he's not issued this thing or he may not be here long enough to receive his boots. You talkin about high-topped shoes? We got shoes for everybody. He's supposed to have em. Every inmate is issued a pair, and his number is stamped on his shoes. He may have had em down in his foot locker. But shoes is no problem. We got a warehouse full a shoes. We got em on contract, you see. Any time we need em we can call upon em. So if he told you there's no shoes, I don't know why he said that.

We have clothin for everybody, like winter underwear. We have the rubber boots; we have the raincoats; we have the winter caps; um, have the shirts, the pants, the jackets. But there's always a problem with clothin: not necessarily not havin enough, but makin sure he keeps it, he doesn't throw it away, he doesn't tear it up, he doesn't sell it to somebody else.

We issue a man's clothes here, and he has three suits, and those are cut to fit him. They're not tailored, I mean, but the length and the waist and the shirt size and so forth. He gets his three suits, and we wash em and put em in a box, and they're issued out to him as he turns a dirty suit in.

ATTICA CORRECTIONAL FACILITY
HERBERT E. PERONE, INMATE

After we wash and dress, approximately seven-twenty, we are fed in our cells. The officers pass the food in. They pass it through an opening in the box. There are bars on the doors. Some mornings we

5.

receive cold cereals, such as corn flakes or bran flakes. Other mornings it's hot cereal. We generally either receive an orange or half a grapefruit or prunes, bread, approximately eight ounces of milk, and coffee. It is getting better. Was very bad up until quite recently but it's drinkable now. I drink the milk and I eat the fruit, with the exception of the grapefruit, because we don't have the spoons with which to eat it. We only have plastic spoons, and you can't eat grapefruit with plastic spoons.

CALIFORNIA STATE PRISON AT FOLSOM<br>
ARCHIE DALE MCDONALD, CORRECTIONAL OFFICER

Well, my job when I get here in the morning is to supervise the seating of inmate population in number two dining room.

At Folsom we do not require what I refer to as forced seating. In other words, if a man desires to eat by himself, that's permitted. If he wants to eat with other people in proper rotation, that's up to him, so long as he's filling the next empty table as we go in a circular fashion in the dining room. Fill up seats as they're empty and keep going around. Tables are square. Four seats to a table. Next empty table. If he wants to eat by himself or if he, like I say, fills in with some friends of his—lotta guys, they eat together most of the time—they come in in a line, they go receive their food from the steam table in a line, they file into the dining room, and follow the seating pattern we have set up.

All I do is to see that the tables are filled up properly, that they're occupied properly. And if a man skips a table, I'll notify him to fill in. They're required to remove their hats in the dining room while they're eating. Sometimes a fella'll forget. I just notify him to please remove his hat. It's just a courtesy to everyone else. I have no conversation whatsoever with them, unless an inmate just comes up, asks a question about something or has some valid reason to speak to me.

There's an officer at the gate supervising the line coming into the dining room. There's an officer, kitchen officer, that supervises the steam line, where the food is passed out. Ah, usually there is a sergeant or lieutenant, who is the overall supervisor of the dining room.

It's very similar to the military. We use the same type of trays that are divided into six compartments, six sections, same stainless steel trays. In this particular type of feeding, it's a constant line. It takes approximately twenty minutes to completely fill the dining room. However, before you have it completely filled up, people have already finished eating their meal and have left the dining room. There are inmate table-wipers that are constantly wiping off the tables to make sure that they are clean and ready for the next occupants. So it's something like a continual line, coming in one way and going out the other. We only utilize one steam line right now, and it moves just at the right pace so actually it's never necessary to stop the line, as I say, to wait for empty tables.

Say that a man wants to sit someplace other than where he's supposed to be sitting—in other words, out of the normal seating procedure. And he asks if he can sit over there, if he can sit with so and so; and I say "No, sit over here." Well, maybe he'll get a little hot under the collar and say something that is derogatory or something like that. Well, I'll have a talk with him. Not right then, no. I'd get him off to the side, because you don't create an incident among a lotta personnel, inmate personnel, especially in a dining room. You might have to take a lotta verbal abuse or something like that, but by taking that verbal abuse, you would eliminate a possible bad situation.

When I got through with my particular assignment in the dining room, then I would call him over to the custody office and I'd talk to him outside.

Say that he did provide a lotta verbal abuse, called me certain names—maybe I was "a dumb bull" or something or that, I'd ask him what his reasons were, the kind of outburst he had. Well ninety-five per cent of the time, he'll say, "I'm sorry I just lost my temper, lost my cool." Then I would explain to him that the dining room is primarily to consume their food. If they wanna visit, they can do it out in the yard or anyplace else. If he wants to talk to the man, he shoulda made, oh, a little bit better arrangements—shoulda come in same time he did and eat with him. Course maybe he's on one job and this guy is on another, then it's impossible. He still shoulda waited to visit or make any comments to the man someplace else, other than the dining room. Now this doesn't mean that talking is forbidden in the dining room. Absolutely not. But we don't permit going from one side over to the other and standing there, visiting and back and forth, a lotta unnecessary traffic of this type.

DISTRICT OF COLUMBIA WOMEN'S DETENTION CENTER
DAISY LA BELLE, INMATE

We eat breakfast about six-thirty. One day second floor go first, next day third floor go. Okay. You go upstairs, you eat breakfast. You get a good meal. Do get a good meal. They feed you regular food. One mornin might eat eggs, the next mornin you might have oatmeal, and they have corned beef hash, somethin like that.

CALIFORNIA STATE PRISON AT FOLSOM
DOUGLAS A. BORSIN, INMATE

Go to breakfast approximately seven-fifteen, seven-thirty. Generally it's pretty good. There's some meals that aren't too popular with guys and everything like this. Hot cakes and French toast are two of em that really don't go over. We have, like on Sundays, usually we have fried eggs, potatoes, toast, and some kind of fruit. Other times we have, ah, not to use the average expression, say, ah, thin beef on toast. And then one mornin we'll have dry cereal, rolls, bananas usually. That'll be on probably Wednesday. And Saturday they have a roll-and-cereal meal. And other times, you might have sausage sometimes or, ah, things like this. Let's say hotcakes, French toast, that's like twice a week.

CALIFORNIA INSTITUTE FOR MEN
COMRADE SIMBA, INMATE

Go into chow, you get in line, you got to watch out for the cups. You gotta go through the cups and the trays, cause they're pretty dirty. You can't wash em. You jus gotta try to find a clean one. Throw the dirty ones down on the floor or somewhere. The mos times you watch the food to see if it's any good.

You might have somebody that's workin on the servin line tell you, "That's no good, this is no good." If you're lucky you know somebody. Then you may pick up on somethin that ain't too cool—somethin that's fucked up. It's a known thing that there's stuff put in some foods to compensate for some food that's missin. Like the menu that's on the line, the ingredients is not usually what it's suppose to be. So when you pick your food, you have to like relate to that. The food is bad, but you get used to it. The coffee's awful. Lotta cats, that have been down here longer than I have, relate to the fact that they don't have taste buds. They jus don't taste the food. They jus eat.

After I get my food I go and find me a place to sit. I usually sit in a regular area. Like if somebody is lookin for me they know where to find me, a community-type situation.

INDIANA STATE PRISON
HENRY WALTERS, INMATE

I'm not really that drove about eatin breakfast. It's just an old service habit. I was always about half-crocked, you know, and always huntin for a little extra sleep. Now when they got eggs, about seventy-five per cent of the guys in the dormitory get up and eat.

Unfortunately you only have em once a week, maybe twice. If we're lucky, we're really lucky, we'll have em twice. Ah, quite frankly, I don't consider what they use to have for breakfast good enough to get up for. I just as soon have a cup of coffee. Well, it was commonly referred to in the service as **SOS**. Here, I don't think they even know what that means. They call it gravy on toast, but it's all shit on a shingle. Just a little worse than it was in the service, if that's possible. They always said that nobody could make it worse than those cooks in the service. Well, they do it here—make it a lot worse, you know. You'll have that. And maybe next day you'll have French toast. I don't know where they got that name. But, ah, then you'll have your dry cereal and milk and sugar. And perhaps two big cookies, big huge cookies. You can call em that. Um. I might say this: I don't think anybody can complain about starvin in this institution. You can complain like hell about the quality of the food. But you can't say they starve you, you see, because they make sure there's enough to keep you from starvin. They're very careful about that.

CALIFORNIA INSTITUTE FOR MEN
MICHAEL COONEY, CHAPLAIN

I live here on the grounds. I have an apartment now. I had a house for a while. I wouldn't advise anyone livin on the grounds—you're too close to the job all the time. Get up about seven o'clock. Shower. Eat in my own apartment. I cook once in a while, but I usually have an inmate do it for me. Eat usual stuff. On the diet now, so I eat very low—practice some table calisthenics. Then the inmate and myself have got to decide what parts of the paper we're gonna read. We both could go for the sports section first, and that always winds up in a row. I have two inmates actually. But one works only part time for me in my apartment.

CALIFORNIA STATE PRISON AT SAN QUENTIN
HAROLD W. BROWN, SERGEANT, CORRECTIONAL FORCE

I been very fortunate. I've had a beautiful marriage with my wife. I have coffee in bed every morning, and that's my breakfast. I don't stop and eat at home.

CALIFORNIA INSTITUTION FOR MEN
JOSEPH A. MCCAGAR, CORRECTIONAL OFFICER

Every mornin I get up at quarter to eight. I got my alarm clock set, day off, vacation, workday, I get up at quarter to eight. I find that I feel better this way. I'm a person who doesn't like to hurry.

9.

If I have to meet someone at a particular time, I would sooner be early than jus slide on in under the wire. This is my individual make-up.

My wife raises dogs. I have some chickens and some doves. I do a lotta putterin around—that's what it amounts to.

The doves that I have at the present time, I have a trap rigged in one of the cages, where they can come in but they can't get out. I have a bunch now that I'm gonna hold until after the huntin season and then release them. They're what they call mournin doves. Actually I don't raise em, cause they won't breed in captivity, so all that I do with the ones that come into my cage is feed em. They're very well taken care of. And then I let em go for the rest of the year. I have a thing about hunters who go down to the sportin-goods store, buy all this equipment—fancy clothes and the gun and shells, and take a bead on that little dove. Probably it takes four doves to make a meal for one man. In fact, if I were in charge of huntin, to even things up, you take the man goin out after whatever he's gonna hunt, let's say a bear for instance, then give him one shot, make him put the gun down and give the bear a chance, even things up a little.

I have twenty-one doves and a backyard flock of chickens. I've got little bantam silkies. They're real nice chickens. I've had em ever since I've been in California. They take up my mornins. And apart from that I run errands, go to the store, maybe write a couple of letters.

INDIANA STATE PRISON
DANIEL ENGLAND, CORRECTIONAL OFFICER 2

Around seven-thirty I take my daughter to school. I've got a car I'm workin on. It's my hobby, you know, workin cars up. And I've got a little Ford I'm workin on now—soup it up and paint it and mess with it a little bit. So that takes up a lot of my time. I spend about three or four hours on it. Rest of the time, I play guitar or else listen to stereo. I like rock.

CALIFORNIA STATE PRISON AT SAN QUENTIN
LOUIS S. NELSON, WARDEN

I arrive at work at or before eight o'clock. I can't believe I can require other people to be to work on time unless I myself am at work on time. And I find already my staff on duty, and night reports are on my desk, so I can see how the night went and check my calendar and begin the day's operation, much the same, I guess, as any administrator does. I don't live the life of a movie-prototype warden, where I stand and look out over the yard and push a button and yell to some guard, "Bring in Joe." My life is more administrative than that sort of action. I have to meet with my staff and coordinate their efforts and their, ah, talents in keeping the institution on a day-by-day operational basis. I do take time out to visit with inmates, interview inmates, get the reactions of my staff, and do the multitudinous paperwork that's today required in bureaucracy to keep anything going. Spend far too much time on paperwork. I've often facetiously said that the State of California wouldn't need to build walls. They could take the paper and make papier-mâché out of it, and effectively corral the inmates just as much as we're using concrete and stone.

I don't meet the staff every day, but I meet with certain people in the staff, and with the individuals that wish to see me. And my door is always open to my immediate staff in the sense that I have seven people in the line immediately below me in the table of organization. And I don't require them to make an appointment to see me, because if they have something pressing on their mind, I want them to come down and talk to me now about it rather than opposed to waiting. It makes for a little chaos of course in the day's planning, but I feel it's important to maintain that sort of easy relationship with my immediate staff.

Let us take yesterday, for instance. I came to work, and the first matter on the agenda yesterday morning was the new employees—we have some new employees who were hired. I meet every new employee for the purpose of not only signing their document, which means that they're on the payroll, but also, I want to meet them personally, and I want them to meet me, and I want to tell them certain things, which I think they must know working around prisons, which have to do with the statutes that pertain to prison operations, because there're certain statutes that are peculiar to prison situations. I think the new employees must know those, because if they don't, then if they violate those laws, then it becomes my problem to report them to the district attorney, and, ah, I wanna know if they've been told what those statutes are, so if I do have to report them, at least my conscience is clear.

We have some employees who are unable to withstand the pressures of the inmate body or the inmate or blandishments of the inmate body or whatever. We apprehended a man last week who had in his possession some Benzedrine. This man was arrested. That was his last day of work. He had quit. His resignation was effective at the close of business that night. He was shaken down, but let's not say it was routinely. Some information had come in that this man was going to be

11.

loaded—going to be dirty. And he had been suspect before. Information had come in saying, "Hey, this guy's a mule. He's a pack mule." And nothing was done. We can't operate that way. But because it was his last night there was some concern on the part of the staff that, well, maybe tonight he will be loaded because it's his last night. And sure enough he was. He didn't have any heavy narcotics, but you never know what has come in before.

CALIFORNIA STATE PRISON AT FOLSOM
EARL STRAUB, CORRECTIONAL OFFICER

Folsom is run on the snitch basis. They have the inmates that will go out and pass a note to an authority, saying that this guy is going to do that or this is going on or drugs are coming in or this guy's gonna get a package with some drugs in it. And doing those means, they reward themselves by becoming a part of authority and assisting the authority into apprehending the drugs, money, or narcotics, whatever it happens to be. But Folsom's run strictly by that. They know usually pretty well what's gonna happen and what's programmed to happen amongst the inmates. And they run down every snitch note and try to keep it in secrecy and run it out and find out and evaluate it, take care of the situation. And the inmates know this, too. They come to Folsom, they say, "Well, you gotta be careful who you sociate with here. A bunch of snitch people in this joint, a bunch of authority inmates and all that stuff."

But they're right. That's the way the prison operates.

CALIFORNIA STATE PRISON AT SAN QUENTIN
LOUIS S. NELSON, WARDEN

I don't get into the center of the institution frequently enough. I used to do it every Thursday morning, but, ah, with the problems that have arisen here in the latter part of nineteen seventy, my guards in blue—I'm talking about some inmates—have told me, "Warden, you better let things cool off before you start wandering around loosely again." And there's a lotta feeling on the part of some of the more obstreperous members of our community that we set out to kill George Jackson, and there's a cry for revenge. I don't say I'm afraid of my life, but discretion is the better part of valor in this case, I think. But it will come along. All things smooth out. Another year, people probably ask who George Jackson was. I know that there's—in mentioning the name of Caryl Chessman, there's a lotta people who say who was Caryl Chessman? Caryl Chessman was a hero about three levels

12.

above Jackson, on the part of the inmates, because of his success in the courts.

When I need to go somewhere, I go. I don't call up a coterie of armed personnel or uniformed personnel to escort me anywhere. By the same token, I learned a long time ago, don't wander needlessly around blind corners, because you might stumble into something that might be a great danger to you. I don't go around there as much as I did. But I can't continue on this long. I have to start wandering around and see for myself what's happening, cause that's pretty important. I have to know the temper of the institution. I don't know a better way to sample that than to go out in the yard and test it for myself.

We get a lotta complaints from inmates in the sense that they'll bitch about something specific: "Why weren't the beans last Thursday well done?" I don't know why the hell they weren't well done. I don't know how I could ever find out. You know, that's the kind of bitching we get.

Somebody'll say, "Well, the mess hall's dirty." And ah, the inmates themselves are willing to live in this sort of a situation, cause supervisor starts cracking down on the men that are cleaning the mess hall, then the next thing you know the inmates are bitching about the harassment of the staff, the brutality, cause they're standing over a guy making him do his work. So we're in this kind of a tightrope we walk. But generally, see, in California, the food is predicated on poundage, not upon dollars. And so our ration remains level regardless of what the cost is. We don't go up and down with the cost of food. In other words, when watermelons are cheap, we can't buy a lot of watermelons, just because they happen to be cheap. We retain the same poundage year in and year out. Same ration.

We put people in isolation, but it's no dungeon, not all dark in there. And we don't just open it up and throw somebody a couple of scraps of bread and a bowl of water. Even the men in isolation get their ration a day. They get two meals, short of dessert. We have to feed everybody twenty-five hundred calories or more even though they're in isolation. And we can't keep em there longer'n ten days. So that's very seldom fatal.

When I talk to new employees, in particular the line staff, entrance-level employees, I comment briefly on the fact that when I sign the yellow appointment document, which puts em on the payroll, by that simple process I have transformed them from normal, average American citizens to a brutal racist oppressive bastard. That's what our

13.

critics say we are. I would suggest it isn't that simple. We don't transform anybody by bringing him to work in prison into something they are not. The people that work around these places are just the same kind of people we find everywhere, doing the best they can do in a pretty difficult job.

DISTRICT OF COLUMBIA CORRECTIONAL COMPLEX
JOSEPH SAKALAUKAS, SERGEANT, CORRECTIONAL FORCE

I worked the control building for a year. I was assigned over there. And the control building—some people call it the hole, we call it the control building cause it's to control the inmates that can't get along or can't behave themselves within the institution itself. They break the rules and regulations, and we put em in there for either an administrative reason or a punitory reason, depending upon the circumstances. The fighters—you have cuttings, and this sort of thing that goes on—well, they go to the hole. And I operated the hole.

And while you're in there, you also receive the inmates that are more or less unstable. Some of em—I won't say they're nuts, but they don't belong in here—they belong in some other type of institution, not in an open place like this.

And while I had that job, I had everything done to me. I had defecations thrown at me and had people spit at me, food thrown at me. I've been called every name you can possibly imagine. And every abuse that a man could possibly get, you'd get in that building. And yet at the same time, you had to continue working there—you couldn't just leave it.

On that assignment, we'd take over from the midnight crew at seven-thirty in the morning. We'd go in, count the inmates. This is the most important thing for you to do, I guess, to make sure that everyone's there. Then we fed the inmates. Then after we fed the inmates, we received that day the rest of the inmates that were coming in—that were supposed to be locked up awaiting the inmate court or what have you—and then releasing, which pretty much took care of the whole morning, the movement part of it.

The only weapon we carried's a pencil. We try not to use any violence at all. That's a thing of the past. Lot of people think it goes on an all. The only time you have violence is, like I say, some of those inmates are a little off their rocker or something, spit at you, throw crap at you, food. But this—maybe he's frustrated some reason. I don't know.

14.

I worked in cells quite a bit, behind the wall. And in the control building, we have the facilities there to contain somebody if we have to. But I have yet to see it done or to do it myself. We have the clubs and we have the claws and the cuffs and things like this. Occasionally we have to handcuff a man. This we have to do.

CALIFORNIA STATE PRISON AT SAN QUENTIN
JOEY WILLIAMS, INMATE

Guards, they are horrible. Some of em jus dumb and nuts. I call em freaks. They have the privilege to say, "Well, I have a pencil buddy. You better be good," you know, or "You better do this," you know. "If not, I can stick my pencil to you, poke you to death with a pencil." And a pencil can hurt a convict.

CALIFORNIA STATE PRISON AT FOLSOM
EARL STRAUB, CORRECTIONAL OFFICER

Adjustment center, you might call it a prison within a prison. These are people that either have broken a rule or they're such a case that can't be controlled in the general population and they're assigned to the adjustment center for a period of time. Might be five days, ten days, might be sixty days.

This is the place they call the hole.

I'm up on the second floor. And that job consists of assisting unlocking inmates out for the yard and bringing them back in from the yard, locking them up, and then any other requirements for visits by inmates or attorney visits—escorting the people out of their cells to the adjustment center office and then on out to their assigned either interview or visiting.

The new procedure that they're using right now is: they have a call for an inmate on the second floor, they wait til the escort officers arrive. The escort officers arrive on the second floor, we go through the mechanism opening the inmate's door and advise him that he's going out on an attorney's visit or whatever it happens to be. He steps out and comes down the corridor. On the second floor, mechanical door has to be cranked open. It's all padlocked and locked in, and you open a panel and by leverage you select the cell door that you want. And at this time you can crank open that one single door. And it opens partially so the inmate can get out. After he gets outta the cell into the corridor, you crank the cell back, close the door.

If the man does everything voluntarily, there's no restraint whatsoever. He comes out of the cell, and comes down to the grill door, which we're on one side of the grill, he's on the other. And he strip-shakes himself. He strips himself down, all clothes off. We go through all the clothes and see he's carrying no contraband or no weapons of any type. And then we body-shake him, visual body-shake him, at this point—look in his mouth, his rectum, ears, and go through their hair and their arm pits and that's about it.

Then we give him his clothes back. He dresses and comes on our side of the grill. Then he's escorted on out of the building with two escorts. Other'n me. I work in the building. Usually send an outsider, you know, an outside officer or officers to escort the individual.

The yard usually starts about nine-thirty in the morning. Prior to letting them out, we do have—the way the system works, one officer goes down and holler "Yard," and you just take down their cell numbers that they say they wanna go to the yard. As you pass there, the inmate might say eighty-five, or you go by eighty-six, he says eighty-six. That indicates he wants to go to the yard that day. And you got a sheet with all the cell numbers on it, and you mark that off as you go down the forty-six cells. And after that is done, then they have medication that the officer's required to pass out—daily medication. And you separate that by cells and go on down the cells and give the medication to the individual, see that he takes it, and proceed on to the next cell, the next individual.

The yard in the adjustment center is broken down to upper yard and lower yard. Lower yard takes care of the first-floor adjustment center, upper yard takes care of the second and third floors in the adjustment center. And if the second floor has the yard in the morning, then the third floor would have it in the afternoon. It's broken down morning and afternoon.

By the time you get the last man out to the yard, it's just about enough time to go back and start running the first man out back in. And it's just about an hour that he has out and it's just about how long it takes to run the yard out and back. So the time is occupied just shaking them down and going out and shaking them down and going back. Sometimes you'll find them taking certain things out that they're not supposed to. You wouldn't consider them contraband. It's not authorized, but it's a lack of memory by the individual, like a pencil, or some cigarettes or something of this nature. But no weapon or contraband in the sense of contraband. They have the smokes and the cigarettes out in the yard for the individuals; checkers and basketball and handballs are out prior to them going out.

Course they go to the yard only on days when the weather permits, cause it's outdoors. There's no indoor yard at all. So it's inclement weather or foggy, then actually they stay locked up.

ATTICA CORRECTIONAL FACILITY
HERBERT E. PERONE, INMATE

Generally we are locked in all day, up until last Friday, when I and five other inmates initiated a civil-rights lawsuit against the superintendent. We were contained in our cell for twenty-four hours a day without any yard privileges whatsoever, and rarely were we allowed or permitted to have yard recreation. Now, since this civil-rights lawsuit was initiated last Friday, we have gotten yard privileges every day for approximately one hour a day. Sometimes we go to the yard in the morning; sometimes we go to the yard in the afternoon. I submitted it to Judge John Henderson, U.S. District Court, Western District of New York in Buffalo, and we are waiting for some determination.

They have a basketball court, and they have two handball courts. And that is the only form of recreation. I walk. I talk to various friends of mine who are permitted to go to the yard. During my yard period, they take out three companies, and there are forty-one fellas on each company.

We talk about the various commissions that are investigating the causes for the riot. We discuss how best we can present what we feel are the inequities. And naturally we discuss whether we consider these various committees are sincere in their efforts to find the causes for the riot and to reform Attica. And inmates who I converse with are aware of their own failures in life, and they are aware that the fault isn't all the administration's, nor is it all society's, but they share in it equally.

INDIANA STATE PRISON
HENRY WALTERS, INMATE

It's a hell of a place, the hole. They used to have chains over there on a slab of concrete. They made em tear it out, some years ago, since I've been here. They tore it out. The last warden that was here had it put back. But I understan now they're not usin it. It is a dank place, in the basement of the deputy's office, inside the walls. And they have what's known as strip cell, which means you only get a mattress, which they were supposed to put that at an end. Whether or not it's been stopped I don't know. But, ah, it's not as bad, I imagine, as the type of thing that goes on at Cummins or especially some of your southern states or out in Montana. I understan they have pretty rough holes out there. But it's bad enough. And the one thing I hate about it, most of the guys spendin time in the hole here usually come down with some kind of illness.

17.

I was locked up for three days in what's known as The Rock, which is the seclusion unit and cell house. That's called I Detention Unit. But it's just a group of cells that has, ah, a toilet bowl, a face bowl, and a bed in it, one shelf for toilet paper or whatever. That's it. No tables, no chairs, no nothin. Change the sheets once a week, three meals a day, and you get out for a shower whenever the officer can afford to let you out for a shower. That may be once a week, twice a week, or once every two weeks. It depends on how they stand as far as assignin the officers to that unit. They only have one officer and he's busy, you can holler for a shower for two weeks and he may or he may not give it to you. It depends.

I was there for three days. I was required to take a lie-detector test, and then I was turned loose. I haven't the slightest idea how in the hell they decided to lock me up or for what. I still haven't found out what kinda big hairy plot was goin on. There was supposed to have been some weapons in the institution. How in the hell they got my name on the list I don't know. Now I find out three or four months later, they found my name on a slip of paper in the inmate's pocket.

I didn't feel lonesome, however. They locked about thirty of us up. Humph. All lifers. And they gave all of us lie-detector tests about somethin that never happened. It was the most ridiculous thing you ever saw. They entered the institution with shotguns, led by the warden. They shook down the education buildin, they shook all of our belongins down, guys that got locked up, and they kept some of the fellas that were reputed ringleaders locked up for three or four months. Nobody ever found out what the hell really happened. Was just some inmate runnin his big mouth, tryin to make a deal with the administration or somethin.

FEDERAL DETENTION HEADQUARTERS (OHIO COUNTY JAIL, FRANKLIN COUNTY JAIL)
GABRIEL POTTER, INMATE

I was locked in the hole at Newark. No restroom facilities whatsoever. They had a cold water pipe that came out of the side of the wall. It was an inch and a half in diameter. Pushed a button and it flooded the floor. There was a round pipe that was level to the floor that you went to the bathroom in. The only way you could flush this was by flooding the floor and let it run through this pipe. I didn't take a shower there for three days. I didn't have any drinking water. What food I ate was passed right through that cell. No bedsheets or anything. I slept on a foam-rubber mattress, and appearance was almost black, nothing on it. There was a hippie in the tank with me. He'd gone crazy, been in there fifty days and he was going nuts. And marshals

18.

moved me in three days, and I left there and went to Franklin County Jail.

This jail is three floors, and it's designed for one hundred and twenty men. The floor that I was on, designed for thirty men, had one hundred and thirty-six. I stayed there about forty days and didn't a day go by that the tension wasn't so bad that inmate's head was busted open or it was nothing to see a guy's throat cut. There was no restroom facilities. You flushed your commode once a day. Way you did this: during the day when you use it, you kept a blanket over it. At night the water would come up about ten o'clock, and it would flush one time. You keep this blanket over it round the clock. The commode was solid black. You cannot get a wash rag to wash your face with, or towel. No sheets whatsoever. I took three showers while I was there—one when I left, the other two, I'd say, twenty days apart.

I got an infection in my groin that I still have now. It's not a venereal disease, it's a disease I caught from the mattresses. On my back I got spots where I got infected, bedsores. They was all over my body when I left there. I attempted to see a doctor. As long as I was there, I couldn't see a doctor. It was nothing for a young man to be raped, violently raped, thirty or forty guys in one night. And every morning they would find some guy.

There was two men on the floor and one hundred and thirty-six guys. And all of these guys knew the conditions in Ohio, the chances were that they would never get out of prison. I had a court-appointed attorney there. I saw him one time and that was it. I sent him over fifty messages to come and see me. He never come to see me while I was in jail, and only time I ever saw him was when I actually appeared in court. And he stood up there with me.

They pass out the water there. There's not a drinking fountain, they pass it out in buckets. I've seen guys fight over the bucket of water. You can't get any commissary, and when you walk in the tank, if you got a pack of cigarettes, you're gonna lose em before you get through the door. After they stay there awhile, they see the conditions and what they have to do to get something to survive, then the animal instinct comes, you know, for survival.

DISTRICT OF COLUMBIA WOMEN'S DETENTION CENTER
DAISY LA BELLE, INMATE

The hole is about the size of a bathroom in a hotel or somethin. You have a toilet. The first few days they put em in the hole, they had em handcuffed, behind their back, they had their feet shackled, and had em layin on the floor, no mattress or nothin. They left em in

19.

there for twenty-four hours. I figured after that they allowed em to go, you know, they took everythin off from em. And then they got this iron door like that. They got this little slot that they might open it once or twice a day, where you can look, you know, look out. And maybe some of the girls'll holler at you or talk to you. Sneak cigarettes. You couldn't smoke cigarettes. You couldn't write letters. I mean they might as well be signin your death warrant when you in there.

It's pitiful. It's rotten. It's just like being locked up in one of them johnny-on-the-spot bathrooms out there, like they be workin, construction workin. That's what it all boils down to. Nobody to talk to. Only time you see somebody is when they bring you your food. That's all. You just lay there. And maybe count the bricks on the walls or somethin. No smokin. They might give you a cigarette bout once a day. This is what they call punishin you, really punishin you.

BUCKS COUNTY PRISON
JOHN D. CASE, SUPERINTENDENT

You know, if we treated dogs the way we treat prisoners in some institutions, the SPCA would be swearin out warrants all over the place. You can't expect a man is goin to change for the better if all you do for him is put him in a filthy cell with three other guys he's never seen before and lock him in there twenty-two hours out of twenty-four. And in some places, he doesn't get out at all—some jails a guy doesn't get out for a bit of exercise. Now, if people think that can produce change for the better, what they should do is lock themselves in their own bathroom for about twenty-four hours and have somebody bring em their meals three times a day, and then you'll eat where you shit. Do that for a while and get some idea that things are not what they should be in institutions.

DISTRICT OF COLUMBIA CORRECTIONAL COMPLEX
GEORGE F. X. LINCOLN, INMATE

Nineteen fifty-nine I was here for robbery and I came in contact with Islam as taught by the Honorable Elijah Muhammed. And at that time we were not recognized by the prisons. Persecution was widespread. So we went into court, filed a petition and what not, and over a period of three years, we finally won the right to worship in prison. Spent three years in solitary because of the court action.

Solitary is like a man in a room. It's like when you're kids, your mother want to punish you, she says, "Johnny, I want you to stay in that room and don't come out." You can't play the radio. You can't play the TV. You jus in the room. And if she really want to punish you, she pull the shade down and tell you don't raise it up. This way you don't have no outside vision of anything. And you only see someone when they come by to feed you or see if you still livin. An that's what solitary's like. And I went through that for three years. And I think that I still have my sanity.

You get a mattress. Sometime they let you stay fifteen days with no mattress—concrete and some water. It depends upon how angry they are with you. And at that time, of course, they was quite angry.

I don't know if I coulda gone through it without my faith in my God, which is Allah.

There was twenty-one of us, all told. However, some of us got out earlier than others for various reasons. I was one of the few that stayed the longest. An it took a court order to get me back in the population.

We do push-up exercise. Maybe once in a while they bring you somethin to eat. I tell you, when I went in, I was weighin two hundred. I was weighin one hundred and five when I went out. So you can imagine what you goin through. But surprisinly the body can take it.

ARKANSAS STATE PENITENTIARY
DEWIE E. WILLIAMS, CHAPLAIN

I believe that yeast can help the bread better'n knockin it down. This is my work. This is the way I approach it. I think love and grace and acceptance and kindness not only will eventually show itself through the lives of the individuals back here who have numbers on em, but also in the fellas who wear the olive drab.

Rather than complain about conditions, I have simply attempted to tell some of the administrative personnel to evaluate that. Not say, "This has got to be done," or "This has got to be stopped," but simply say, "Now, what did this cause? What effect has it had? And how can we remedy this situation so as to prevent somethin like that in the future? How can we change the attitudes?" I don't deal with that concrete act. I'd rather deal with the emotions and the attitudes. I think it's better'n the long run.

I would not file a specific complaint, I don't think I would. Because I believe my future work would be severely hindered, and I think that through the years, by followin this course of action, my ministry will be stronger and more effective. I think if I can work behind the scenes, workin with the emotions and attitudes of the individuals with whom I come in contact, that will pay dividends much greater than runnin out and saying, "Now this has got to stop."

CALIFORNIA INSTITUTION FOR MEN
DONALD E. BAILEY, SURGEON 2

Six o'clock in the morning before they go to work, they have sick call. The nurses run it. If there's something the nurses can take care of, and the patient is satisfied with this, okay. If not, he'll hold him for the doctor depending on what his problem is. Then we see them when we come in. Nurse'll give him a special pass at six o'clock so he can come back and see the doctor. We see them somewhere between eight o'clock and nine o'clock.

I get to work about eight. First thing I do is get the records, see if any new patients have come in, anything that has to be done right away. Fellow that's on call will have done the emergencies. But it's up to me to order any special tests. So I check that first, and go back to the ward and see the patient. And routine patients I wouldn't see first. The new or the acute I'd see right then to set up any testing or any special order I had to write before I start my sick call.

Night before last, man came in with a high fever. What we do in that case—they ordered aspirin and sponging if he hadn't cooled down the fever, routine blood test and urine test. Then I came on and I checked his throat; tonsils were enlarged and inflamed, so I ordered a throat culture for bacteria, and then I ordered an antibiotic sensitivity—so we'd start him on medication but then we'd have a check to see whether we had the proper antibiotic. Takes about twenty-four hours to get the culture back. That would show us what bacteria and would also show us what particular antibiotic that particular infection was susceptible to or which ones it was resistant to. Normally we'd start him on penicillin, which is what we did. And then the culture would show us whether that particular infection happened to be resistant to penicillin. We do a double check. We are able to do that. Every doctor doesn't do that, because it's expensive unless you have your own lab.

That set him up—his treatment was started. And then I looked at a pysch patient that was havin some trouble. Hadda give him an increase in medication.

We have some real bad psychs come in. We get them from the county jail directly. Lotta the people that are picked up are psychotic. The big problem of course is that they get involved with the law because they are psychotic. Unfortunately the psych hospitals have had these people, but they put them on treatment, which means heavy tranquilization. And if they're controlled on treatment, then they discharge them, and they discharge them as cured. It's cut down on the psych-hospital population, but it's made a problem for the public.

This kinda person does crime: the ones on medication. After a bit he thinks he doesn't need it or he doesn't take it, even if his family's checkin on it. First indication you have is when he reverts, and then you have an episode of some sort that involves the law. And most of the time when he's arrested, they say, "This man's psychotic," and they put him back in the mental hospital. Hospital won't take him. So then the court has him, and they send him back here as a Z number, which means they're supposed to get a ninety-day psych work-up here. Then an evaluation. And they go back to court, and the judge has that to guide him in deciding what to do. One of those cases, he was hallucinating—visual hallucinations and auditory hallucinations, and he was getting messages, and he was involved in a conspiracy, getting messages through the air that would tell him about the entire situation politically here and around the world. He was in the military area and he was getting messages about what to do about this person, that person. He was writing articles for Time magazine, Newsweek, L.A. Times. But he was getting a little bit violent. He decided one officer was on the other side, for no reason. The officer walked in to bring him his breakfast, he went at him. He didn't hurt him. So we had to increase his medication.

Most commonly used medication for this type of bring is Thorazine. We had him on Thorazine and Artane and Stelazine, all three. But it varies with the patient.

CALIFORNIA STATE PRISON AT SAN QUENTIN
PRESTON S. SMYTHE, INMATE

Valdez hung himself the other day. It'll be in the paper this week. This is stupid. The man tried to commit suicide three times. They put him up there in the psych ward with a twenty-four-hour suicide watch on him, take all his clothes. So they give him all his clothes back. Half an hour later he's dead—hung himself by his clothes. Where was the suicide watch? A known suicide-prone person. Hell, they had to cut him down, East Block. They had to cut him down, he was hangin all black in the face. Things like that. It's a shame.

CALIFORNIA INSTITUTION FOR MEN
DONALD E. BAILEY, SURGEON 2

When they first come in, you have to classify them according to their physical ability. They've had a physical before they get to the guidance. They come over here, and they're evaluated for their phsyical ability and what restrictions they have as far as working and where they can work. People that have been assigned, if they don't like the job, they'll come in and tell you why they shouldn't be there. Then you have to decide whether they have a legitimate medical reason or not. And if there is one, then you notify the assignment office of what their physical restrictions are. That's one problem. The other problem is about medication. Of course if they're asking for tranquilized medications, sedatives, this kinda thing, of course you have to be careful about starting them on it or getting them going on it, because then they get outta hand, and it's hard to cut it out once you started. We try to keep that at a minimal for their own good, really, because you don't solve any of their problems by giving them a pill. This is what they're used to doing on the outside: soon as they get a problem they want a pill to make them forget about it.

ARKANSAS STATE PENITENTIARY
ROBERT TALBOT, INMATE

When I first came here I had some arthritis pills. They took em from me and threw em away. Had operation on my finger. Couldn't bend it; still can't bend it. Told me to see a doctor here. He gave me some more pills. So I went out to him, told him what kinda pills I had. He didn't give me the same pills, jus gave me some type of big red pills to take. And I took em and I said these things are not gonna do me no good. So I didn't even try to go back and get any more.

Went to the dentist a couple a times. Had a tooth pulled. Need a couple pulled now, but I'm not gonna go back up there. Too rough on me. Dentist, he tear your gums all up and don't stitch em. He'll pull the wrong teeth. I wouldn't go to him if he was in the freeworld.

BEDFORD HILLS CORRECTIONAL FACILITY
MICHELE PEREZ, INMATE

There was one dentist, he used to bring girls goof balls and stuff in from the streets. He was a nasty pervert, cause anybody that went in there, he would feel em up, you understan. The girls that would let him feel on em, he'd bring em pills and turn them on. But he was wrong—he was testin everybody comin in. But some of the girls didn't like that, especially the boondaggers, you know, like bulls that come offa the street that they dress in men's clothes and all that, you know, hard. They might break his arm or somethin like that, you know. So they was complainin about him and they had to put officers in the thing, and the officer couldn't turn around to write your name down cause he'd grab you. This man was crazy.

I know, you know, cause he's done it to me. One day I dug it cause he kept pattin my chest with his towel, and he kept goin like this and, you know, pushin in on me. And he seemed to be doin it for about five minutes. When it dawned on me, I said, "Man git offa me."

He said, "Lay back," you know. He had a attitude, cause I didn't let him feel me, I guess, you know. Then when he started pullin the tooth, he was tryin to put his balls on my elbow. He was pullin and grindin in on my elbow. And then I pushed him away. He was crazy. He didn't have no class or nothin, you know.

CALIFORNIA INSTITUTION FOR MEN
SANCHO SUAREZ, INMATE

We had an individual here who was from the Brown Berets. His last name was Ensisco. He had a fight with the pigs on the outside. He shot one, and they shot him about four or five different times. He's a paraplegic now. In here they didn't give him any medication whatsoever. Inmates that were tryin to help him were kept away. It was not their business. It was the medical staff here at Chino to handle him. Okay, a person bein a completely paraplegic, he has no way of gettin down from his bed or from his wheelchair that they have. So because he had dusted a few pigs off, a pair of scissors were planted in his wheelchair at the bottom base. Now the only way he coulda done that is either he picked up the chair, put it in there himself, or had gotten flat down on the floor to be able to do it. So the pigs here go into his room. They bring one of those gurneys to remove him from his room. They shook down the gurney. Nothin. So they removed him out of his room where he was in the hospital. So they sent him into another room, so the pigs could shake the room. They didn't find nothin. So when he comes in, you know, they set him right there on his wheelchair. So right away there's a lieutenant, a sergeant, another officer, right away the sergeant went directly to the wheelchair. "Ah. What's this?"

Now, by law, this is illegal search and seizure. On the report that they made they said they had found a pair of scissors cut and made into a form of weapon. Now what is a paraplegic gonna do with a pair of scissors? He can't get up and fight. They were givin him medication. Every time they took him out to court—he had a bladder problem, urinalysis problem—he'd urinated all over himself. They wouldn't change him, they wouldn't take no extra clothes for him. He'd be in the county jail for maybe three, four days like that. Now if that's not degradin the dignity of an individual, then I don't know what it is.

25.

And yet they had the audacity—the administration sayin that they had one of the finest medical administrations.

ARKANSAS STATE PENITENTIARY
SAMUEL LEXINGTON, INMATE GUARD

The hospital is about as quacked as I ever seen for a hospital. I mean, they got a man over that's a homosexual. Doctor is a homosexual queer, you might call him. Now he ain't no more a doctor than I am. He's a freeworld man. And you can go over and ask the doctor to do somethin, and you ain't gonna get it done. Now they give you physical examination, sure. That ain't an operation or nothin you need. I went over the hospital, it took me two years to get a pair of eyeglasses. They put me on a list about that long to see eye doctor. And you get over there to see an eye doctor, and they've got equipment over there that's outdated. And, ah, if it's real serious, they'll send you to Little Rock Hospital. And when you get up there, they're not gonna do too much for you up there.

They got a little x-ray machine over there. It don't work. It don't halfway work. And then you got nobody that knows how to read a x ray. There was a guy, worked on this tower up here, fell off the tower one day into the runner rail and broke his leg. And he was hollerin and yellin, they thought he was drunk, so they throwed him in the hole. And then he tells em, "My leg's broke, have to go to the hospital."

"Yeah, we know it's broke."

"Man, it is broke. I ain't jivin you."

So they took him over to the hospital, took a x ray, couldn't find anythin wrong with him. He's screamin his ass off, gettin in pain then. It was broken. Poked through. So they took him to Little Rock Hospital. They put a cast on it. It was broke, you know. They put a cast on him. He could still walk on it. They had it fixed where he could walk. Then you know, he did light work.

CALIFORNIA INSTITUTION FOR MEN
DONALD E. BAILEY, SURGEON 2

What you try to do is give them the benefit of the doubt without going overboard on it. In other words, you try not to give them everything they ask for if you're a little suspicious about it, but you give them a full benefit of the evaluation—you test for whatever they said—you go along with it as if they really had it, and then you test. And then the next time you see them, you have a better idea of it. And of course they have a better idea of what you know about them. And usually it levels off, and you figure out what's really going on.

26.

For example an epileptic. Epileptics are hard to treat, hard to diagnose here. A lotta these people that are narcotics users claim to be epileptics cause they like any kinda medication. Automatically they're put on Dilantin and phenobarb, which are not any big picnic to a narcotics addict, but it's something. So you have to decide if they really are an epileptic. Usually you'll have a record the first day they come in. Talk to them, try to get a history outta them, try to decide whether they tell you the truth or not. That's probably your biggest adjustment to make when you treat patients in a place like this, because you have to be able to evaluate what they're tellin you. In a private office, you figure a patient come in, they're gonna tell you the truth what symptoms they have. But here you don't know. They'll give you the symptoms depending on what they want. If they don't want to work, why they'll come up with some reason why they should work in a special area or why they think they should have a certain thing that's a privilege.

CALIFORNIA STATE PRISON AT SAN QUENTIN
RAFAEL HERNANDEZ, INMATE

Now especially, now since August the twenty-first, it's pretty hard to get anything in there. If you're sick and wanna see the doctor, it's hard to see him. They won't let you in there. I remember one time I went in there cause my back was hurtin. All I wanted to do was maybe get some heat on it. So I went in there, and I seen the doctor. I don't think he was the doctor. He was an MTA—Medical Trainin Aid. Well his job is, you know, to distribute medication—if you need somethin for a cold, you know, to give you aspirin or whatever. I went in there one time with my back sore. That's when I was a tier-tender—jus pass out hot water, and from bendin over a lot, pourin the water in the bucket, you know, back gets sore. So I went in there. I explained to him.

He says, "Turn around."
So I turn around.
He says, "Well, I don't see no blood on you, man."
Say, "Get outta here."
That got me hot, you know, blew my mind.

CALIFORNIA INSTITUTION FOR MEN
DONALD E. BAILEY, SURGEON 2

Another complaint that's very common—Dr. Anderson sees those—is back problems. Legitimate ones are probably pretty rare, but they complain of back troubles cause they wanna get outta this job or get on special duty. It's an area where it takes a while to discover whether there's really anything wrong. It's easy to say there isn't any-

27.

thing wrong. You can't see anything superficially. We usually try to do a work-up on em so that we do know whether they really have any problem or not.

INDIANA STATE PRISON
EARL GRADY, INMATE

I could say there is no hospital. That would say it. That would just about say it. There is no hospital. This sounds strange, but I had TB. I was in bad shape. I got well, but I think of the guys that go over there and die, useless. Inmates administerin medicine, inmates using a needle, givin men injections, medicine that they are sposed to have and not sposed to have, or accidents made, you know. They buy manuals from Department of Corrections, United States Government. No inmate is sposed to administer medicine to anyone. I think they got one doctor. You figure it out.

CALIFORNIA INSTITUTION FOR MEN
DONALD E. BAILEY, SURGEON 2

None of the inmates are allowed to give medication. They're not allowed to give any type of injection or medication. That's all dispensed by the nurse. The inmate wouldn't even give out aspirin. They have no responsibility for medication. The only responsibility the inmate attendant would have is to give general care—make the bed, give him water, help him up and down. He wants something to read, bring him a magazine. If he has any complaints, report them to the nurse. Baths and heat treatments, that sorta thing, they can supervise.

DISTRICT OF COLUMBIA JAIL
CECIL MASTERTON, INMATE

Now the hospital. We have a good hospital here. If you sick, you go to the hospital. You have nurses and doctors. Dr. Beldon, he'll write out anything on the chart that you say is wrong with you. Then he diagnoses and puts it down. He give you cold medicine, give you aspirins, stuff you can carry in your pocket. He'll give it to you to take and tell you when to take it, how to take it. But if it's any narcotics or somethin that you're not supposed to have, somethin that makes you sleep, they give you under lock and key. You draw on it from the medical department. Some of em have a little trouble with the charts gettin changed by someone unauthorized, some inmates do. They complain that they're not gettin the right medicine, that they give you somethin to take the place of what they have been givin you, because, you know, they run out of that, they run short of it. And they do run short of medicine here in this hospital for what reason I don't know. It has been done. I've heard em say, "We're short of it. We're out. And you'll have to wait til we get it, and then we'll give it to you." So that's the way that went now.

BUCKS COUNTY PRISON
RAYMOND WARD BURNS, INMATE

Well, guys that wanna try'n get high, if they're placed on medication—they can go to the doctor and tell the doctor he can't sleep, and the doctor might put him on Seconal or Noludar or something like that for sleep. And he could save two or three of them. The doctor will look in your mouth—the doctor or guard, whoever give them out will look in your mouth after you put the pill in your mouth. But he can always hide it under his tongue, in back of his tooth or something like that, save two or three of them, you take them all at once. And this will get him high for a little while, you know, take his mind off the whole prison. Something like that. And sometimes they give it to you liquid form. You can put it in your mouth and just hold it without swallowing it, and get back in your cell, put it in a glass or something and save that two or three times and get high on that. And that's what the majority of these guys do, you know, just to get away from it for a while. This isn't being a junkie, you know, or nothing like that.

CALIFORNIA INSTITUTION FOR MEN
DONALD E. BAILEY, SURGEON 2

We don't give the patients any drugs that are sedatives, tranquilizers. If they're on a medication like that, they come in and get the medication at the hospital. We give it to em in liquid form, so they don't fake a swallow. If they've been somewhere else, they think it's a nuisance to come in and take each dose in liquid medicine, but we established that, and we stick to it. Drugs are locked up. Any narcotics are double-locked, and one nurse on duty has a key.

BEDFORD HILLS CORRECTIONAL FACILITY
MICHELE PEREZ, INMATE

Sometimes a girl'll have bad pain, and because you a junkie, they think you wanna get high, get up on medication.

There was this doctor, and they wanted to get him out and have a new doctor come in, because this doctor, he used to—you think you're pregnant and he's lookin at your toes. And if I'm lyin—this doctor was crazy or somethin, you know, and like he's a Christian

29.

Science, you know, and they don't believe in healin people with medication. But everybody's not a Christian Science.

CALIFORNIA STATE PRISON AT SAN QUENTIN
RAFAEL HERNANDEZ, INMATE

I've been in the hospital two times, I think, for hepatitis. It's nasty in there. Nasty. Like especially in the ward, the hepatitis ward, they're suppose to change your sheets every day, they're suppose to clean your room every day, and they're suppose to give you a lotta juices. And none of this is done, you know. Floors are dirty, sheets are dirty, got cockroaches crawlin all over.

CALIFORNIA STATE PRISON AT SAN QUENTIN
PRESTON S. SMYTHE, INMATE

Oh, Christ, that's a snakepit. That's the most horrible place. Well, people'd rather be sick in their cell and buy the medicine they need from the guys that work over there, than go there. I did four days for an ulcerated foot. And time I was on that thing, except for one black ward lieutenant—he was a gas, he really did his job, the only one, all of em up there—I'd change my own dressins, did my own medication. And the four days I was there, I was beat for five meals. They come in and say, "Well, you want somethin to eat?"

Say, "Sure I want somethin to eat."

"We'll trade you your food for your pills tonight."

I can't get out of the bed, man, I'm all wrapped up, I told em, "Stick it in your ass." I didn't eat, but they didn't get the pills.

The hospital, it's dirty, it's raunchy. The medical treatment is the worst possible as far as I'm concerned. Men have been known to be raped on the God-damn table after comin out of a God-damn anesthetic, while they're in the recovery room.

The hospital used to have a wonderful reputation, bein one of the best in the penal system. No more. The guys, like I say, would rather be sick in their cells than go to that stinkin hospital. It's no good. And I put it all in one seat—right in the head guy. Because you can't talk to him. I tried to talk to him when I was president of inmates. He wouldn't talk to us.

And they've got contract doctors over there. There's one over there can't even see. Tell him your foot hurts and he's liable to be lookin down your throat. We got a couple that are damn good, but they haven't got a twenty-four-hour position. Men have died there just because of lack of care, because the MTA won't take the responsibility. And the cons can't because they won't let em. Man's layin bleedin there.

30.

Maybe sittin there with a shank stickin outta him, man for both hands, holdin him, ain't gonna do but lay there an die. They got a good doctor on call, but, hell, he might be out the country club or some damn thing, you know.

And they lock people up that are gettin IVs. Damn intravenous'll infiltrate arm, just start swellin up. By the time they get a custody man up there to unlock the damn door, that guy is hurtin. They've had blood transfusions back up. Well, so many things.

I would no more let one of these guys whittle on me than the man in the moon. And bein seventy-per-cent disabled, I always think this: I got a pile of iron in me, I got bullet holes in me. I'm shot—got all kinds of holes in me. And, ah, I don't know if VA doctor'd be allowed to come out here at all. I know they won't let VA representatives in here to talk to you. So I really don't know. Boy, it worries you. It's a worry, believe me. Spose my insides go bad. There you are. They're just bad. Right now, I got a ruptured stomach—it's poked up in the esophagus, which gives you one hell of a case of heartburn. You have to watch what you eat cause when you lay down at night it backs up on you. Take an operation to cure me. No way. I'd rather have the heartburn than go over there and let them take care of me. No way I'm gonna let em do it.

CALIFORNIA INSTITUTION FOR MEN
MICHAEL COONEY, CHAPLAIN

I see everyone in the hospital. Just pop in by the door and say hello to em.

A fella's in very serious condition, well, of course, you try to preserve a serious mien. But for the fellas that's maybe got over an operation, he's comin along in good shape, might have been a pretty serious one, quite frequently I'll say to em, "You're not dead yet." And of course, that's always good for a laugh anyway.

I generally have an idea of who are Catholic and who are not. If they're Catholic I ask em if they want confession or Communion or somethin like that. Or if they maybe want their families notified, if they need cigarettes or somethin to read. You always have to be careful when a fella's seriously ill how to approach him, too, because maybe they have the idea when the priest walks in, "Oh, my God, I'm gonna get the last rites—I'm finished now." He must be thinkin the doctors are keepin somethin away from him.

Actually you don't give em the last rites. You try'n explain to em that it's the sacrament of the sick—it's actually a prayer that's bein said for your recovery. Puttin it that way, it makes it much more acceptable.

31.

I spend an hour and a half or so. That's in the main hospital; then we have two sections—the contagious disease ward that's in the maximum unit, and we also have another section in the maximum unit, where we have any of the men that are in maximum-security guidance center. They get sick, they're brought into this section. Then those that are psychotic or paranoid, they're locked up there, too. When you go in there, you must be accompanied. The maximum unit you have those so-called dangerous ones. An officer must come along and open the door for you. Up to about a year ago I could do it myself—they give me a key and I walk right through. But there are some problems that arose. Besides, they have female nurses there too, and it's better to have someone go along, and for my own safety.

BUCKS COUNTY PRISON
PRESLEY MIDDLETON, CAPTAIN OF OPERATIONS AND
SECURITY

We got somethin in our control center we call The Redbook. It tells you all the things that's sposed to happen, say, within the eight-hour period: dressin guys out for court and so forth. It's like a set rule, what we're sposed to do. And I jus make sure, bein the captain, I make sure this is done by use of the other officers.

CALIFORNIA STATE PRISON AT FOLSOM
ARCHIE DALE MCDONALD, CORRECTIONAL OFFICER

When an inmate has submitted a writ of habeas corpus to the courts, it's necessary for us to take them to the superior court by our transportation. And quite often I do that—take them into court and return them. We use our state vehicles. It's a screened vehicle. These are sedans. They sit in the back. I drive. The inmate or inmates— no more than three—are in the back seat. We use what we call a belly chain around the waist with handcuffs attached to this chain and then leg irons. They can walk with the leg irons—the chain, oh, it's approximately twenty-four, twenty-eight inches. I'm not sure the exact length of the chain on the leg irons.

FEDERAL DETENTION HEADQUARTERS
CHAUNCEY O'SULLIVAN, INMATE

I'm comin downstairs late to go to court. And I'm goin to trial. I'm representin myself in court. My wife is havin a baby so I'm under all sorts of pressures, you know, from here, from there, from the court, and he tells me, "What are you doin late?"

So I sluffs it off: Oh well, ah, "I had to write out some more papers for court."

So he looks to my papers and he starts readin it, you know, and I said: "What are you readin, man," you know. "You see it's notarized, so you don't have to read it."

He says, "Well, I don't have to give it to you because that's supposed to be here like the night before you go to court."

And I told him, "Oh, you're gonna give me my papers. You're not takin em."

And he says, "Well I'm not gonna take em this time."

I says, "This time, no other time," you know, "cause if you do, man, I'm gonna jump across that counter on you."

So he tells me, "Well get dressed."

I said, "I don't wanna wear my personal clothes cause they're dirty. My wife didn't get a chance to bring up some clean ones. And I'll wear greens of course."

"Well I'm not gonna get them."

"Well, I'm not gonna get dressed til you do."

So he called lieutenant, and you know, a little argument, but he can't lock me up then, you know, I gotta go to court.

BUCKS COUNTY PRISON
RAYMOND WARD BURNS, INMATE

You go into a courtroom, it's a big chess game. You've got a lawyer saying one thing and district attorney saying another. And the king, that's the judge, he's the big decider. You gotta pin him, checkmate him. You can't do it cause you got the district attorney against you. You got a public defender, who is paid by the state or the county. I mean, that's like fighting the hand that feeds you. A public defender's gonna defend you, he's only gonna defend you so far. Then when it comes time for appeal, it's gonna cost the county money. You're a pauper, you can't afford it. It's just unfair, the whole system. Judicial system's unfair. Government is unfair.

MANHATTAN HOUSE OF DENTENTION FOR MEN
HERMAN W. GREEN, LIBRARY OFFICER

Requests for law books, well, it runs up to an average of more than three hundred a week. The problem I've had, since there's such a shortage of law books, I mean the proper law books, the most I can take during the course of a day is about ten men. And we're steadily getting new admissions, so I'm steadily behind. That's always been a problem.

So to get to use the law library, inmate has to put in an interview slip. And an interview slip is addressed to the library or social service, whichever, and he states what he wants to do. Now these slips are put into a box on the floor and it's locked. Every morning, the house captain will go up and unlock the box and take out the slips on all the floors. And he in turn will take them down to deputy warden's office and sort them, because they might have slips in there for the chaplain, slips for social service, slips for library, slips to join certain recreational groups that we have in the institution, such as arts and crafts, music club, drama group, things like that. So the slips are sorted and the person in charge of a particular project will get the slip.

I must determine who can come up. You see now, it depends, you might get a man who simply wants to know why he was arrested or he has a charge—he wants an explanation of his charge. Well this might take five minutes or three minutes or what have you. But this is all he wants to know. So when this man wants this information, I will get rid of him and get another man. Now, if it's urgent—now, generally the inmate might say on the interview slip that it's very urgent—"Can I come up the library because I have to go to court the following day?" or "I have three days to put in this writ," or what have you—well, then I'll give him a priority. And sometime you have a case of an emergency nature, he'll have the floor officer call me and then I'll handle that direct. This is not with an interview slip, this is just a direct contact that the floor officer makes with me.

Well, firstly I would ask him, when they come in, what does he want to know; and he'll say, well, "I have to put in a habeas corpus," or, "I'm fighting extradition," or so forth. Well whatever it may be, if I have the book to help him, I can. So if he wants to read about extradition, okay. Well, I'll get the law book and I'll turn to extradition and ask him, especially if there's a language barrier, I'll ask him if he reads English, because the books are in English and sometimes we get Puerto Rican inmates or Spanish-speaking inmates who cannot read English. Now if there's any trouble along these lines, well then, sometimes I would be able to find my library help or assistant to sit down with him and read the passage for him.

Now say we get a man from state prison, who is fighting his case. In other words he might wanna be retried. Now he might've spent maybe from seven to ten years already in prison. Now evidently when studying the law books upstate he found there was an error someplace in his trial, so he comes down here—he's been granted this writ—to fight it. Now a man like that, it take quite a bit of time in the library, because there's a lotta research that has to be done. And I have a few books that can help many of em, and they're mostly working on Supreme Court, take time. Sometimes it takes several days. When I get a man like that, well, I just let them come until he completes his work, because there's no point in having him come for one day and then bring him up the following week, because it doesn't help.

FEDERAL DETENTION HEADQUARTERS
ANTHONY CORCIONE CORRECTIONAL OFFICER

You go up the floor. Eight o'clock we have a count. You lock everybody in their individual cells. They can lock in anyplace; they don't have to be in their own corridors. I mean, they might be in with a few friends of theirs, watching television or playing cards, as long as they're just sitting in one spot. We'll go and we'll make a count at eight o'clock. We call it into the count room. Usually takes about fifteen, twenty minutes. Once the count is clear, then we open up our tanks and we let the individual people out to their work detail.

Some people work on the first floor, in the clothing room, in the kitchen. Then we have our own crew. Each floor has its own clean-up crew, sanitation people. You let them out and they'll start in, strip the floors, buff them, sweep up.

People are considered what they call adjustment-and-orientation-assigned, just coming in, like safe-keepers and all, from different agencies that bring them in; all they're required to do is to get up in the morning and clean their own personal area. Then the rest of the day it's up to them.

BEDFORD HILLS CORRECTIONAL FACILITY
MICHELE PEREZ, INMATE

I clean the lobby. I chose that job because all I do is sweep and dust, then I'm finished and I can do what I wanna do on the campus here. This is in the units where we live, you know. The lobby is not big and it's not small, you know, it's in between. And when I first came here and I got that assignment, I used to do it real good. But since I feel like I'm goin home, I just sweep all around instead of under the tables, you know, dust, just slap the rag around. And then on Mondays I have to mop, cause the recreation area Saturday and Sunday I don't have to work, cause the office takes days off, you know, so the rec is really dirty by Monday, cause they use it Saturday and Sunday when nobody's cleanin. And Monday you have to get swept and mopped, you know, and the lobby too. Then on Tuesday all I do is sweep and dust the tables, water plants.

ARKANSAS STATE PENITENTIARY
MICHAEL JOHNSON HAWKE, FIELD MAJOR

First thing I do, I come over here to the back gate, pick up my three trusty inmates that saddle my horses for field officers. And I take em down to the horse barn. And I go out there with em to see if maybe we had a horse las night that got kicked or got crippled somehow.

I check the horses, make sure there's none crippled or what we can't ride. And I leave there, leave those inmates there to saddle the horses, and I'll tell em what horses, what officers, you know, so forth, and I leave there.

After I been to the stable, I usually come back here to the count room, to my office, which is in the count room, and I'll make up my roster as to what officer'll be carryin what squad today in the field and what each squad will be doin, because the day before I will check with the farm man, the institution farm man, and ask him, "What work do you want done tomorrow?" And he tells me, and I arrange for it to be done. And then I'll turn it over to my captain, and he'll check with me, make sure that he agrees, you know, because it is actually his line, and he'll be over em, as far as personal contact with the officers, more than I will be. And then I'll usually leave outta the building and go down to the dog kennel. This is for no particular reason. I started out in this business as a dog sergeant for two and a half years in Texas, and I don't know, I jus happen to go down there. And usually see how the dogs are, how the inmates are that keep em, you know, if they need anything—the inmates.

Then I'll come back up here, and I'll start arrangin my equipment for the day. I'm talkin about trailers to ride the men on or hoes or if it be cotton sacks or if it be gallon buckets to pick up pecans in, you know, jus whatever, you know, necessities we need to make the day right—water cart, and these type of thing. It needs to be done in advance because, ah, make the day go on.

Well, when we start turnin out, I'll go over to the back gate where the inmates come through, because the buildin major and buildin captain'll take care of gettin em out of the barracks, and what have you like that. They come out the back gate while I count em out the back gate, each individual squad, to the officer. And I'll probly say the count, like twenty-five. He'll say twenty-five in recognition that we're in accord.

At the present time we're workin under a two kinda line situation. We have the inmate guards and the freeworld over the long lines, the field-work lines. We turned out this way. Hopefully in twenty more days, it'll all be all under one, under the set-up of free-world officers.

And durin my workday, well, I'll bounce back and forth wherever I'm needed, occasion rises. And I'm not on any schedule but just a constant checkin basis from one line to the other line to the other line, tryin to help, tryin to be of service. Service is not the right word—might say, ah, supervisin these people, these freeworld people that are over the inmates. Because there is no doubt in my mind that somewhere down the line that some of-these officers, now, what you might say, mistreat an inmate. But might I show him the way like they should—and here is where I come in—jus criticize em. I'm not the most popular person here, as far as freeworld or the inmates are concerned. I don't say that I can't be. I can be to the right type of individual. But durin the day, this is why: I know how the farm manager wants his job done. I usually tell these people before they leave how I want it done. And they tell me that they understan. And then later I go along and check, and perhaps it is that they didn't understan, and perhaps it is that they're not gettin the inmates to do it the way that—they're jus lettin em do it like they, the inmates, want to. The job gets done, but it's not how the farm manager wants it. I'm sure he has his reasons, I don't question his reasons. Only time I question the farm manager about his work is when I think it involves a security risk or a hazard to the inmate. Then I'll question it. But I won't at this time, you know. I'll probly criticize his captains: "Well, look, that's not it, that's not what's happenin, that's not what I want. Jus stop. Start over. Get it like I want it. I'll be back in a little bit, and I'd like to see you doin it."

We'll take a person is pickin cotton. Maybe I want the cotton cleaned up real good. Maybe this farm manager has gotten on me and said, "Now listen, I went by where you pickin at yesterday, and I couldn't tell which end of the row you culled it on."

Well, that's a slam on me, you know, not personally toward me—I know how to pick cotton; I picked cotton several times before, several thousand times. But some inmates'll pick it right and some won't. And a lotta times, it's the supervision. For that, all you have to do is walk up tell the inmate, "Look, you're not pickin clean enough, I want you to get it cleaner."

Okay, you get clean. But if you don't tell him, see, he's gonna do jus what he thinks he can get by with. I think you would or I would either if we were in the situation. But if we were told to get it cleaner, well, we would probly get it cleaner. This type a thing, this type a thing. Maybe he wants the cabbage planted every six inches apart. And maybe I got down several rows and they're planted three foot then two foot then one foot, and jus scattered and junky lookin, you know. This is poor supervision, see. I don't blame it on the inmate. Not at all. I usually get on these freeworld. It's poor supervision, that's what it amounts to.

This is not a job to come out here and sit on your can and keep em from escapin. An outside officer on a farm-type situation we have in this institution has acquired twofold purposes—well, actually, three: security officer, times and types of counselin, third is to get some work done, because, to be honest, and I think everyone knows it, we try to make it some part of a payin proposition, you know, as far as supportin the institution, and also your foodstuffs and your garden.

ARKANSAS STATE PENITENTIARY
SAMUEL LEXINGTON, INMATE GUARD

We pick up our guns, go out, and we wait for a freeworld man to pick us up. We got Major Hawke out there, he's a major over the whole squad. We count the men outta the area. When we get the proper count, we load the men on a big truck specially made to haul long line. When we get to the field, all the inmate guards set up a line. We more or less surround them. Everybody gets in a place where we can watch em, and after all the guard are in place, then the rider—he's an inmate like the rest of us, he's in charge of workin em, tellin em what to do. They get a bucket and pick up the cotton. Take it up, load it on the truck. That's all they do all day long.

ARKANSAS STATE PENITENTIARY
ROBERT TALBOT, INMATE

Go to work. Go to the sally-port gate—that's the gate of the main building. They count as we go out. Wait little while til the truck comes that goes up and takes you to the field. Gets to the field. We'll pick the pecans, everyone gets a bucket, a gallon bucket, an start pickin pecans. Some dudes climb the tree, shake the tree. We pick em up. An the bucket boy, every time he bring a bucket, we'll give him one bucket and so on like that.

It's not hard. Jus like, early in the mornin it might

be cold. Your finger might get cold and stiffen up on you and no way of warmin em. That's the only hard thing about it.

CALIFORNIA STATE PRISON AT SAN QUENTIN
HAROLD W. BROWN, SERGEANT, CORRECTIONAL FORCE

My duties as assistant training officer range from setting up the civil-service exams—giving the tests, coordinating the appraisal panel for the oral interviews, doing all the necessary paperwork, a lot of red tape—to after the men are hired, I participate in their instruction, in their indoctrination, in their classes throughout their probationary period. I act as an instructor for the institution in various subjects, such as search, transportation, use of restraining gear, the laws pertaining to these fields. I participate in setting up visual aids and the making of movies, like depicting search, contraband, explosive devices, weapons. I am engaged at times going from the institution on investigations. I am engaged at times in leaving the institution for the purpose of public meetings and gatherings for public interest. Of course, this ranges from schools to organizations. I'm sent out in the field many times to evaluate new kinds of equipment that could possibly be used here at the institution.

Our officers are trained, and it's planted pretty stiffly in their head, that any force that they do use has to be and will be justified. So if an officer overreacts and uses more force than what's necessary, he's held accountable for it.

I've seen several times down through the years where an officer was suspended for five or ten days for using too much force. When you put a man down, you've got him, you can control him, and you go ahead and break his arm, this is not necessary. It's too much force. And the officer doing this should be punished for it. If all the force that's necessary to move a man is to take him by the arm and say, "Let's go," then that's all the force he'll be allowed to use. If he's fighting you, he's coming at you with a knife, you have to use tear gas to get him out of his cell (I've had this undesirable experience many times), you do it. But you do it very humanely and never with excessive force.

We have the regular batons, but I've never really found it necessary to poke anybody with them. You can use a baton as a come-along by holding it properly on a man. You can do many of these things. Many times that I've had one with me it was really to preserve order where I was at. And sometimes having it with you is threat enough.

With our inmates that we have now, with the new attitudes that are being reflected in off the streets—this new quote unquote revolutionary attitude—things are changing considerably. These men don't really need an excuse to be violent. In the eyes of their peers, they become a big man if they can kill an officer or cut an officer or put an officer down. They don't really worry about the consequences. They don't really worry if they're caught, if they're killed. It's just the idea that they are then held high in the eyes of their peers. And this is a most difficult situation to contend with.

There are no weapons on the ground whatsoever. You can't carry a weapon on the ground. You're outnumbered hundreds to a few many times. And if you had weapons, they could be taken away from you and the institution security would be jeopardized. And this couldn't be. The thing a man carries for his own protection, if you can call it protection, is a whistle. Standard police-type whistle. And this is a summons for help in case you get yourself in a bad position or find yourself in a bad position.

There are areas in the institution that are covered with gun coverage—gun walks—and by no means are there a lot of em. These are strategic areas, well placed, that tend to cover most activities. In an honor unit, normally there is no gun coverage. During the times of emergency, yes, we're going to call guns in and the gun rail is there. But by virtue of the fact that it is an honor unit, we don't have gun coverage. In the one main-line unit I spoke of, they do have gun coverage in there part of the time. When the men are finally locked in their cells at night, the guns are removed. They don't keep em out on twenty-four-hour day basis. Yet in segregation unit we do maintain gun coverage there twenty-four hours a day. Each area, by the activities of that area, denote how many guns and how much coverage they will have.

In the institution we primarily use thirty-thirties and thirty-eights, M-one carbines, for the most part.

INDIANA STATE PRISON
HENRY WALTERS, INMATE

We feel we don't have to do anything to have em start shootin at us. They've been tryin to provoke these inmates in here for two or three years. And man, it don't work. Because these guys know what they're doin. And most of em figure, you know, you watch a thing like Attica or George Jackson, man, and you know that we're sittin in the same situation. The only thing that's been improved aroun here recent years, man, they spent money for the armament room. They spent big money to take care of them weapons down there. And they built a tower, a gun tower inside the walls, which was unheard of here. Boy, they got one now. Just built it last year. And everyone knows what it's for. They got a tunnel leadin from this buildin inside to that tower, where they don't have to be exposed to inmates. And it was put there without any sort of provocation. We consider it provocation. We think they done it as a slap in the face to say, "See, we don't give a damn about you. And if you say anything we'll kill you. See?"

ARKANSAS STATE PENITENTIARY
SAMUEL LEXINGTON, INMATE GUARD

I haven't fired my gun in, well, three or four weeks. But a lotta these guys see a rabbit or a squirrel, they wanna bust a cap at it, see. Take it in, give it to somebody to cook it. Give it to the warden. If they see a deer out there, they'll shoot it. But as far as shootin at men, now they told us jus cause a man gets on your guard line ain't no reason to shoot him. They give us thirteen to twenty-five feet. If a man's that far outta the guard line then he's illegally out. He's escaped. You fire a warnin shot. If he doesn't stop, if you think you can shoot that man, go ahead and shoot him. If you think you can't, then tell The Man you couldn't do it. Then they'll take care of it from there.

But it's hard to beat these people. It's well mobilized. They got units and two-way radio. Can't beat the two-way radio. They got airplanes. Can't beat em either. Dogs and men on horses. No way you can beat em unless you got wheels, and very few people got a wheel here.

ARKANSAS STATE PENITENTIARY
A. L. LOCKHART, SUPERINTENDENT

Compared to nineteen hundred and seventy, February, we only had twelve employees, security people; now we have like seventy. And we're phasin out inmate gun-carriers—we will, the next thirty to sixty days. To my knowledge I don't know of any inmate that's ever gunned down anyone tried to escape. I know they've shot, but not intentionally to kill. And a lotta times the bullet's ricocheted and hurt someone. But far as jus out-and-out shootin em, I don't know of any of em. And I don't think it goes any deeper than an inmate jus tryin to do his time down here, and that's the easy way to do it, as far as he's concerned, if he doesn't have to shoot anybody. He gets extra privileges for it, more time off from his sentence. And other things go along with particular job he may have.

It's jus somethin we've gotta get away from, from inmates handlin guns. When you start trainin employees to be correctional officers, then they're naturally gonna make mistakes, too. You could terminate every employee that made a mistake. If you did, you'd wind up with no one here or you'd wind up with a new crew every mornin. I suppose you've got to live with some of the mistakes that are made if they're not severe, and let em prosper and learn by their mistakes. And hopefully you can cultivate a good correctional officer.

ARKANSAS STATE PENITENTIARY
SAMUEL LEXINGTON, INMATE GUARD

Well, I'm a prisoner guardin these prisoners—I'm an inmate guard. Guard the long line, east line—field work, work one hundred men to two hundred men. You got eight inmate guards with anywhere from twelve-gauge shotgun to a thirty-thirty heavy-caliber rifle to a thirty-caliber carbine. We used to carry pistols, but they didn't have enough pistols for chases, so we quit carryin pistols. We jus carry rifles and shotguns.

They have imaginary guard line between two points. Like, say, I'm over here on this corner and a man's facin me over there is the other corner and in between this line, imaginary line, that's our guard line. And if a man tries to go through that line, we fire a warnin shot. And if he don't stop, we have orders to disable a man but not to kill him. Try to hit him in the leg, some place where you can stop him.

Well, I been guardin now for about five years. Back when it was pretty rough under Lee Hensley, Dan Stevens, Bishop, Roberts, Murton, all down the line, way it was with me, I worked out on the line two, three years before I gotta break. Worked my way up to trusty—and then they turn me to trusty guard. Lotta people say that trusty guard is sorrier than the rest of the inmates, but I figure this way: you got your own time to pull, but pull it anyway you can. They had thirty freeworld people here. They had to depend on the inmates for help, see, help guard the inmates here. And for that they would give us our furloughs, extra good time and passes and visitin privileges.

ARKANSAS STATE PENITENTIARY
WAYNE E. MIFLIN, INMATE TRUSTY

They're a lot more careful screenin em now. They don't have as many shootin accidents, but the guy stands there all day, tempers get pretty bad. They used to shoot at you to make you work faster. Now they got older-type inmates, it's a little bit better-type people for guards. They're not pushy or rowdy. Nearly all the jobs trusties have now are long—they're twelve hours. You can be on call twenty-four hours a day if there's any trouble.

ROAD GANG, ARKANSAS STATE PENITENTIARY, CUMMINS PRISON FARM, 1943.

Bout the only benefit is the thirty-days-a-month good-time. You're allowed to have visits every Sunday all day long. We all live on the West Hall. Little easier to walk in and out of your barracks. With permission you can go into other barracks, sociate with other inmates.

We have to show a little responsibility, or if you have some kind of talent, some skill that's handy here, not an escape risk, have more to gain than you have to lose, then they go ahead and make you a trusty. They need gun guards now on the line. And gun guards now are classified—you got a A, B, C. And a C-type trusty still wears white clothin, but he works at regular jobs and he's under lighter supervision, but he's still under supervision. And your B, he's allowed to do private jobs, move around free and all that stuff, but he's still not allowed to carry a gun. And your A trusties can do maybe any job nearly a free man can, but they're not allowed to supervise the inmates.

ARKANSAS STATE PENITENTIARY
A. L. LOCKHART, SUPERINTENDENT

Inmates. There's a mixture weak and strong. I'd say your strongest individuals gonna be your leaders, and either your trouble or your best inmates in most cases. You get a strong inmate and he's a troublemaker, and if you leave him in a particlar situation long enough, then he's either gonna have a lotta followers, or he's gonna be the loner in the group. You know, either he's gonna cause you a lotta trouble or he won't cause you any. There's no in-between in most cases.

We can use the strong ones as leaders for the other inmates. At one time the strong individual may have been a trouble-maker, a hell-raiser, and he may be in here a few years, and all of a sudden he changes. Somethin inside snaps and he's jus reversed. And after he goes straight for a period of time, then you might put him in a particlar job, where he would be workin with other inmates, that he could lead em, show em where he might have made his mistakes along the way, and hopefully let the new inmates realize sooner what he has realized, you know, his mistakes, and therefore cause them to, I say, snap a little sooner than what they might normally. Cause a lotta ways you can use the strong inmate. Not for brute force, but jus to set example that way.

DISTRICT OF COLUMBIA CORRECTIONAL COMPLEX
JOHN O. BOONE, SUPERINTENDENT OF ADULT SERVICES

Some of the southern prisons, I'm sure that the super-intendent or warden had a strong white clique or a strong black clique or a leader that he could—he jus call Joey in and say, "What's happenin," See? "You and I runnin this place, you know. And you're a big black and I'm a big white. Now what's happenin out there in your culture?"

So this was the thing. And a lotta time it meant corruption, too. "You can run the gamblin games just so you give me my kickback." And, "You can run the prostitutes in the white section." "You can run the gamblin and the prostitutes in the black section"—that's conjugal visits. And this actually happened in a jail.

I was workin for federal prison system. I saw white kid come in, skin and bones. I said, "What in the hell is wrong with you?"

He said, "Well, I have eaten very little for a month."

I said, "Why?"

He said, "Well, I was in this jail, and this big black inmate was issuin the food. And if you didn't have money, you didn't eat."

You had to buy your food. And he didn't have any money, so he didn't eat. An black guy'd get that money and naturally kick it back to the jail. Otherwise he couldn't do it.

Now, it costs us about a dollar and a half per day to feed a man. A warden from Alabama came up here, and we said, "How much a day it cost you to feed your men?"

He said, "Thirty-eight cents."

"Thirty-eight cents? How do you do that?" You know, we said, "Boy, we must be doin somethin wrong."

Guy hunches over me and he says, "Beans and fatback, beans and fatback."

So that's how they could pay thirty-eight cents.

So what I'm sayin, they payin a thousand dollars a year in Georgia or Alabama or what have you to keep a prisoner, or in Arkansas, where they have thirty inmate guards in towers with guns that are trusty. When they start havin to pay civilian guards and all that, and that cost go up, five thousand dollars, you think the people gonna pay it? Impossible. So all I'm sayin, you've got to change tracks. We've got to look for a new way.

CALIFORNIA STATE PRISON AT SAN QUENTIN
LOUIS S. NELSON, WARDEN

If you would ask me if we got some kingpin convict in here that run the place, hell no. We haven't got any. Certainly there're groups, pressure groups spring up every once in a while. We have a Mexican group, called the Mexican Mafia, who became so obnoxious, their own peers tried to put them out of existence. They started a war, and in one day they attempted to kill every one of them. There are what the blacks call low riders, these people who run around pushing their weight around, threatening the weak and the single people (I say single in the sense that they don't run with anybody), trying to pressure them into paying protection, this protection racket. But they're not based on any ethnic grouping. These are hoodlums. These are prison hoodlums.

We generally know how to deal with those. We put them in our own jail within the prison. We generally put them out of circulation. We react the same way as the community on the outside when they become dangerous to our population. We get them out of circulation. We lock them up. We lock them up in a segregated area.

CALIFORNIA STATE PRISON AT SAN QUENTIN
PRESTON S. SMYTHE, INMATE

My routine day, is gettin that silly paper together. I have four men. I have the reporter. Then I have a sports editor, been here a long time. Then I have a circulation manager, takes care of all our circulation. And myself.

I do what they call show the flag. I like to go down to different areas and talk to people, talk to staff, talk to inmates, whatever. See, this is how you get the little interestin, little inch, two-inch articles. And this guy'll tell me somethin, I'll say "Wow!" you know. And pull out the book, write it down, and bang, and get a little two-bit story. Or I make it part of my editorial or somethin along those lines. Only trouble I have with staff is job-conscious free people, what I call civil-service hacks, because they are. I'm workin under a man right now, I could do his job in my spare time, and I don't have any. And I know that I'm smarter than him.

Now the warden, I told him, "Mr. Nelson, I'll put my name and number behind everything that goes in this paper. I'll be responsible for it, every word, every word. If I overstep the limits, and I know the limits, sack me up and ease me in the hole."

He says, "I can't do it."

They won't give an inmate the responsibility. Even though I know I can do it.

I've just sent out some fifteen hundred pink slips. What they are is askin our readers, our subscribers outside, what they like, what they don't like, who they like, who they don't like, and blah blah blah, you know, opinion poll you might say. And I've got about a hundred of em, got em all in the office. And they like to see certain things. They like to see more stories about the difficulties we have here, which I can't write. They'd like to see more stories about what has happened to men who have left, which is extremely difficult, cause I can't get the word out. They keep sayin, "Well, why don't you tell it like it is?"

I can't. Quite frankly. I write them personal letters to tell em, "I'd love to, but I can't do it. I'm censored to death." And I refer em back to the October first editorial I wrote, runnin down just exactly the limitations that are placed upon it.

And of course it does no good. They still ask the questions. But with censorship the way it is, I mean, you really can't do much. I call this damn paper Bowl of Jello, and that's what it is. There're only certain things I can put in it, and there's a great deal I can't.

Absolutely nothin about George Jackson. I had a complete front page story ready for that darn thing, five-column spread, the whole works and, ah, it was censored out of there. I mean, they wouldn't let me print it. I tried to write an editorial in The Bastille, which is my column, about it. No good. It won't go in there. The old head-in-the-sand bit. And it's that way today.

Dr. Kleimar, our—one of our psychiatrists—he writes a column, Still Small Boys. And he wrote one, an open letter to the staff of San Quentin, and I okayed it on my own, cause quite frankly I knew that the censor wouldn't okay it. So I went and ran it. And, oh boy, Monday mornin I got my ass chewed out for a solid hour over that one. And he said, "Well, maybe we better start lookin for a new editor." When he got done chewin me out, I just picked up the phone and called the warden. I've always found Nelson fair. He's a tough old bird. But he's a fair old bird. You got an argument, you're all right. He's a politician. Ha, ha, you better believe he's a politician. Him and I have had some pretty good nose-to-nose scraps, but he's never held it against me. He never jangled the keys, like so many of em around here.

But, ah, it gets difficult. It's a matter of lack of communication in staff, just as it is among inmates—we have our lack of communications. Like Mr. Nelson, he doesn't know what's goin on out there. He doesn't know. He's sittin there in an ivory tower, I mean, and til it's brought to his attention by somebody, he doesn't know about it.

If you go inside, when you walk by the Four-Post there, you'll see two parallel white lines. They were printed on the damn street after this August twenty-first thing. I looked out—when we came

47.

back to work, I looked out and here's two guys out there paintin these damn lines on it. And boy, I snapped what it was, cause we had a red one up in Oregon. And all the guys walk like a bunch of ducks between those lines. Well, I got on the phone to Mr. Nelson about it. And I was extremely emotional about it, cause I walked between the damn things for six and one half years up in Oregon, and I don't want them white lines. But he didn't know about it. He didn't know a thing about it. And you'll notice that it comes all the way this way, but goin back it stops rather abruptly. And that's where the communication—see, when he found out about it, he said, "Oh, hold it." Cause I was in Oregon when we burnt that damn thing down, so I've had a lot of experience. In fact, there was a little guy out there in the rain with a cuttin torch burnin that red line off that asphalt. Guess who it was? That was my contribution.

DISTRICT OF COLUMBIA CORRECTIONAL COMPLEX
JOHN O. BOONE, SUPERINTENDENT OF ADULT SERVICES

You got to get somethin to get their attention and channel this great drive that they have, this drive. I don't see, keepin em in prison, how this drive survives. They're stronger than many people who don't come to prison. Only thing about it, it is in destructive means rather than constructive. We should hire some of em. I think they'd make damn good law-enforcement people. And they'd like this kinda stuff. These guys would take lower salary to do somethin where they would have a sense of worth. Lot of em are in trouble cause they've felt worthless and rejected. Put em in a white coat and give em a mop in the hospital, so when they put down that mop and walk aroun, someone'll mistake em for an intern or somethin. Or when they can look into this thing and feel that they're really doin somethin with somethin. The services, they would be very successful.

CALIFORNIA STATE PRISON AT FOLSOM
DOUGLAS A. BORSIN, INMATE

My job, I go to work. They call it lead man, chief clerk for accountin office, where we buy and pay bills for everything that's usually in the support area. Industry has their own accountin and things. That's divorced from us. But everything else that's bought and sold in the institution, we buy and sell through here. That goes for our canteen, all food, materials and supplies to maintain the institution, clothin, etc. We have the business manager's office up there. We have no custodial staff, strictly civilian. We work right outside the West Gate, and there's a building as you come around the drive called the OG

Building, and we work up there, those flights of stairs up to the porch there. So outside one wall but still within main walls of the institution.

Primarily we have to, ah, take care of issuin all these purchase orders. Then when the purchase orders are issued downtown, we in turn get a copy back out here. We file these. We do all postin of our accounts of what we've spent and what we've received in debits and credits, and as I say, correspondence. We have one clerk works up where he does, handles all the purchasin for the canteen. We have one man posts all the so-called stock-receipt reports. In other words, when our merchandise comes in from the outside, it comes into the receivin warehouse, just located outside the walls, and we get in most cases, you know, informed that this merchandise has been received. So then we in turn can collate this and relate it to the individual purchase order. And then keep our records up to date this way. And we buy any special purchases that inmates might wanna buy, like radios or shoes, books, magazines, and hopefully television sets. That's a little thing that they've been investigatin, and Mr. Craven has it now on his desk to either approve or disapprove. Most of us hopin that they do approve it.

Generally it's pretty routine work, so the guys sit around, we break for coffee, do our work and shoot the breeze back and forth a while. We got a pretty good work group up there, I think. Everybody relates to each other. And it doesn't seem to be any personality clashes, etc. I've been there right now about twenty months, and in that length of time, I've found that the relationship between the civilians and the inmates is more or less like you are workin downtown. We don't have custody around to bother us, you know.

One thing I think most of the guys up here agree with, I would say, that all procurement does have importance because you do have to purchase supplies and merchandise. And I think it's one of the hard jobs of the institution, as such, cause you don't stay up with it, and your supplies don't come in, especially chow and things like this, why, guys'll be pretty shook up behind it, and I can't blame em the least on that.

We can do little favors now and then—like a guy might want something typed up, you know, might wanna write a letter or, ah, actually some of the guys have even done legal work up there, you know, guy hand-writes something out and needs some typin done, he doesn't have access to a typewriter, or it's a necessity, the final factor involved that he has to get this legal writ into courts by a certain time. The little typin section we have here isn't equipped really to handle the volume of work involved, so a guy has got to have something. And there's occasions I've typed em myself, other guys've typed em. And most of em say, well, you know, three pages of legal work is worth a pack of cigarettes. If a guy pays me or not—if he makes an offer, I'd be a fool to turn it down—he's just payin my services. But if a guy come in and say, "Hey, I need this favor personally," this is the way we work, too. Because what the hell, if you can't help your fellow convict, who the hell can you help?

CALIFORNIA INSTITUTION FOR MEN
SANCHO SUAREZ, INMATE

Up here, if you wanna have what we call your good set of bonaroos—your good clothes or your dress-up clothes or whatever, your new pants or new shirt—usually the people that we know that work in the clothin room or the other guys that work in the laundry, if you wanna have press a jacket or pair of pants or a shirt, couple of packs, you know, starched, got your bonaroos waitin for your visit for the weekend. Or maybe, let's say for example, this guy works in the laundry, this other guy works in the clothin room. Some of the new things will go through there, so you make an exchange. Here's a box of new T-shirts or whatever.

Like myself, I work in the print shop. Sure, you know, there's other groups here that have to have material printed. Myself and two other dudes do it. Just because we want to help em. We are all one, one class, and that is, we are all convicts. So we try to help each other as much as we can. Actually what we call it, rip-off time. We say, "You scratch my back, I'll scratch your back." Anything we need, buy.

Maybe it'll be cigarettes. Or maybe this guy is workin let's say, for example, in administration office and all of a sudden let's say a dude comes in from up north, say that dude has a jacket of bein a rat. We have ways of findin things out, if he is or he is not. Dude in administration owes me a favor, well, "Hey, man, here's so and so, look it up."

Maybe this dude has a bum jacket and maybe he's not. Things like this we clear. Goin into records that we need or statistics that we need, somethin like this that is beneficial to the convict himself or to the chicano or to the black or to any of the other groups here. When I say we, I do not just mean me or any other chicano brothers or black brothers, but combined as a mass. That we believe that this will be beneficial.

You know, I'm a correctional officer. I could just as well work as a garbage man. You know, it all depends on—I work here. Basically, my job is to keep a guy here til he's released by due process. That's basically what an institutional guard—I mean, they can say any way you wanna look at it, but basically I'm responsible for preventin a guy leavin before his time, you know.

Now, there are a whole lotta ways that you can do this, you know. You can be the hard-nosed guy with the gun over in the tower keepin the guy here. Okay. If I'm up in the tower, I don't communicate with inmates. I don't talk with any of the residents, you know. I'm up there, and my sole purpose for bein there is to keep em here. When I come down, I'm not in the tower, I'm here.

My function here is the issue of clothes and seein to it that a guy is properly dressed. I mean, people have gotta have clothes. And that's my function. I am sposed to be able to take care of the clothin needs, you know. This is like dinin room is sposed to be able to feed everybody, dormitory officer's sposed to be able to house people.

Right now I'm out of coats, and it's cold. And I got about three hundred more people to clothe. We're goin on a new system of clothin, and this mornin, I ran out of coats. And I still have about three hundred people. There's sposed to be twelve hundred more coats somewhere, comin, you know, in transit. They've been in transit for the last six weeks. I just, I'm just out. That's all. Instead of tomorrow me bein able to come in here and work on Sixteen-Dormitory, Seventeen-Dormitory, instead of me bein able to have these guys come in tomorrow and give em an issue, I'll have to tell em, "Well, you're gonna have to come back again," you know. "You can take one of these old coats I got over here to wear, to keep you warm. Eventually I'll be able to give you another coat, new coat."

But there's never enough for inmates.

I've been on this assignment for better'n a year. Before, I worked in the kitchen, I worked on the labor squad. I like labor squad better'n anything else. In here, you're doin somethin, but not like out there. Here you don't get a chance to do really anything physical. And right now, I'm gettin a little weight on. When I had the labor squad, I was in good shape. I used to tell em, "Well, I'm not gonna tell you to do anything that I can't or won't do."

And when I had labor squad, we used to unload boxcars, you know, sand, little boxcars full of sand when they were runnin the foundry up there, to dig ditches and stuff, you know. And I used to work, too, you know. I used to tell em, the men, you know, "My job is supervision. My job is not really on the shovel. So don't let me see you doin less than me. I don't care if you do just about as much as me, but don't do less than me, cause that might irritate me, cause you're sposed to be doin and I'm sposed to be watchin." But it helps keep you in shape.

Hey, do you realize that right here, right in this clothin issue, I could get absolutely nothin done without the help of the inmates who work for me. It's all I got workin for me in here is inmates. I got twenty-eight inmates and they work for me, you know. Together we get done what we have to get done. We get these people clothes.

There's not enough officers here to run that stampin machine, you know, issue those pants out and cut em off, the cuffs. Inmates doin it. They do it. We do it. The clerk, he's an inmate. It's kinda hard for me, I guess, to explain this to you because you don't know what prison's all about. But there's a rapport that you develop, you know. And just because a guy's an inmate, he's still, you know, a human bein, and he has feelins you know, loyalties. And he has emotions just like everybody else. Because the guy happens to be in blue denims and because he happens to be convicted of crime, he's no different than I am. The only difference is that at four o'clock, I go out the gate and he has to stay. But when his time's up, he goes out the gate, too.

You rotate jobs. You're sposed to rotate every— usually, but not necessarily now, but every six months you change shifts or you change jobs or you change somethin. I been on this for like, say, a year. I stayed here. After my first six months was up, I stayed here for another six. It was given me as an assignment and there's nothin, no guidelines really, to go by. And most of what goes on here, it pretty much comes out of my head, you know. And I appreciate the fact that in the years I've been in corrections, finally I've gotten somethin to do where somebody don't tell me exactly how I gotta do it, you know. And if this place works out here, it comes out as a real good operation, then I can go look at it and say, "Hey, man, you did this," you know, "you put it together."

And it's a challenge. I'd like to stay here long enough to see it work the way I think it should work, way the administration thinks it should work. We should have a real good system on clothes, where everybody has got the clothin they need and they're able to get their laundry done the way it should be done. I'd like to see it work.

I am the clothin girl for the population in R and D. My work: women come in like from courts and go out to the court. Their clothes—like if the women make bond and leave, you know, within the night, their linen and the clothes they were given when they came in, they have to bring em back. And they're goin in Dirty Clothes. So I count the linen, the clothes, and then I issue clothes to the floors. I go through the clothes, clothes that I feel are raggetty and can't be used any more, you know, they go in a bag and they're surveyed—throw em away or make rags outta them. Um. That's about it. I, you know, keep my area where I work at clean.

Hey, you think it's fun liftin them clothes baskets out there? Draggin them baskets up and down the floor, somethin happen stop the girls from ridin elevator, you know? And if you think it's fun, it's not. And they load it with clothes. Three motherfuckin baskets the whole institution with rollers on em. And you got about twenty-five of em downstairs in the basement. What you do, you walk to the basement, put em on the elevator, an walk back upstairs and take em off the elevator. Then walk back down to control if you're not through with your work.

I make thirteen dollars a month.

I work in license-plate factory, but my regular job is not in connection with license plates, it's in connection with metal desk parts, file cabinets, and desk files, index boxes, all metal. My job is fairly complicated. I take blueprints, take orders, get the blueprint, figure out the material required from the order, and set up the shear, make the layouts on the material, and then cut it to size.

When I get in in the mornin I look at the orders, present day, what orders I'm behind on, what order is the most pressin, and, ah, set it up.

I find out what help I need and get them to give me a couple of helpers. And this mornin I needed two. Just as I got em and started to work, they called me to come down here, so nothin happened. Yesterday I did work—no, yesterday I went to group counsel. Day before yesterday, those reflector-out plates for divided highways, you know, had an order for one hundred and thirteen thousand of those, eight by twenty-four. And we cut those all day. All day, the same thing

LICENSE-PLATE FACTORY, PENNSYLVANIA STATE WESTERN PENITENTIARY, 1971.

all day. It's precision work. And it's not hard. Machine do the work. We make file cabinets, no trespassin signs, occupied signs, state property signs in here.

It's very noisy. I wear—minute I walk in, I put earplugs in. In there fifteen minutes without it, without the earplugs, I couldn't work. I'd be a nervous wreck. I think this is what's happenin to some of the fellas, unaware of it, like stomach problems. It annoys your teeth, stomach, nerves, rash. I did have a rash. I don't know where it come from. It's gone now.

CALIFORNIA INSTITUTION FOR MEN
DONALD E. BAILEY, SURGEON 2

Neurodermititis. They'll break out with a skin rash or sometimes they'll break out with hives. You'll see a case, maybe—I got two now. It tends to recur. It's usually the same individuals.

CALIFORNIA STATE PRISON AT FOLSOM
CHARLES AMITY, INMATE

I just can't stand it, the noise. I constantly wear earplugs. Lowers the noise level, but doesn't hamper my hearin conversation. Crew can talk to me, and I'll hear em, but the noise—see, you get all kinda metal around, and it's constantly scraping against the shears.

I make sixteen cents an hour. I like this job in a lotta ways, but that's, ah—well, the guy that had it before me was one of the kinda fellas who secured everything that's here. And he was a cop-killer, he killed a couple cops, and he was a journeyman. He was a methodical-type fella, pretty good friend of mine, too. He had them convinced that the job couldn't be done without him, that he had set it up that he would be reemployed by the state to work here in that capacity and live at the ranch and so forth. Just the day before it was to come through, Sacramento disapproved it.

So they put me on it. I had never seen a shear before, but I knew the parts, and I got a math background. So I like the job. Pays about twenty-five dollars a month.

INDIANA STATE PRISON
WILLIAM SIMMONS, INMATE

I'm the institutional radio operator. I go to work and set the radios for the daily schedule. They have three stations, three radio stations, that are piped to each cell. And I work in the master control unit that controls the programs.

I'm not allowed to carry keys, so the officer on duty

has to unlock the radio booth, and then I go in and check the radios and reset them for the day's schedule. And actually that's all there is to do until four p.m. Then there's another change. Mr. Devereux outlines the schedule for the institution. He tries to program it by the majority.

We have, well, it's a regular radio receiver with an amplifier. Actually there's nothing to it. AM-FM, that's all there is to it. You have three different radios and the music's piped into each cell. Resetting radios takes about five minutes, then nothing until four p.m. So I sit around, go to my cell, play chess, read books—well, mostly magazines—Time magazine, news magazines, Reader's Digest, Esquire. Playboy's been banned. Fortunately there's a TV in the radio room, so I have access to that.

There's two radios that are changed at four—the jazz and the news radio. And after that's set, it doesn't require another change until seven. At that time, sports come on, some kind of sports, pro or college. Then another change at midnight. All three radios are changed at midnight for the real late hours. Then there's not another change until the next morning, about nine-thirty or ten o'clock.

But my job, it's pretty boring job. It's a good job in the fact that nobody bothers me. I come and go as I please. I have twenty-four-hour count so I can stay out as late as I want to at night. But actual work, there's probably about a half-hour a day.

Sometimes it gets pretty lonely there in the radio room, but I am, I guess, pretty much of a loner. Not that I shy away from crowds or I'm afraid to communicate, it's just that I found that while in here, it's better for me if I isolate myself to a certain degree. I don't really wanna get out and move around a lot, because—I don't know, I've always felt, ah, if something occurs in here, I don't wanna be in the middle of it. I used to go out and play basketball once in a while, but I was always afraid of an injury, cause facilities in here aren't too—well, if you get hurt, chances are you're gonna be up pretty tight for medical attention. So I kinda quit doing that.

This place is—there's no doubt about it, it's hell, but after watching several shows on TV about corrections, I just know that the average citizen just doesn't give a damn, unless they have a relative or a loved one, someone close, involved, they just don't care. And most of the time, when you talk about corrections or helping the con, they'll say, "Well what about the victims?" I don't think they're ever gonna make any progress until they realize that this is a responsibility—that they have to put some money into it and help the ones that need help and want help. Otherwise if they don't do this, crime rate gonna go up, cause you get back out in the population what you put in, maybe even worse. So I would like to see more places—there's a place in Illinois that was opened up recently, no walls, no fences; it's an honorary system. And it's true they're trying it out with minor offenders, but I think it should be expanded to eighty per cent of your population in prisons. About twenty per cent wouldn't work out properly. Until they start treating a guy like a man and giving him self-respect and the things he needs to feel like a man, I don't see how they can hope to gain the inmate's respect. But they probably don't want it. Probably not.

INDIANA STATE PRISON
HENRY WALTERS, INMATE

Durin the day from eight to four I work downstairs in the casework office. I can be called on to do anything that anyone workin in casework office wants me to do. This includes the filin of the paroled inmates' packets in the parole vault, which is vault four. This includes filin of the discharged inmate. You understan that when an inmate is discharged he is no longer obligated by the State of Indiana to report to a parole officer. He is completely free of that charge. If he should commit another crime and return, it will be under a new number. Therefore his packet can go to vault seven, which is much larger than vault four. And they have packets over there datin back to the twenties. Those records are very seldom disturbed. But on occasion people call up to find out if a certain individual was an inmate in this institution and what was his, you know, the conditions of his confinement, what did he do while he was here, what kind of an individual. You get these kinds of queries from employees and probation officers and from parole officers, federal and state, all over the country. Plus you get inquiries from people wantin to know if this man could possibly be their relative, you know, from children lookin for their dad who came here in nineteen-ten and they haven't seen him since. Perhaps he was discharged in nineteen-twenty but he didn't go home. They may never find him, but through some record that is in his discharge packet, they may be able to track him down. A lotta cases they do.

This is a position that no inmate's held in here before. It involves workin in close proximity with people in casework office. And as you notice, most of em are white. They don't like that. The officers don't like it. There's only one woman that objects to it, and I can understan that. Her husband has gone off somewhere three years. She's very bitter, and I think I just happen to be handy, and she takes it out on me. But the counselors don't like it; the custodial officers don't like it. Now it doesn't make em any difference that I have the vaults in better shape than they've ever been in for the parole packets and the discharge packets, and that I'm very conscientious about puttin em up and keepin em in order so that they can be found in a moment's notice. They don't care about that. Jim Devereux was about the only one in a position of authority who really appreciates that. The rest of em resent it.

You think we're paranoid? These people that work here, I've never seen a more suspicious bunch of people in my life. Somebody says, "Go get me a packet," and there happens to be a lady in the vault when you go in there, here comes three or four guys peepin aroun the corner, see what you're gonna do. You know, and you wonder, how do you ever get any work done? And why would they give you the job in the first place if they're gonna react like that? It's a hell of a curious thing. To the extent that they make you feel uncomfortable, and pretty soon you find yourself lookin over your shoulder all the time. You know, they call you trusty, and then they show you how much they distrust you. This is what it amounts to. Everybody out here has felt it. It's a hell of a thing. Now you're not really a trusty, you're just on outside duty. The trusty bit, they give you that name because you don't walk through there and hit the road. So I don't know if you're really a trusty or not. Because if they took em out of those towers, I don't know how many would stay here. You see.

It's no big job to go over that fence. I mean, it's not electrically charged or anything. And, ah, I'm an athlete. It'd be quite easy to get over there in about three bounds. It's got barbed wire on top of it, which could be handled. Wear gloves. That isn't the thing that keeps most guys here. I think most men have the desire to be free strong enough to make em run, but they also wanna be free legally.

They don't have any real resentment against the ole, black, Uncle-Tom nigger, that's traditional in these places. They don't have any resentment against him. Hell, they'll give him a job anywhere, you know, warden's house. He can be a clerk anywhere. He can be a porter in places where vital matters are discussed. They had one brother in here that worked downstairs helpin the officer that's in charge of the riot squad. He handled guns for em. See, they was good niggers. They're basically very ignorant and very predictable. You can almost down to a detail predict what they're gonna do on any given day. And, ah, that type of black is no problem for these people. And he's desirable.

It's that black man that has the intelligence that sets him apart from the common criminal element—is intelligent to the point

58.

where you can't browbeat him and you can't offer him a job, a good job, in exchange for his manhood, you see. You've got some guys in there that are so intelligent that they can do any job in this institution. I think some of em could run this institution very efficiently. But they are so politically aware of what is happenin and so against this system that sometimes a brother can't get along with them. Man, he's gotta be awful sharp to stay with em.

But I don't think they get the point here. And that is that when you bring men in here and mentally browbeat em, when you subjugate em to all sorts of mental pressures, you know, and you make em do your thing, which is you take all of his manhood away from him and demand that he be a statistic and that he fall in this line and never get out of this line, you are making zombies unfit to exist in society. They don't have to make decisions. No, hell no. They make all of em for you: what time you go to chow, what time you get a break, what time you go to work, what time you go to sleep, who you see, who you write, what you hear on the radio, what they can write to you, what books you can read.

The name of the game is corrections not punishment, or this wouldn't be the corrections department, it would be the punishment department. And what they're doin is they're creatin people who can really stay in tune inside a penitentiary. They know how to do time. Official point him out and say, "That's a good boy, there. Ain't never had no trouble outta him." Man, when he comes out them gates, you better be cool, cause he's gonna stick up or kill the first thing that moves. He's just that bitter. All the frustrations he's experiencin in here, he's gonna take em out the minute he's released.

CALIFORNIA STATE PRISON AT FOLSOM
GARCIA PEREZ, INMATE

I'm disciplinary clerk in the custody office, medium-A security. On Fridays and Mondays they have disciplinary committee, and I have to prepare the paperwork involved, like the one-fifteen actions and things like this. The paperwork has to be ready for each man that's been beefed.

I check the lockup sheet to see if any inmates maybe were put on segregation status durin the night, in which case I run down the paperwork, nature of the offense, the chargin officer, other pertinent information. Then type up rough drafts that may have been left durin the night on a regular one-fifteen form—it's a pink sheet. I make one original and three copies, and one is for the inmate. This is a new policy they have now, where the man is entitled to one copy of the offense that's signed by the officer that's charged him with the violation of whatever rule it is.

Most often I would say it's B-twelve-oh-one, inmate's behavior. That can be many things—altercation, a fight, just about anything. And maybe contraband would be second. This is just a guess.

ARKANSAS STATE PENITENTIARY
CLARENCE JAMES LEE, CORRECTIONAL OFFICER 1

You don't jus write a person up jus because they're here. Depend, really, I guess, on how much the inmate does before you write up disciplinary on him. Cause you got your minor infraction, which is jus you go in and get a good chewin out, you know, go in and the supervisor might fuss at you for a while, and that's all there is to it. Three of these minor infractions, it goes on your record. But jus get one or two minor infractions, it doesn't go on your record. But, ah, you get jus disciplinary, ah, this goes on your record. So somethin like insubordination to an officer, that would be minor infraction. Or disciplinary be somethin like, ah, strikin an officer or assault upon him, you know, somethin like this. Somethin what you really call serious.

ARKANSAS STATE PENITENTIARY
WAYNE E. MIFLIN, INMATE TRUSTY

You don't have a lawyer or nothin. Even if you get caught and sayin you were doin nothin, even if you weren't, there's no defense. Might as well jus go ahead and say, "Okay, I'm ashamed a that, probly won't do it again. Lemme slide some." I've never had a disciplinary so I don't know what I'd ever do if they caught me dead wrong. I'd probly jus cop out to it, cause there's no defense. If an officer writes you up, you might as well jus cop out. They'll jus pull anybody in on it, anybody standin roun the hall—"Come on in here, have court, hold court." If you have one hundred days' goodtime, you lose it; a year's goodtime, you lose it. The buildin major, he's been here long enough that he knows how to handle situations and how to conduct court. The newer people here, they write people up for petty stuff. People that's been here, they deserve a little credit, too, cause they know when a guy's out here in the field and he's draggin along. You can't even get away with that in the military service.

When you first come here you don't see how in the world you can get in worse trouble than comin to the penitentiary.

That's the end right there. After you get here you find out that's jus a minor thing. Boy, you can get in worse trouble after you get here— maximum security, stabbed, killed, worked to death, whatever.

DISTRICT OF COLUMBIA WOMEN'S DETENTION CENTER
LUCILLE MCNEAL, CAPTAIN, CORRECTIONAL FORCE

As I said, we have a disciplinary board that has to be handled daily. Because if a person is put in control cell, we have to bring them before the board at least within forty-eight hours after they've been in maximum security. And we also have the classification board that meet each Wednesday, and we have to go over each girl's assignment and so forth. And also we bring up people who are coming up for parole.

We usually try to hold the disciplinary board in the morning. The administrator come here around nine-thirty. And then about an hour after she comes in, then we get together and hold it, usually until about eleven. Usually we break up about lunch time. If there're any more, we take them after lunch. If not, we go into something else. Maybe I will go into writing up reports, some of these reports that I have to write, such as an officer is not doing well and we held counsel with her and she hasn't corrected sufficiently, now we need to get certain things on paper. Or any of the other things that come up. There're so many of them.

Girls' disciplinary offenses: well, um, they didn't get up on time, they weren't dressed at seven-thirty. That's one of the first ones. Lack of cooperation with the officers. Maybe the officer told her to do something and she didn't do it. Or maybe she used—it's the way she talked back to the officer, that really didn't communicate right. Or maybe the girl is outta bounds—she was supposed to go one place and she went another. There was a fight. Homosexual activities. A girl using profanity to an officer or using profanity on another girl. Refusing to work.

DISTRICT OF COLUMBIA WOMEN'S DETENTION CENTER
JANE MASON, INMATE

Usually board meets practically every day, because there's always a stack of disciplinaries for somethin. Like I got brought up for sayin "God damn it," you know, because officer heard me say it. She said I was being disrespectful. And by me not likin her anyway, I said it again and told her I wasn't talkin to her. So I got a disciplinary for this.

Some of the beefs that the guys get, I'll crack up behind em, you know. "God, damn, this guy got a beef, so and so and so and so." It gases me you know. And I'm workin in here in warden's office by myself, so I can crack up. Nobody sees, you know, but me.

We have this locked box, where a prisoner can put a note in it, and I have the only key, and I call for these people, come over and see me and so on. So half of my day, anyway, is usually taken up with this and then tryin to solve some of the problems that are presented by the inmates. They'll come to me with complaints. Like one of the men this morning was complainin that he's sposed to be on methadone and the methadone had been stopped. There was no reason for it. It was a mix-up, really. But he was upset about that and also upset about the fact that he didn't get down and see the counselor because the corrections officer wouldn't let him off the block. And of course I had to call up and tell the sergeant, who, you know, wasn't happy with that, because he felt—I'm sure the sergeant felt that this didn't happen on his watch. You know. But it did. And what should have happened is the corrections officer should have called down to the counselor's office and said, "Can you see this man now?" Actually, if there wasn't a counselor in the office time he wanted to see him, there'd be no point sendin him there. But see, this is one of the things that correction officers have to learn: you never deny a man a reasonable request, and you follow through on it. So you could get on the phone, and if you can't get the counselor, say, "Look, I'll check with him later. And I'll get you down there." See? But it's easier to just say, "No. You can't go down." This is the attitude you have to keep constantly changin.

You have counselors that are downstairs. You can't get out the gate to get downstairs to see the counselors unless one of the guards say, "It's all right, you can go through." Then it takes ten minutes for—everyone who gets in this cage out here, all of a sudden they get busy. This goes to their head, you know. They think they're really something now—they get behind the cage, they got power to push buttons. They push em on their own time. They stand there and look at you for five minutes before they push the button. They know you want to get out. I think they take a course in agitation.

Well, to get through the gate: if you get the guard's attention, you can tell him you wanna talk to him on the phone. Now once you get out of the gate, you can talk to him on the phone, give him a phony excuse, such as, ah, you'd like to go see Mrs. Sneed about your records. And he might tell you, "Mrs. Sneed's not in." You might know inside she's not in, but you're through the gate.

Now you can stop over on the way, talk to another guard about—"I just talked to him about going down to see the counselor, and I'm going down."

The guard say, "Oh, okay."

Well, in the meantime, this guard in the center might see you talking to the other guard. And he automatically assumes you're talking to this other guard to get permission to go down. So you just go on down. They allowed you right on through.

And they usually don't check on something. And yet they're petty enough to keep you behind the gate and not let you get down there or go where you wanna go.

ATTICA CORRECTIONAL FACILITY
ANONYMOUS, CORRECTION COUNSELOR

Before the riot I had interviews in the morning, every morning, with inmates. Now it's different. First off, I don't have use of my office. It's difficult to conduct interviews. Our offices are temporarily being used by these various committees, in and out of here. Something comes up that's real important, I'll go out into the jail and see the people, you know, things like social-security cards for people who are going out, and you have to get their signatures and that. But now most of the work is done through court assignments between the inmate and us, which gets away from one of our basic reasons for being here, which is that of a guidance counselor.

Normally, the job entails setting up programs for the men while they're here—educational programs, vocational programs. And there're inmate problems, inmate correspondence, inmates not hearing from their families, things like that. We try to act as a go-between. Coming up shortly, I'll be doing all of the inmates' income-tax returns. Inmates requesting transfers, I'll sift through his various records to make sure he's qualified for transfers to these various places.

Generally I would classify this job as something similar to what the Red Cross guy in the Army tries to do for the

63.

soldier. It's a very frustrating kind of work, because the failures are the only one that you see—the people that come back.

One man that come in here was a very heavy drug user, so that his coherency and everything was quite bad. And we established quite a good rapport. And he left maybe eighteen months later. I don't really recall how long he was here, because time and days just turn to—you know, in this situation. But the day he left here, he had tears in his eyes, talkin to me. He credited me with changing his entire outlook on life. But as things happen, I've read in the paper where he was again arrested for same use of drugs. Whether this was true or not, I think in a situation like that, whether you are successful or not in the long run, you have given an individual who is completely down and out, you know, something to hang onto in life. And although maybe this time it didn't work, maybe he'll come back to jail, maybe the next time it will work. But he's had something else to think about besides those things that got him into this originally.

Counseling is a funny thing, too. You never know what it is that might appeal to someone's mind, say, in a rehabilitative-type process. I might just make some strange comment to a man one day that might cause him to start thinking and maybe in the long run could change his whole philosophy towards life. That rapport that people have to come up with in order for there to be any even conversation is something that has to be worked on for a while.

Before the incident here, average counselor's caseload at this place was about five hundred men. We're very understaffed to actually do the job. There're three counselors now. You get to see them all, but actually it's not a very thorough process. Cause you have people here that I'm convinced have no desire for rehabilitation at all. They will talk to themselves: well, they're serving their time and they're gonna go out and do something wrong again, you know. But being as understaffed as we are, you have to almost, you know, come up with a certain amount of people that there might be some hope for. Of course there's a lot of people that aren't interested. They come down to talk to you because it's mandatory they come down to talk to you at least when they come into jail. Often times we see or hear nothing from a lot of them after that. Ever again. I don't go out of my way to talk to them, first off because of the large caseload. I don't go out of my way to force anyone to talk or anything like that because, you know, number of people would like to sit down and talk to you every day. Whether it does any good—the only knowledge you have is your failures. You come in contact with so many people over the years, you just forget when they leave.

Actually what most counseling is is suggestion. On a couple of occasions, I have made recommendations to the board. What I do in a situation like that is get together with his parole officer and give him my opinions on how this man has progressed in my opinion. And he in turn, you know, in his preparation for the parole board meeting, includes this in his summary.

INDIANA STATE PRISON
EARL GRADY, INMATE

Counselors don't really see the inmate. Counselors don't really know the inmate. They're stuck up front in the administration buildin. You got some decent guards. They got decent men on the educational staff. Counselors are kinda far-fetched, man. Counselor's like a glorified mailman. If you got a letter you might want mailed out, person might not be on your correspondence list, he'll handle it if it's suitable letter.

You know, that's a hell of a thing: counselor isn't allowed to help a man out. A lot of em's function's drinkin coffee, I think. That's it. Out front. They're kinda weird, you know. They give you a good frontal image. They do this and they do that, and the best end up, you know.

Your counselor takes a two-week vacation. You have a problem durin that time, you jus got a problem til he comes back. I don't know. It's like you remain a child the rest of your life in here, you know. There's no room for maturity. You try to act like a man, they slap you down. And this is pretty well constant every day.

CALIFORNIA STATE PRISON AT FOLSOM
ALEXANDER M. GALBRAITH, GUIDANCE COUNSELOR

We can't do anything to them until they're ready. When their attitude gets to the point where they genuinely wanna change, then we are in a position so we can offer some help. We know how limited this thing is. And we're trying to—you know, we got a prison system, an antiquated thing that's been around for centuries. And the public, you know, they shove this all off on us with a minimum budget and say, "Here, do this with them." They want them out of their hair. We have limited resources, almost impossible task of handling a vast range of type of offenses and people with a single device, which can't be done. It's gonna take a lotta money to do it right. But with our immediate institution psychiatrist last week this matter came up: can you rehabilitate anybody or can't you? And of course, most of us are of the opinion: not until they're ready. And then the question got to the point of how do you get them ready? Can you? Can you really influence

65.

some of these people? And there's varying opinions. Sometimes, you know, you just don't think you can get to them, but I think you can. But what percentage of them, I don't know. When they're ready, okay, then you can do something.

And there're dangers, you see. Like, they had a warrant out on my life—I think it was the Mexican Mafia or something. We had snitch information they were jealous because the Black Militant Front or Panthers had killed so many staff people in the department that they wanna get a few, just to get some. They picked myself and two others, we heard, at least. I'd kinda watch where I was going for a while, be pretty careful. But ordinarily I never even think of it.

Now, Galton, the guy that killed the laundry supervisor here, was one of my cases in the adjustment center. And the day before he killed the laundry supervisor, he was in the counseling center. Now, he's a demanding individual. He's not the kind to sit in there and wait. And he loitered out there. We have a door with a grill lock, and we just open it and leave it open all day. So anybody could come in or out.

Well there was a big crowd in there, and I saw him out there, Galton, and he's loitering. It's atypical. "What are you doing? What do you want, Galton?"

"Well, I wanna see my counselor."

I said, "All right. Sit down there and wait for him." I think he was casing it to see whether or not he could get one of us without being detected or apprehended. That laundry was set up that time and the supervisor was alone, but in our offices, because of the fact there are windows in between the offices and there's so much traffic, I think he passed that up. Oh, he wasn't too fond of me, naturally you know, you don't give him what he wants—either don't or can't—cause he was a very demanding, arrogant sort of guy.

CALIFORNIA STATE PRISON AT SAN QUENTIN
RAFAEL HERNANDEZ, INMATE

I had a counselor, if that's what you wanna call him. I went in there with a problem one time, I think it was an outside problem with my family. And I went in there, and I ran it all down to him. And I went in there with an open mind, and he looks at me and says, "You jus wanted to come in here and talk."

I don't know where they get this wantin to help men inside, "men in blue," or the convicts, cause they can't even help themselves.

People want you to make phone calls to their relatives. And that's quite a big thing, too. You just don't do that—I don't. Other chaplains do. Well, because I don't usually know enough about a situation in order to make a phone call, understanding you're not supposed to make a phone call unless you feel it's a very pressing emergency. And these situations are not pressing emergencies, although they are sometimes in the minds of men. And I think that you get into misunderstanding, and you don't really help the situation a great deal that way. And the phone calls have to be collect calls. You're sort of pressing a collect call onto somebody. And things of this sort as a rule should be taken care of in terms of correspondence. Many of these represent a breakdown in the communication between two people and very often this is the fault of the men here, and so you want to weigh this thing a good deal and determine the necessity of doing this particular thing. And it takes time, and it's often not very satisfactory to the man who is very demanding and who feels this is very important.

I feel it's more important to try and help a person to understand his responsibility in the matter and to maintain his relationships in such a way that these crises don't seem to come up so often. Much of the life of the person who's inclined to get into an institution like this is, I think, a life that's being led on a sort of a crisis basis. And if you fall into that pattern, why, I don't think you're helping a person very much. It's hard, very hard. It's much easier, of course, to cut through the tape of responsibility and assume it for the person. But I wouldn't consider that responsible on my part. Most of the calls are concerning problems having to do with their family lives and sometimes even their criminal life or their legal situation. Things of this sort I don't know much about. But counseling doesn't have to do so much—at least my type—doesn't have to do so much with knowing that kind of thing as it does with helping people with their attitudes and their approach to things. The degree to which, of course, you use the Bible is just different with different people, I think—even with different chaplains. One man will find all his answers literally stated in the Bible. Another man will use the Bible as a means of understanding things. And of course, religion itself can be seen as a part of all aspects of life, like this problem of responsibility I spoke of a moment ago is a religious problem.

I think of one I worked with intensely quite a long period of time. And he had a real problem with authority. And we

67.

simply talked about these things. And the main job I had to do with him was to allow him to hate me as much as he wanted to without hurting. And this is quite a job.

I remember he went out on parole finally, and he came back, parole violated, and he came into my office, and the first things he did were angry. He stuck his head in the door and says, "I'm just here to tell you you're a failure."

And I said, "Well, that's not the way I see it." So we had to begin again. This time he made it very well. And again, you see, it was a matter of responsibility. The answer to me was: I can't make you a good man. You've got to do it by changing your whole feeling about life. And this is primarily a religious matter. And the best thing I could do at that point was try to demonstrate to him that he was forgiven, and also that God doesn't take the responsibility for these things. If he wanted to make God of me, which was what he was trying to do, I couldn't be God. Even if I were God, he'd still have to be a good man for himself. And I can't do anything more than God can do, certainly. And many failures occur in spite of God—no, not in spite of Him, but this is a part of creation: you fail, and you fail, not God.

In short-term situation it's where someone comes in and says he wants you to make a phone call. You say, "Well, I'm sorry, I'm not going to make that call."

He's angry; he says, "Well, you're telling me you can't make that call?"

I said, "No."

"Well, who are you to say that?"

"I have a telephone and I have to make that decision."

So he's very angry. And I realize how important it is that he not go angry. You can't always stop them. But if I can stop him, maybe simply by encouraging him to talk some more—or maybe he hasn't sat down, inviting him to sit down. "Somehow or other, even though we're not going to make the phone call, maybe there's some way I can help you or something that we should talk about here." Somehow or other, he's started and we'll talk.

After half an hour of this: he's been very demanding, very demanding about it, really putting you down, he may get up, time comes for him to go—what that time is, it's usually by his selection—he'll say, "Well chaplain, I know you wouldn't make that call," and by now he's smiling, "but it helped an awful lot to talk to you and I feel a heck of a lot better." And he goes out.

68.

I'll say, "Well, come back if you feel like it, some time or any time."

FEDERAL DETENTION HEADQUARTERS
GABRIEL POTTER, INMATE

Every telephone here is tapped. Every outside phone. You can't make a confidential call to your lawyer. I put the wire in for the phones. It runs from the floors through the parole office, and they have a flip switch on one phone, they can listen to any conversation takes place on any phone. Now legally this is not a tap. But they can flip that switch, it's like picking up an extension and listening in. Those phones are put in on an extension. I say every one. I might be wrong. But I can almost prove three of them are. As you go in the warden's office, there's a glass office there. With two desks in it. On one of these desks there's two phones. If you look at one of them, you see it's got five white buttons on top of it, it has a switch on the side. A flip legal-switch. If you look, you'll see that. If you flip that legal—there's a phone sitting right up the front, that the inmates use, number seven-four-one-one-oh-two-one or seven-four-one-one-oh-four-nine, one or the other. Those two phones are tapped. He can switch the switch either way and listen to the inmate's conversation. So if they have a man that they think is planning an escape, instead of letting him call from the floor, they maneuver him to the parole office and listen to his conversation, if he's not aware of that.

BUCKS COUNTY PRISON
PRESLEY MIDDLETON, CAPTAIN OF OPERATIONS AND
SECURITY

Durin an average day, it's pretty rare for any officer to actually sit down and talk. The only person who got, you might say, the time is your counselors. But I think your security man, man in uniform, comes in contact with the inmates more'n the counselor. He has to go out of his office, type the sentencing letters and everything else. And jus by givin a man an aspirin or jus tryin to answer some of his problems there—he might want a phone slip or something like that— now this guy in uniform handles that immediate problem, you see. Possibly this inmate might get attached to you. He'll figure, well, you're a good guy, you know. You understood he needed to make a phone call cause his wife is sick. So this guy is great. Even though he didn't see the counselor. So jus by close contact every day, I guess—we get the guy up in the mornin, we make sure he gets his meals, we make sure he gets dressed in his clothes, cleaned and everything else—we're like, you

69.

know, the father image for the inmates. And the man in uniform is always in close contact. And these guys sometimes respect it, sometimes they don't.

BUCKS COUNTY PRISON
MAJOR JOHN D. CASE, SUPERINTENDENT

It's what goes on in the interaction between the guards and the counselors and the inmates that makes the real difference. With the inmates you find out that many of em, they sleep most of the time. They withdraw like into the womb. And what you have to do is keep agitatin em: "What are you goin to do about yourself?" Right? I don't want any inmates sittin quietly in the corner goin to sleep, you know.

Now I don't have maybe enough people, and I don't have enough trained people, but any time I can, I'm puttin that needle into the guard or into the counselor: "What are you doin about changin this guy?" And I'm puttin it into the man: "What are you doin about changin yourself? I'm not happy with you."

It's a constant battle to train officers so they don't keep thinkin of inmates as somethin beneath them. You know, in other words, that they're not tryin to be the judge and the jury, and decidin that guy's here and he should be punished, you know—because he got locked up, he should get the punishment, see? And of course, you know, some of the people who are locked up are innocent. Not too many, but a few. But then, there are others who are so damned inadequate that they're really socially ill. I'm not a great believer that everybody in jail needs a headshrinker, but I know a hell of a lot of people in jail who are social misfits and need to be led around by the hand. And their braggadocio and their bluff and their belligerent attitudes are all a big cover-up to hide a little frightened boy, black or white, inside, you see. But you can't expect the average guard is goin to have that kind of understandin. He has to understand that he will treat that inmate with respect in my institution. If you don't do that, if you don't believe in it, if you don't believe that, there's an old Marine Corps sayin, "You either believe or you get relieved."

BEDFORD HILLS CORRECTIONAL FACILITY
ELIZABETH LYNCH, SUPERINTENDENT

Selection of staff is terribly important. If we had a more fluid way of getting staff out who shouldn't be in these places, who shouldn't go up the ladder, you know, who shouldn't continue the same old pattern, I think it'd be a lot easier. But today everything has taken a

GUARDS BEATING INMATE, QUEENS HOUSE OF DETENTION FOR MEN, NEW YORK
CITY, 1970.

swing in the opposite direction. Labor relations have gotten so tough that the labor unions are telling us how to run the institutions. It's almost impossible to get an employee out who shouldn't be here. And this is bad, because one or two bad numbers can indict a whole group of people. And we've got one heck of a bunch of employees, who are doing a good job day in and day out. But for a few hard-hats, a few of the wrong ones in there, they indict the whole system. And this is what's bad. I think it's too bad we don't have an easier way to ease them out.

And we don't have the money to hire, but I suppose any administrator of any kind has got money problems, and that's where it is.

### DISTRICT OF COLUMBIA JAIL
#### ANDERSON MCGRUDER, SUPERINTENDENT OF DETENTION

Our biggest problem here: there's not enough money. Costs. For example, I think it cost us, last month, a dollar and twenty-nine cents a day to feed each inmate. So you can see what that will run to, having twelve hundred here. And it's not only food, but programs, personnel, modern facilities—they're necessary, too, to attempt to help the person while he's confined.

Here in this country, money seems to be everything. You can be the greatest gentleman in the world, and if you're broke, you're generally John James. But you can be the biggest robber in the world, and if you have a million dollars, you're Mr. John James. You can be guilty of a crime and have enough money to hire the best attorneys, your chances of going to jail are far less than a man who may be innocent and is without funds, inadequate counsel. I think the system there leaves much to be desired.

### DISTRICT OF COLUMBIA CORRECTIONAL COMPLEX
#### GEORGE F. X. LINCOLN, INMATE

I'm familiar with the system, and I know that there was a time when people like myself—what they call the radical or the militant Negro—we were took out and lynched. But now they're usin the prison to keep us outta the public. They know that there's a natural difference tween the black and the white. An integration's nothin but a farce. They know this won't work. It hasn't worked. And I think that the people that are skilled planners, these people know: keep us locked up, keep our women free—another method of birth control, same as the pill.

My charge is second-degree murder. Life sentence. But I have always maintained that it was an accident, and, ah, I think that the evidence showed that this was not only possible but probable. I think that my guilty conviction, the guilty verdict—I don't think there is any doubt in anybody's mind but that it was racist inspired—all-white jury, and to top that off, one of the witnesses for the prosecution in my case was a former girl friend of mine, who happened to be white. And about the only questions the prosecutor asked her were, was she in the room when this happened, to which she answered, "No."

Then he says, "You don't know if he stabbed Frank or not?"

She said, "No."

And, ah, he said, "Well, you can't actually say whether or not he committed this crime?"

"No."

"But do you think he did?"

"Yeah, I think so. When I came out of the room, Frank had a knife in his chest up to the hilt," she says.

Later testimony, she testified that she took the knife out of his chest and washed it off in the sink. But prosecutor's next question was, had she had sexual intercourse with me? And my trial seemed to, you know, it seemed to pivot right then, as far as the attitudes of the jury were concerned. After she admitted that she'd been sexually intimate with me, nobody seemed interested in whether or not I was innocent of second-degree murder. Everybody got hung up on I'd been havin an affair with a white girl.

I've never been involved in anything of serious nature before, and I was tryin to get the lawyer to tell me what the hell was the difference between two to twenty-one and life sentence. Do you get out after two years or—my lawyer wouldn't even tell me the difference between two to twenty-one and life sentence. He said, "Look. I'm gettin paid by the state; you're not payin me, and I don't have time to come over here every time you send for me and explain things to you. Now the prosecutor wants to give you two to twenty-one if you'll cop out. So you either cop out and you let me know right now or you take what they're gonna give you."

And that's what I got: life sentence. Second-degree

murder. Trial lasted forty-nine days. It's taken me six years, I been in court. I got here in May, and I filed my petition in June, my first petition, a movement for a new trial. I've been in court ever since. And I'm jus gettin a chance for a review, the federal court. I've never even made a trip out for an investigatory hearin. This is the first chance I've had. I couldn't get any action on my contentions that I was denied, ah, due process and that there was a violation of search and seizure and the Escabito rulin applied in my case. I couldn't get any kinda judgment from the—everything I sent to the Indiana Supreme Court was denied, you know, arbitrarily. I didn't get any kind of consderation until I got in federal court.

And I think that's a pattern here. Unless one has the big dollar, you know. If you have the money, the whole ball game's different.

The only wealthy or well-to-do or politically connected people in this institution are those who have become the victims of other political people or other wealthy people or who have so outraged the public with the viciousness of their crime that their money can't save them. There are a few of those here.

I used to spend a lotta time readin law. For about four years that's all I done. In fact, I used to have dreams about cases, you know. And it's good. But I, ah, after I got my case in the federal court, I found myself, you know, gettin involved in cases, in what I considered the fairness of the court's rulin. And that's bad, you know, because you get hung up on whether or not you think a certain court made a proper rulin. Unfortunately, in most of em you can see that the rulin is slanted in favor of the prosecution, you know, the state. Now this is jus one of the facts of law: once a man has been incarcerated, it seems that all agencies are attuned to keep him there, rather than to expedite any sort of release, even though he may be innocent. The emphasis seems to be on to keep that man in the institution, unfortunately.

There's impartiality in the law. They say this: she's blind. Justice is blind. That's probably the biggest myth, you know. There is—let's face it, Justice is a long way from bein blind, you know. There's the colored thing involved, but mainly there is the financial thing involved. Law must be one of the biggest businesses in the country. And I think therein, you know, the financial aspect of corrections, I think, sort of gives you some insight if you look into the problem with corrections.

### DISTRICT OF COLUMBIA CORRECTIONAL COMPLEX
JOHN O. BOONE, SUPERINTENDENT OF ADULT SERVICES

Attorneys are bad. They charge these exorbitant fees. You could see mothers washin and husslin to pay fees to get a son, who's a pain in the ass, outta trouble, at the same time she may be puttin a daughter in school. This is criminal and inhumane punishment. The whole criminal-justice system has reinforced criminality, as far as I can see, automatically.

They're all political prisoners. You can't help but consider that when you see em here. All of em are poor and black, to oversimplify. This tells you somethin. When I came in January, the make-up of the staff was about eighty per cent white and twenty per cent black. And the make-up of the residents, the inmate population, was about ninety-eight per cent black. I often wonder where the white prisoners go. District's about seventy per cent black, and I know that out of thirty per cent population white, you have to have more than two per cent whites in this institution.

I have an idea they're gettin probation, and that's all right. It's good to give people probation, but let's give some blacks probation, too. And some of em are bein introduced to federal prisons by the judges, who honestly feel that with a large population of blacks, that it would be threatenin for whites here.

### CALIFORNIA STATE PRISON AT SAN QUENTIN
JOEY WILLIAMS, INMATE

You hear a lotta guys say bum beef. Well I'm one of those that say bum beef.

It's a hell of a thing to be in here, you know, especially for somethin you didn't do. My father always told me, if you done somethin you're guilty of, you know, why lie about it? If you didn't do it, stick with you didn't do it, regardless what a person tell you, what they gonna promise you, anything. Don't say you did if you didn't do it. So I think that's the thing that's hold me back, cause every time I go to the board they say, "Well, you were convicted by a jury," you know.

I really wanna tell the adult board, you know, "Jus fuck you and your fuckin ass," you know. I don't give a damn what that twelve panel says. They made a mistake, you know. I didn't do it, you know.

I address em in a manner—I put em on the same level that I'm on. They're not supreme to me, you know. I talk to em, I'll say

75.

jus what I feel. Like my counselor told me, he says, "Well, I think what got you shot down was you talk yourself out of that deal."

I said, "That's life." I says, "I express myself, that's all that matters to me. I told em what I want em to know."

"So I think you talk yourself outta that deal."

When I went before them the last time, they said, ah, they felt that if I came to a stop sign, and the stop sign said **STOP**, I would get out of the car and turn it aroun and keep goin. I told em they were crazy.

Any time I go before the board they talk to me about philosophy things. They don't talk to me about my case. They talk about the opposite thing, you know, somethin else in my life, you know—oh, some little minor beef or somethin that I received—anything but my case. So this pisses me off right there. I tried my best to tell em, "You know what I'm in here for as well as I know." I said, "Let's discuss this. What are you lookin for me to do? What kind of program do you want me to bring you?"

They say, "Well what kind of program do you wanna bring?"

What in the hell am I sposed to know what they want, you know, unless they say this. These little guessin games, you know. These guys can be pretty rude when they wanna be. I have nothin personal against them, jus, damn. Some of the things they do are jus so idiotic, you know. If this what you have to do to get a date, you know, first thing you know you gonna start fuckin up, you know. Cause this has entered my mind several times: why the hell should I be over there on a block and have all these fuckin privileges and those other guys are bein locked in their cell, whole fuckin day, you know— they go to work, don't do a fuckin thing, you know, then get a date and go up there. Gee, I'm workin, I'm goin to school. I don't have any beefs—good work record and everything. Boom. Down again. It's pretty funky. Three times. This'll be my fourth time goin back up there. They shot me down two years the first time. Then a year. Then nine months. This'll be my fourth time.

I think I'll make it this time. I'm hopin like hell I do, you know. I go positive, you know, I don't think negative, because, um, everybody lookin forward for that date. It's a hell of a thing, you know. You never know when you get out, specially if you're doing five to life. You do ten tops, you know, "You can go kiss my ass." If you got five to life, you can't say, "Kiss my ass." Or nothin else. Jus have to bear with em.

They put different labels on you in here. Radical. If you wear your hair too long, you're a radical. If you wear your head shaved, you're Muslim. Same with the whites. If they wear their hair long, they're hippies or radicals, you know. Or wear dirty levis and strip go across their heads, well then they're radicals, you know. Jus doesn't make sense, because they put labels on you.

The parole board, they only look at the bad things. I went to the board the las time where everything The Man tells em was bad. I tell em, I says, "Wait a minute. Wait jus one minute. Listen now. If you turn the pages back, I know there's somethin good about me." I said, "Let's talk about some of that." The Man told em what's derogatory about me, you know. So I said, "Lemme hear somethin good," you know, "cause everybody like to hear somethin good about themselves, don't nobody wanna know nothin about the bad," you know. I said, "I already know the bad things." I said, "I'm here," you know. I said, "That's bad enough," you know. "So let's talk about some of the good things," you know. I'm a wise-ass, cause I make this statement.

Try to maintain your cool over there with em. They do things to try to make you blow it, you know, say things to you, you know, see if you will blow up.

"I don't think he's ready yet. He can't control himself."

I don't know what the hell they expect outta guy after bein in this fuckin place so long, you know. Everybody talks to him like he's a doll sometimes, you know. Then they get you up here, and they might just touch that old southy gentleman—or touch you somewhere where you don't wanna be touched, and then, Wow! you blow up.

"Aw, he's not ready. Come back an see us next year." You know. Walkin off another one.

You got a lotta guys in here that's academically smart enough to hold different positions and things. They won't let em do it, you know. They come in here, "We need some guys down in polish factory, gonna put you there," you know. Guys work a lotta places they don't wanna work, you know. Can't get into. Then you got some guys here that say, "I'm gonna do this, cause the board'll like this." And those guys get in those damn things and then they—jus for the board, you know. I say the hell with the board. I'm betterin myself in education here. I don't care about them. I'm goin to school. As far as a college education, the hell with the board. The board is not goin to do me no good when I get out on the street.

"What kind of an education background you have?"
"I got the board," you know.

CALIFORNIA INSTITUTION FOR MEN
JAMES M. CURTEY, INMATE

You go in sit in these very rooms before a member, and the first thing they'll do is start harassin you, get you mad, try to push the button. They never look—I've never been to a board meetin where they really look at anything constructive. They never said, "Why did you do it? How can we help you? What would you like?" They start hashin over things that's happened years ago—your past record that you've already served time for. They wanna chop this up and chop you up with it. They wanna get you so mad you wanna jump across the table at em.

Same thing around the joint. They have these group-counseling sessions—guys just sit up there and bitch about their troubles. They don't really get down to anything constructive. I have a counselor, and I don't care if you put it in all the newspapers—tell him, and he knows I say it—but the guy, he don't like a three- or four-time loser, he don't like a guy that drinks or writes checks. So here's a guy that's come up through the ranks from an officer to sergeant, lieutenant. When he goes into the parole board, he'll tell you, "I've gotta protect society—I can't let you out. You'll be swindlin somebody outta their money." Who is this guy to go in yakkin to the parole board, who's already prejudiced against me?

And parole board, for instance, Mr. Edmonds, goin before him a year ago—he's ex-district attorney from Fresno County—not only me, everybody—he sends men outta the room with tears in their eyes, they're so mad. Doesn't ask em one question: what can we do to help. Sends em out so mad they wanna kill him. The counselor writes reports that you don't see. He tells these people, "This guy's prognosis is not good, he's not ready for society. He's drunk and writes checks." And he don't really know you. He sees you on the yard every couple days. Speaks to you. He sits down to write a board report with you. He's got a hour, hour and a half he spends with you, asks you a few foolish questions. And this particular counselor asks you questions, and before you can answer em, he'll take you on a trip to New York where he lived when he was a kid, about a drunken brother-in-law he had, or somethin. So you never get an opportunity to tell him what you want.

They've got one board member who used to be a lieutenant across the street, Mr. Hoover, the most progressive man on the board. This guy'll overturn other people's decisions. He'll turn the people out. My prediction is, he'll go a long way. But he knows convicts and he's not afraid to put one on the street.

While we're talking about doin time, I think California has one of the most vicious parole systems in the world. For instance, you're walkin round the yard, you have a date, somebody agitates, you get in a fight, this fight can cost you a year. Or you don't have a date, and you're close to the board and you get in a fight. Or some guys'll make home brew, or some guy'll get high on pills, gets arrested for it, gets a disciplinary, and so he goes to the board, and they say, "Well you're not ready." That's a year sentence is what they're givin you. Now, I don't say I'm the most shinin example in the world. I've got a past record don't look good, but here I go to the parole board, I'm takin a year for a violation. I don't think that my counselor was qualified. He didn't represent me right. So as a result I come up with a eighteen-month date. Why all this time for nothin? In this system, in the State of California, they have a lotta guys come back, and they say the percentage is down now, but you can rest assured that fifty per cent of the guys that go outta here, if they could turn em out completely free, then they'd leave the state and they'd never hear from em again. But they send em out there on parole, they keep em under a tight supervision. The guy gets in a fight, and here he is back doin a couple of years for that.

INDIANA STATE PRISON
HENRY WALTERS, INMATE

The parole packet's kept handy because, you know, they have a high rate of recidivism. A lotta men are out of here only thirty days, and they're comin back here on parole violation. Could be anything. He could get a ticket for drivin while drunk or somethin. That's enough to bring him back. It could be sociatin that would bring him back. It depends. And in that case I jus run from vault three to vault four and get out the parole packet and bring it upstairs to the casework office, where it is immediately put back into the active file.

DISTRICT OF COLUMBIA JAIL
JOHN A. KNIGHT, INMATE

When you in jail, that's punishment any kind of way you go. To me it become almost just like a disease. Once you get out, you're put back in the same environment. If you can't have the proper trainin, you'll try and probly get a job an figure you can't make it on

79.

this job. And you know, it's environment that really cause the hassle. The guys here in the District—I can't speak for no other place bein here in the first place—it's environment that's causin em to be in here. So they go back in the same environment. If they don't have the proper trainin, they can't get nothin. And the worst thing about prison life is that it's no prison, I don't care they feed you steak three times a day, is a good prison—but the worst thing about prison, as far as I'm concerned, is the concern of the judges that sentence the man, the district attorneys that sentence a man. Like I got sentenced to twelve years, and actually, I believe the probation officer sentenced me. He told the judge I had one of the worst records he ever had, and that was the second offense that I had at the time, you know, other than my juvenile record, which they say don't count a whole lot against you.

There's a lotta guys in here need individual treatment, you know, really need individual treatment. Lotta guys in this field are really lost, lotta guys in this field. Psychiatrist told me over Saint Elizabeth once, I feel safe in jail.

I said, "I hate jail."

He said, "You know, you feel safe in jail. You have no trouble to go through."

An I been in the street. Actually been scared, you know, wonderin will I make it this trip. You realize, this last Christmas that went by was the first Christmas I spent in the street since nineteen forty-six.

When a man leave jail here—like a halfway house is what some of the best thing could happen for somebody to do. But most of the halfway houses which are, accordin to the zonin laws, is put right back in the environment what I was in. I had nothin against halfway house, some of the staff there. Which I was one of the first members of a therapeutic house, you know. But you put right back in the same—the guy's right back in the same place.

"I ain't got nothin. What else is there for me to do?" when he's back, I say, if he's not properly trained. An the people actually don't have money here for proper trainin.

The courts send you here, you know. Now why can't the courts—why don't some judges come here? They had some judges come down to Lorton when I was down there last. An a couple of em got sick, suffered from claustrophobia an everythin. They know bout jail. But, I mean, judges that give you the time, half of em never been there. Half of em never study a man's case an wonder why's this man keep comin back an forth to jail, why's he can't make it. What kinda problems he got? Is he alcoholic? drug addict? Or what is he? He jus can't adjust? You know. So what?

I'll say this here: anybody has to spend over five years in jail an come back for the second an third time, is somethin wrong with him. I went over Saint Elizabeth, sent over there by the court, an I talked to a doctor for fifteen minutes the whole time that I was over there. Fifteen minutes he gave me. The guys that see whether you sane or insane or what problem you have is their attendants.

Las time I got sentenced, I was out, I was helpin my older sister. I sent the probation officer aroun to talk to my older sister. My mother come over an visit me. I said, "Have the probation officer come roun to visit?" I said, "Have he been roun to see Mary?"

"No. He haven't been roun to see her yet."

That next week I went up an got my time. He still hadn't went roun to see—to interview the people out there. He jus took my record an look at it, you know, this man been through so an so. An that was it. That's the same way the judge looked at it.

I got out las time, I had a housebreakin. I got another three-to-nine in nineteen fifty-seven, which I'm presently doin. I also have a charge pendin. I did three years an somethin an was released by the parole board to a halfway house. I was makin it fairly good at the halfway house. I got an out-count, you know. But I had a problem up there. Problem was drinkin. I would drink, you know. I had used drugs. I tried to give that up, so I turned to alcohol. Then when I started to drink, I'm jus like a Dr. Jekyll, and I got a Dr. Jekyll and Mr. Hyde personality. This's it, you know. There's things that happened to me drinkin, I really don't even know how they happened or did they really happen, you know. I was tryin to struggle. I know if I keep workin, I would had to make it some kinda way, you know. But as it is, I got locked up on this charge and this is it.

You know, they twisted my mind for twenty-five years. You gotta get twisted mind. You away from everythin that you love, that you need, that you really want. You know you can't have it here. This is some of the punishment of bein locked up, you know.

A lotta people tell me that I don't look like I'm forty-four years old, you know. I don't know what in jail preserve you, but —some days I'm wonderin, you know, wonderin what's all this gonna come to. I get to the point where I get tied all up inside. So I don't know. It's jus like, I guess, a sentence to death. A death sentence. If they would be sentenced to death and go like that, all right. But a person's sentenced a long time in jail. You can believe he died a thousand deaths.

81.

One way or other, one way or other. An I've been in jail with some guys been in a long time, you know, they actually afraid to come in the street.

Mos thing that been on my mind: is there anythin that I can do to make it? Can I really make it if I try? You know, can I cope with the problem if, uh—in the long run, will I be one of the squares, that they say is in the street? Cause everybody here, they say everybody in the street—say, "You know so an so an so an so?"

Say, "Yeah, I used to go to school with him."

"I seen him an it's first time I seen him in twenty years."

"That square's still workin."

You know. But he never been in jail, see. I'm beginnin to believe that all the squares is really here, you know, an the hip ones, smart people, is in the street.

An when a guy get out, if he make parole straight—if he don't go to one of those work-release houses—save his money, he has some money when he get out, he has fifty dollars, he get out with that. Average guy get off the bus ain't got a hundred dollars when they get off the bus. An supposin they do have people that love em, but they don't have the place to put em, you know. So what is you gonna do? Say, "Well, it's all right?"

"You know you can't stay here. Go to such an such a house. I got ten kids."

Mama say, "Well, I don't have no place for you to stay here," you know. Try to help you, you know.

So now what are you gonna do?

If you ain't got no trade an you do get a job—you see, you gotta room, but you can't make it or you ain't makin ends meet, and the pressure get too tight, you gonna start usin drugs or drinkin. You gonna do somethin for pleasure, you know. And from then on—then you gonna say, "The hell with this. This is too hard." The struggle is hard, you know.

If I stay out late to a party, I gotta try to make it up in the mornin. Then I'm not at my party. Do give a man a good day's work, man'll still say somethin to you. An then if you gotta record, a lotta people might figure that the man is ridin you a little harder than he do the others. So you say, "The hell," you know, say to yourself, "why don't you take a five-minute walk in the place with a pistol and stick it up, or ten minutes of break-glass in the joint and go in there an steal something outta that cell? Or go in the shop, lift somethin an come out there?" Anythin, you know. Yoke a man, somethin like that, and say, "It ain't but gonna take a few minutes." You know, "An I don't have to work at this drudgery if I get away with it." That's the thing: "If I get away with it."

Like you read in the paper every year it snow up in Detroit for two or three days. It snow so deep, the bears an deers an stuff, they're comin to town. Animal or no, when you get hungry, he's goin any place he can to find some food, you know. So it's the same thing about a person out there in that jungle. That's all it is. Ain't nothin but a jungle. You know. He's gonna do what he can to survive.

I come outta Atlanta, I had a nice bit of money. Where I was raised up at there, it was Southwest. I don't know if you remember old Southwest? Wasn't nothin in it. It was mostly tore down. So there wasn't a whole lotta drugs. Nothin like that pushed around. So I started drinkin, drinkin, drinkin. Now an then I smoked some pot, you know. An now, like when I got out this trip here, I drink. I drink at the house, an the people I was stayin with was tellin me, "Well, you keep drinkin like this . . ."

I was workin. I said, "I am keepin a job. I'm drinkin an workin." But physically I wasn't doing nothin but killin myself. Because I'd come in—I got to the point where I wouldn't even sleep but maybe a couple hours. Then go to work. I worked down in Bethesda Hospital. Then I was workin at Washington Hospital up until I got arrested this trip here.

An many night when I was workin at Washington Hospital, I didn't come in. Like I'm on out-count, I mighta been in Southeast somewhere, so all I had to do was go back to the house-meetin maybe once, twice a week. So I'd go in the Southeast somewhere, you know, an stay up there til two-thirty in the morning, three o'clock in the morning. I had to be to work at seven o'clock. I could walk where I worked at Washington Hospital. But it was a struggle. I'd get up an try to make it, you know. I would make it. Try would make it. You know.

I was really scared, you know. An it's a thing where you ain't really into no crime or nothin like this here. If I had any intention to jus put my mind in crime, goin in the street an put my mind in any kinda crime, I wouldn'ta got a job in the first place, you know. Because I can't call myself no professional criminal. I haven't did nothin professional since I come to jail. Nothin. You know. I mean, these jobs is nothin professional.

So. I don't know. I needs some help from somewhere.

Maybe I jus wind up doin some time or get so old I jus probly won't come back to jail no more. You know.

Even me. Everybody say, "What could I do out there to keep from comin back to jail? What could I do? "Win some big money in a crap game?" You know, "Get me a nice apartment or a bed." An so an so an so. "Then I can make it from here, once I get a good start." You know, once you get that start, say, "I can make it from here." But can I make it from here? If I started drinkin or usin drugs, will I get this Dr. Jekyll, Mr. Hyde complex? I get sick off drugs, I gotta go somewhere steal some money. Drugs is takin up all the money. Physically I'm killin myself one way or the other. Or if I get drunk, I get to the point where I think that if nine hundred people is watchin me, I can steal somethin an get away with it, you know, cause I'm sick. I know I'm sick.

An you've actually got guys here right in jail that they can't get along—they can't adjust. You know, it's a certain thing to feel out if you don't know a thing. They never will ask. Well, I've always been curious if it was somethin I didn't know. I don't even read a book that I don't understan—if I don't understan, I go an ask anybody what is so an so. Jus like they found two young girls dead in apartment here about a week or so ago. An a young guy comes up, "What does decompose mean?"

I say, "It's rotten," you know. I say, "That's the best definition I can bring. It's rotten," when he came'n asked. But there's a lotta guys like that. He knew how to spell the word an know how to pronounce the word decompose, and he would jus go an he woulda never looked in the dictionary, you know or followed it up.

ARKANSAS STATE PENITENTIARY
WAYNE E. MIFLIN, INMATE TRUSTY

The people that come here, they can't adjust to this kinda environment, people really make clowns outta them. And not only the inmates tease em and harass em, but the freeworld people, too. It's better now. Some of the ones that are goin through the trainin school realize that these people really belong in a mental hospital. We had one guy, I think they interviewed him before they decided to get Mr. Lockhart for a superintendent or Mr. Hutton for a commissioner, I don't know which, ask him somethin bout would he like to work here after he took the tour, and he said No. He said he didn't have any background in a mental hospital. He said that's what it resembled to him.

There's a lotta people that are really sick. We have

one ole colored man, works out at the trash incinerator. He's only got three years. But he's been teased and harassed, beat on and jus cause —he's not an idiot, he's jus an old clown that enjoys everythin, anythin. He's so far out, he jus picks up—if they have pork chops bones with a little meat on em, he'll collect em all up durin the day, and he'll stick em in his pocket, and he'll go in and eat em late at night. He finds em in the garbage can. He doesn't know better. And he'll see a old dirty sock layin on the floor that belongs to somebody, and he'll grab it and run with it jus like it was his. They'll get mean, beat him up, take it away from him. He don't need to be here.

BUCKS COUNTY PRISON
MAJOR JOHN D. CASE, SUPERINTENDENT

Your jail is cluttered, any jail, with people with family problems, drunks, drug users, mentally ill, who are not the responsibility of the corrections system. And we are not really set up to treat those kind of people. But we get em, cause if you're a cop out there, and some guy is goin beserk, or he's drunk, or he's under the influence of drugs, or he's fightin with the old lady, if you don't have some alternative solution, the only thing you can do is bring him to jail. He goes to jail and, you know, in most places nothin's done for him at all. Just makes him bitter, and next time, instead of just beltin the old lady in the mouth, he's gonna kill her. You know. Then he's back for murder.

BUCKS COUNTY PRISON
PRESLEY MIDDLETON, CAPTAIN OF OPERATIONS AND
SECURITY

The warden's philosophy is to treat all these guys as patients. So if a man is a patient, he should be in a hospital. Not in a jail. This is not a hospital. This is a cage within a cage, I guess. You lock a man in, it's like lockin an animal into a cage, and that's it. And the way it go here, poor guy goes to court, some guys go through this sixty days of observation, I guess, in Byberry State Hospital down here in Norristown. And from what I gather from some of the guys that came back, for sixty days all they did was give em drugs. Had em all pepped up for sixty days and that was it. The doctor seen em one day outta sixty. Send em back and say, "Okay, this guy's ready for trial." And you need hospitals is what you need—clinics, lotta clinics for the drug addicts. And maybe that's the answer. That is the answer. But again, there's no funds, no money. "We're in the red," they say all the time. We're never ahead, we're always behind, I guess.

And the strange thing about our law, so funny, that a guy can snap out down'n the community, the cops can arrest him, but the cops have no authority to put the guy in a hospital. The only place they can bring him is right here. The guy who goes beserk down there'n the county, handcuff him, stomp him to death, bring him up here, leave him in our jail—he's our problem. We can get him into the hospital. But it seems kinda ridiculous. Sometime it takes a little while to get a man processed—paperwork, judge to approve it—to get a guy—if he's insane or he's really strung out, we cannot get him to the hospital, but we go through nine hundred ritual of gettin him in the hospital. And we got a lot of guys on over'n there now that shoulda been in the hospital months ago. People, they are bein neglected. The outside is not thinkin about the guy on the inside here. They're bein neglected. The guys should be in hospitals.

CALIFORNIA STATE PRISON AT SAN QUENTIN
LOUIS S. NELSON, WARDEN

Rehabilitation? I don't like that word, cause I don't know if that ever happens. In the first place, rehabilitation means returning to his former state. I don't know that we wanna do that. We don't wanna return him to society as a criminal. That's what it came to in a sense. But if you think it's some sort of modification of attitudes, hell yes. There's some changes in people's attitudes and behavior patterns and life styles that occur within the institution. So let's look at it coolly. Seventy per cent of our people that go through these prisons in California never return in two years. So something has happened to them. Something has happened to people while they're here in our institutions. They didn't come to us that way; they left us that way. There's been some transformation. I think it's utterly ridiculous our critics to say people that succeed succeed in spite of the prisons, those that fail fail because of the prisons. I think if we're going to get the blame, we must assuredly get part of the credit. So we must be doing something right if seventy per cent of our people stay out.

DISTRICT OF COLUMBIA CORRECTIONAL COMPLEX
JOHN O. BOONE, SUPERINTENDENT OF ADULT SERVICES

Prison has completely failed to rehabilitate. You will find isolated instances of success, where a man more or less pulls himself up by his own bootstraps in prison. We got token vocational trainin, and we are better than average. We have twenty caseworkers. The average prison don't have any hardly. Six psychologists. But even with what we have, we admit that this is just a beginnin.

ATTICA CORRECTIONAL FACILITY
MATTHEW BAKER, INMATE

You just can't treat people like animals and expect to accomplish anything. You can't rehabilitate them by beating their heads against the wall or having them beat their own head against the wall continuously, because there's nothing there. You're not really taking anything away; you're not really giving them anything. You're giving them plenty of time to think, right? Right. But just what's this guy gonna think about? How bitter he is? How bad the system is? What the hell. A guy starts reasoning with himself, eventually he'll grow bitter. He'll say, "The hell with it. When I get out I'll just do the same thing over again."

I'm institutionalized to a certain point, but you get guys here been in jail five, ten years, you know, and they're doing life. What the hell kind of chance has this guy got to make it on the street? And so he figures, "What the hell. I might as well just go ahead and be here"—nothing about rehabilitation. And they get adjusted in their own society, calling a penitentiary or jail a society, which it actually is.

DISTRICT OF COLUMBIA CORRECTIONAL COMPLEX
LOWELL MILLER, INMATE

I think that prison life slowly works away at a man. And I seem to feel that it's aimed at destroying people. You have to fight this feeling of ineptness. When you're in jail, you feel so worthless. You don't feel like anything at all. You can't accomplish a thing.

CALIFORNIA STATE PRISON AT SAN QUENTIN
LOUIS S. NELSON, WARDEN

First and foremost, of course, the prisons are established here to do what society wants them to do, that is, to take these people out of their midst. Society gets uncomfortable with a man, and they no longer tolerate him. Then they banish him somewhere. There's no place to banish them to anymore, so they put an island like this to banish them to. So they want themselves protected from this individual. The thing we don't talk about very much: prisons are meant to punish people. They're set up to punish people. The penal code is to inflict penalties on somebody, or sanctions. You can call it anything you want. You can talk about taking sanctions against a person, inflicting discipline upon him, all those are mealy-mouth terms for the fact that you're gonna punish the guy.

Discipline means other things, too. But in the final

analysis, society needs to feel, I think, in their own conscience, that when a guy violates our laws we're gonna punish him. And they feel a little better because they've punished him. They feel better. It may be tragic, but nevertheless, it's true. And I don't really think it's too tragic by virtue of—if we drive down the highway, why do we drive at sixty-five miles an hour instead of a hundred? We drive because we're afraid somebody's gonna punish us. If a highway cop stops us, he isn't gonna talk to us about rehabilitation; if we go in front of the judge, the judge isn't gonna try to plan a big program for rehabilitation; what he's gonna say is, "It's gonna be sixty-five dollars," or "thirty-five dollars," to remind you that it shouldn't be done again. That's punishment. That's hitting you in the pocketbook. It punishes us. It doesn't really benefit us. It may be corrective, but primarily it's meant to punish us for violating the law.

So. We do punish. And anybody who thinks we don't and prison people who say, "Hell, no, we don't punish," are talking out of the wrong side of their mouth, because we do punish. And we have to be free to admit that prisons do punish. And I don't care if you establish a prison in the center of San Francisco, for instance, in the Hilton Hotel, and you threw a cordon of people around it and kept everybody in there, punishment would ensue as a matter of course—they're held there against their will. You don't need to go further than that, incidentally. You don't have to take somebody out and put him in the pillory or the stocks or whip him every day, to inflict punishment. You do have to regiment as a matter of course in order to have some orderly flow of movement. And to get people up, for instance, for breakfast in the morning, there has to be some regimentation. So all these things do afford some system of punishment, or some semblance of punishment, because you're talking about people who don't necessarily have good judgment and part of their punishment is association with each other. That's built-in punishment, too.

That sort of punishment is not my doing. Society sets that up. See, we can run prisons any way society wants us to: if society wants us to lock people up and chain them to the wall and throw away the key, we can do that. It would be tragic, but nevertheless, we could do that. It's done in some countries. This is what society's ordained. I'm a civil servant, and I'm paid by the members of society, and they have a right to dictate what I do as long as I can be within my own conscience. I couldn't do that sort of thing—just lock people up and forget about them. But I fully subscribe to the philosophy that if a man does wrong, society has a right to deal with him. And if they take sanctions against him, which includes punishment, I don't think this is wrong. I don't think that vengeance is all the right of the Lord's. I think society has a right to rise in their wrath and say to a man, "If you do something, we're gonna punish you by doing this and that and the other thing, including capital punishment." I think the state has the right to go all that distance.

I think society doesn't really owe these people inside very much. I think that we owe them certain things, because we are what we are, not because they are what they are. We owe them the right to be treated like human beings, to give them the dignity and respect to which human beings are entitled so long as they act like human beings. And it's difficult to do in many cases. When somebody spits in your face, it's difficult to smile back and say, "Thank you." I say literally, not figuratively but literally spit in your face. But I think we should treat them like human beings because we are human beings. They're entitled to that sort of treatment. We should afford them the opportunity to improve themselves. We cannot force them to improve themselves. We can only make it available to them. We are only part of it.

I've spent much time and effort in attempting to study the motivation of people behind these walls. And nobody has come up with a satisfactory answer, how to motivate people. They're motivated by many things. People are motivated by so many things that you can't write any specific or any general plan for motivation. I think the thing that I am more concerned about than anything else is: we need to research what we are doing. And if the things we are doing have no effect, then we ought to have guts enough to cut them out. And if we find that some things are more effective than others, we should increase those—we should direct our efforts towards that end. But I don't know. If somebody was to ask me, "If you had a million dollars, how much more good could you do?" I'd have to say the same thing that the President of the American Corrections Association said: "Don't give us any more money to spend until we find out what we're doing."

There's one hundred and two on our death row. One hundred and two sentenced to death in California. Ninety-two here, five out to court and five at the California Institution for Women. So there's ninety-two on the death row in the residence and five out to court. That's a new high.

The pressures have diminished over the past—really since nineteen sixty-three. See, there's only been one execution since January twenty-third, nineteen sixty-three. There was one in nineteen sixty-seven, but there was intervening nine years now, there was only

DEATH ROW, CALIFORNIA STATE PRISON AT SAN QUENTIN, 1969.

this one execution. So the pressures have been diminished. I think the men in death row today are living in a sort of limbo. They don't believe that the death penalty is ever going to come back, yet they're fearful that the Supreme Court is going to rule that it's constitutional. So the pressure's not as great. I can remember here many years when the number of people on death row varied from seventeen to twenty, went about like that, and we got the feeling that if it got up to about twenty-two, we would about reach our maximum. Over seventeen, the problems in death row increased in greater number in relationship to the people received. In other words, if it was eighteen, there was more problem than seventeen, but lot more than one more problem just because one more person came in. So it's certainly a lot of pressure. But the pressure is nothing at this point until such time as the Supreme Court decision comes down. If the Supreme Court decision happens to uphold the constitutionality of the death sentence, then there will be pressure on men in death row, and they will feel the pressure. And it still won't reach a climax until the first person's executed—one is. Then they'll feel the pressure, because the flurry of legal activity and the strain on the nerves of the men will increase one hundredfold.

I think the Supreme Court can't fail to uphold the constitutionality of it, because the founding fathers, when they wrote the Constitution, provided for the death penalty in certain instances.

Under the law I have to attend. Well, it's a hell of a poor way to spend a morning. The only reason that I stay away from death row as much as I do is cause I don't want to become emotionally involved. Because for a number of years I was directly in charge of the people on death row, and I got to know them all as individuals. And that time we didn't have very many, so you could know them all. So it was a much more difficult thing. And I was not the warden at that point. But I had to be present at every execution. I was second in command and I was standing by in case the warden keeled over. The attorney general had ruled that the next in command had all the authority of the warden in a case like that, so the execution could proceed. And it's a difficult thing. The difficult thing is the part leading up to the execution: the few minutes of preparation, the few minutes you're there that—and having to tell the man that there's apparently no legal action pending, there's nothing to stop the execution at this point except for a phone call from the governor. And that's the only thing. Or a phone call from the judge. But there're no legal matters by this time. We have generally got all those matters out of the road before we go to the gas chamber. Always the most dreadful part for me was waiting about seven or eight minutes to the point of time until the clock's hand gets around and the warden nodded his head, which started the execution. Everything beyond that was anticlimactic to me. Because once the man is strapped in, and the chamber is sealed and tested, that action was kind of remote then—it was kind of off in another room. And aside from offering a prayer for the repose of your soul, there was nothing to do except stand and wait until he was pronounced dead. Because, I say, that was over the hump. Once the pellets were dropped, it was over the hump. You leave there, of course, there's a tragic thing, but you don't have to do much more than go back and read the circumstance of the crime and you could see generally why the citizens, State of California, said he should be put to death. I don't think I'm any more responsible for the death than the judge, the jury, the district attorney, or for that matter, the defense attorney—all as citizens of the State of California. I think if it came to a vote, they'd uphold it by about eighty-five to fifteen out of every hundred votes. I'm not opposed to death penalty. I'm sure as hell opposed to the way it's administered. Man should be up on death row twelve or fourteen years, it's utterly incredible to me the law would insist now in 1972 we execute a man for a crime committed in 1958. I don't see any justice in that sort of administration of justice. If there's any justice to the death penalty, the man should be executed within a relatively short period of time after his case goes up to the California Court of Appeals. Then it's held his legal rights were protected, and the evidence showed beyond the shadow of a doubt he was guilty, then I think the execution should be carried out as swiftly and as quietly as possible—not allowed to languish up there forever. That seems terrible to me.

CALIFORNIA INSTITUTION FOR MEN
JOSEPH A. MCCAGAR, CORRECTIONAL OFFICER

Well, I've been lucky over the years. I've had a few times that I've been scared, tried not to show that I was scared. Let me start from the bottom. When I was up at San Quentin I knew that I would only be up there until such time as I get transferred down here, because I had my home down here. At that time they were usin the gas chamber quite a bit. I was livin on the grounds up there in what they call alimony row, because my family was down here. Every time they would hold an execution they had to have, I think it was, thirteen or seventeen civilian witnesses. Then you have to have a certain number of officers to supervise the visitors. In order to keep them from holdin over some of the guys, waitin to go home, I thought that long as I lived there,

ELECTRIC CHAIR, OSSINING CORRECTIONAL FACILITY, NEW YORK, 1940.

I might as well see the whole show. So I witnessed four of em while I was up there. I don't think it did a bit of harm, I think this was a real good experience.

The civilian witnesses up there, when they congregate at about a quarter to ten in the mornin, the second-watch lieutenant comes out and gives em a talk, and he explains to em in a very nice manner that they are gonna see a human bein die, and they need not have any reluctance about this, they need not fear, because they are not takin the man's life, it's the state that's gonna take his life. And the state requires—that's all they're there for, is to witness the act. And they have to sign the ledger, of course, as a witness.

This seems to settle the people right down. Now, when you're in there as a spectator, and these civilians in that area, you have one or two that'll get sick, and you have to escort them out.

You see a man out on the street get killed, like in a car accident, this is one thing. When you see that a man is almost gonna be brought in and die by the numbers, it's no accident. It puts a whole different face on the thing.

There was a notorious case out here many years ago. Man named Billy Cook, out here in California. He used to hitchhike, and whatever people would pick him up he would kill em, bury their bodies, go on with the car. He had one indictment in California, and that was the one they happened to get him for. This was all written up in Life magazine. This was a pretty horrible crime, and the state had no trouble that time gettin thirteen witnesses. I think there were fifty-seven people witnesses in there. The amazin thing: usually outta your thirteen witnesses you'll have one or two get sick, and I saw fifty-seven people that day stand and watch him goin, and nobody got sick. It shows how much public feelin was against this particular individual.

Probably the first one I saw was the most profound. This was a guy who'd been picked up as a drunk. They put him in the drunk tank in jail, and they hadn't segregated them. And he got in an argument with somebody else in the tank and stomped the guy to death. Now here was somebody who was just a wino—didn't have anything. So he got the gas chamber for that. This was the first one I saw. When they dropped the cyanide pellets, when the man first gets a whiff, it's a very strange thing to watch. He'd take a big breath like that, and his tongue would begin to come out. It doesn't take many minutes for a man to die that way, and I guess it is pretty humane, because I think after the first lungful I don't think they're still alive or functionin in any way. They're alive, that's all.

94.

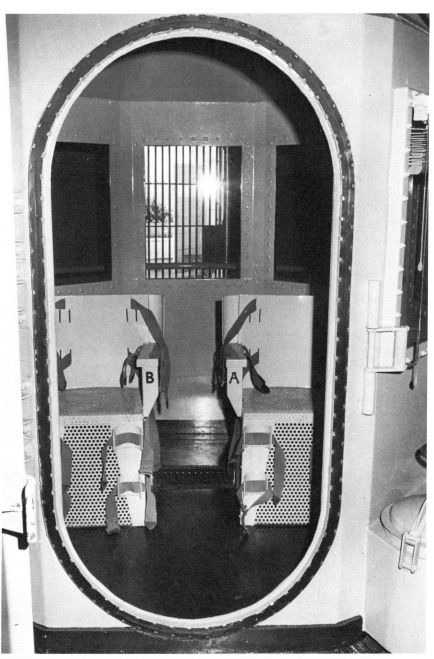

EXECUTION CHAMBER, CALIFORNIA STATE PRISON AT SAN QUENTIN, 1969.

Well it was profound in this respect: that I never seen—like a man be brought in and put down in the chair and be strapped down there for the explicit purpose of dyin—I had never seen this before. In the service you see a guy that gets hit by fragments of a bomb and he's dead. They're in an airplane—guys got crashed in their airplane, and their skulls are only that big around when you see em, all burned to a cinder. Accident. But this is not accident. You ordinarily would have a lotta sympathy for this man, but then when you remember the pep talk that they give to the witnesses, then you also remember, well, this guy is not in here for stealin hubcaps. He's in here for takin a life. It kinda puts you emotionally neutral.

The fallacy of it accordin to my feelin is this: usually the guy that winds up in the gas chamber is the guy that has nobody and no money behind him. Now there are murders committed every single day. A lotta authorities will say, "Well, the gas chamber is no deterrent. We used to put people in the gas chamber and we still had murders goin on." But I like to look at it another way. Supposin the President of the United States right today was to come on television, radio, and in the newspaper, and he was to serve twenty-four-hour notice on the American public to say that every murder in the first degree, startin tonight at midnight, if the murderer is caught he'll be executed within thirty days. Now if you knew that to be a fact, and if I knew that to be a fact; then let's say we still find this hard to believe, but lo and behold, after thirty days this state executes five, this state executes seven, this state executes eleven. It's really bein carried out. Now, then, I think you're gonna find it's a terrific deterrent. It never really has been carried out.

CALIFORNIA STATE PRISON AT SAN QUENTIN
GEORGE RUSSELL TOLSON, CHAPLAIN

I've only had a couple of executions since I've been here. The last one I had was a very beautiful experience. This fellow was considered to be a monster by the papers and so on and so forth. From my point of view he was an exceedingly soft, sensitive person who was as outraged by his behavior as the society was. And he honestly maintained that he did not want to live if this was the kind of thing he was capable of doing. And he didn't think that he really was conscious of what he was doing, but he was convinced that he'd done it just as the rest of us were convinced he'd done it. And he didn't want to go on living if that was possibility. But he certainly wanted to get himself right with God.

And we talked a great deal about that. We had a baptism. And we used a fellow mate as the deacon for the baptism in the cells. And that man is today one of my best friends.

Very moving and beautiful experience. This man I attended daily almost until his execution, and I went with him as far as I could go. And he was such a magnificent demonstration to all of us of courage and faithfulness that even the warden said it was one of the finest experiences he's ever had with a person. And of course that made it a fine experience for me. It did happen, and I'm very grateful that I've had that experience. It will always make that aspect of my work easier, I am sure, to know that it's possible.

I take the statement in the Bible about " 'Vengeance is mine,' sayeth the Lord," very seriously. I don't believe there's any place in life among human beings for punishing one another. I like to think in terms of consequences.

CALIFORNIA INSTITUTION FOR MEN
GUFF A. ROREX, CORRECTIONAL OFFICER

The convicts write letters. It all comes down to the mail room unsealed. We have a Pitney Bowes machine there, that either seals or seals'n stamps, whatever's necessary, and we run it through and gettin it ready to go to the post office, which I pick up about eight-thirty or eight-twenty. Up until recently, why, a certain percentage had to be censored. But there's no censorin done either comin in or goin out anymore. But it still comes in—the officers out there don't have the time to seal it, and of course, runnin it through that machine, doesn't take us very long to seal it. Mail to courts or assemblymen or senators, governor, any of that, they can seal it themselves. But the other mail has to be left open. I don't know why. We don't look at it. We jus dump it in a big bunch and we jus run it through the machine and seal it up.

Somewhere's around eight-thirty or eight-twenty we take it up to the post office, pick up all the convicts' mail, California Institution for Men minimum security, and for the guidance center, which is maximum–close security. And that mail is left over at the guidance center, and the other mail is brought over here—convicts' mail and institution mail both. Takes, let's say, roughly an hour to make that run.

Then we have to take and separate that mail and open it and check it for contraband or money—mostly money. Any money that comes in, we keep in the mail room and sent it down to the business office so it can go on their account, cause they're not allowed to have cash, jus scrip. Then they're issued this scrip, that they can spend out at the canteen.

It has to come in as a money order. They have a rulin here that cash cannot be accepted. We have to return to the sender and explain. We have a regular little form that we put in there and mark what's wrong and explain it. And they can send it back as a money order made out to the California Institution for Men with the man's name and, if possible, his prison number.

They can write to anyone they want to now, and the mailin card is out in the unit where the fellow lives, and the only thing that they keep track of now is legal mail. And they lay out legal mail. Then that is supposed to be registered on their mailin card. We don't keep track of any of it. What we do keep track of is if he has money in there that has to be returned to sender, we keep track of that. We have a record of that and we have a record of all money comin in.

Personally, I think the courts are wrong goin so far. I think they've gone too far. But that's their problem and the heads of the institution. This freedom of speech and freedom of constitution rights, as far as I'm concerned, has gone too far because they've forgotten about the constitution rights of Mr. Average Citizen, who pays the bill out there. I think sometime they go so far on these others it impinges on his rights. And he hasn't done anything to cause these rights to be infringed on. So I think, as far as I'm concerned, they've gone over backwards on these constitution rights of the fellow that commits the crime. I mean, be fair with him but I don't believe in mollycoddlin him.

CALIFORNIA STATE PRISON AT FOLSOM
EARL STRAUB, CORRECTIONAL OFFICER

Like today, inmates' checks that come through the mail have to be endorsed by the individual to be deposited to their trust fund. So they have a procedure whereby the checks or the money orders that come through the mail, they are set aside, and then on Thursday these people that have checks will be called into a certain office to sign their checks. And they give me that responsibility of taking the checks down on Thursdays and having the individuals come in and sign them. And that takes sometimes an hour and a half, sometimes two hours by the time you get ten or fifteen signatures. Of course if they're over there in adjustment center, they're in the hospital, you carry the check to the hospital, or out at the ranch, you know, that inmate may come in from the ranch. But that's just one of the other activities of the week for a utility officer.

CALIFORNIA INSTITUTION FOR MEN
GUFF A. ROREX, CORRECTIONAL OFFICER

On Sundays, by nine-thirty we have the outgoin mail all ready to go out, and I go out to the main gate and work out there. That's when the visitors come—Saturdays and Sundays. Saturdays I stay in the mail room all day. But Sundays I have that time where I go out there.

We have to process those visitors. Visitors have to register. We have visitin cards for all the convicts. The names are on the visitin cards of who he wants to visit him. And if they haven't been there before, they have to fill out an application and be interviewed, and if the convict wants him on his visitin card, it's up to him to have em on his card. And if they bring in packages the man in here has requested—he has sent them a form that has been signed by the officer sayin he's still allowed this much stuff. We have to check that in and take just a rough look to see they don't bring in any liquids. They can bring in picnic lunches, but any liquids they want they can buy outta the canteen. And once in while a bottle'll get by, I guess. You can't run a place like this without stuff gettin in that's not supposed to. Jus impossible.

Most of the people that come in to visit are real friendly, and once in a while we'll get one that tries to cause trouble. We had one woman that'd come in and make up stories. She had a chip on her shoulder. Put in complaints on various officers. They'll come in sometimes mad, because they can't bring in this and that, and clothes they can't wear, like coats that match the color of our green uniforms or our khaki uniforms—tan or white shirts they can't have, they can't have neckties, tan jackets.

They're allowed only a certain amount of goodies they can bring in from the visitin ground to their unit. They got too many cookies or that type of thing out there it causes ants and roaches problem. Anything extra is picked up, confiscated. That's on Saturday and Sunday. Then Sunday afternoon that's all taken to the mail room and listed, and it's taken and donated to the Boys' Republic—that a boys' home, which is a home over here about a mile and a half, two miles.

99.

MESS HALL, DISTRICT OF COLUMBIA CORRECTIONAL COMPLEX, LORTON, VIRGINIA, 1933.

# LUNCH.

CALIFORNIA STATE PRISON AT FOLSOM
EARL STRAUB, CORRECTIONAL OFFICER

They're all back in adjustment center. Approximately ten-thirty, quarter of eleven, we go down and bring up the lunch food to our particular floor. It's brought into holding boxes, that are heated downstairs, and we bring it up in trays and buckets that they have from the kitchen—they call em flatheads—and whatever happens might be in the serving trays. And that's carried upstairs and portioned out on a moving cart. We put the food on the cart, push the cart down the tier, and serve each tray right there. It's put on metal trays with compartments for each food and served directly to the inmate off the cart. Officers serve. There's one inmate that passes out the coffee, and sometimes if he gets through with the coffee soon enough, which is ahead of the cart, he'll come back and help, assist in serving the food out to the tray. But the officer carries the tray to the cell.

It takes approximately twenty minutes to serve forty-six people on one floor. As much as they eat, which is usually very little, it doesn't take them any longer than ten or fifteen minutes. The first man starts eating, and twenty minutes later we're coming back out. So normally he's just finished his tray and have it set up on the cell tray area, and we go through and start to pick it up, pick up the garbage and tray and clean it up and on to the next one. He has approximately

101.

twenty minutes to eat. We count the trays. The man is issued a plastic spoon when he comes into the institution. So all we would pass out with the food would be a bowl, soup bowl, and metal cup for coffee, metal tray. We count these coming back, make sure that we have exact number that went in there.

After the trays are back, we clean up the trays and carry the empty utilities and the garbage down to the first floor to be let out of the adjustment center when it's all accumulated from all three floors. And about, I'd say around twelve o'clock, we're all through with the feeding of the inmates, time you start to feed them and time you pick up the trays and clean the garbage, let the garbage out. And they have one inmate out who is a worker, he stays out all day, and he does the mopping up and the cleaning up of the pushcart, the food cart.

Officers, we have no lunch, we have no lunch period. When you eat, you bring your lunch in. It's strictly an eight-hour position, that you be in your position. I never eat. I bring an apple and I have for the last six or seven years. And that's what I eat at lunch time.

DISTRICT OF COLUMBIA CORRECTIONAL COMPLEX
JOSEPH SAKALAUKAS, SERGEANT, CORRECTIONAL FORCE

When inmate's in control cell, the instructions we have is to give a full meal, a full meal. And at one time they took em off the full meal and gave em Metracal, a full ration of Metracal. I guess everybody's heard about the bread and water thing. I've heard from some of the people over here twenty-five, thirty years ago, how it was. But for ten years I've been here, it's never been that way.

The only restrictions we might of had is if a piece of meat had a bone in it or something like this, we'd try to eliminate that part of it, so he couldn't get a weapon. Cause you can make some nasty things out of bones. I don't know if you've seen some of the devices they've made. But I've seen one of the sharpest instruments I've ever seen made out of a toothbrush handle. That's hard plastic. And I mean, you could shave with it. This is something that you assume a man needs, but when you give it to him, you have to control those things. But we do try to give boneless meat, this sort of thing, you know, here.

FEDERAL DETENTION HEADQUARTERS
ANTHONY CORCIONE, CORRECTIONAL OFFICER

Count recall for lunch is ten-thirty in the morning. And they normally open the chow line about ten forty-five, eleven o'clock. We have early chow here. Normally the boiler room eats early chow—the guys that work on the detail I do. First-floor sanitation, the receiving area, and the people that work in the kitchen eat early. Then they start moving the population down around eleven-thirty. Normally about an hour to eat. And they feed around two hundred men here, and the chow seats about forty men at a time. They move them in. The reason you have count recall, they lock everybody up and they move like thirty men at a time. They call up and say, "Send thirty." As soon as these people start leaving the chow, they send thirty more. And most of the guys understand that you only have a short time to eat, so they don't sit around and talk, they move on and let somebody else get it.

CALIFORNIA INSTITUTION FOR MEN
GUFF A. ROREX, CORRECTIONAL OFFICER

For the last year they've had the mail officer go out to the dinin hall and watch the line on the outside so these fellas don't keep jumpin in front of others and causin trouble. Well, some of these fellas will come up to the main kitchen, they line up longside of the buildin, and when they start to feed, why the doors open and they start in. So if the line's been there and another man comes up and gets into line, sometimes they'll jus be talkin to a friend of theirs til they get almost to the door, but if they try to go in to eat, then that man is sent back to the back of the line for jumpin line. So that's what causes some of the fights. Fella will say—maybe it's his friend—will say, "Sure, get in here," and save him a place. But the fellas in back that aren't his friends take objection to it an there has been some pretty good fights out there over it.

I might say, oh, "Fella, you jus jumped line back there and that jus doesn't work, so you'll have to go to the back of the line." Oh, sometimes they'll give you an argument, but they'll always go.

Lotta the time I jus bring a couple of sandwiches and eat em. If we're real busy I jus eat it right while I'm workin. With a little bit of slack, why then I'll take ten minutes, fifteen to eat my sandwich. Sometimes I'll get somethin outta the lounge.

The personnel have a lounge that they can go to. This is run by the California Institution for Men's Employees' Association. And they have convicts that do all the cookin, a manager that oversees them, and they put out pretty good food there. At noon they have a regular meal. Then the rest of the time it's jus sandwiches of different kinds, coffee, milkshakes. Well, the other day we had—I had a little time so I went down to eat—and I had a Spanish plate which was real

103.

CHOW, DEATH ROW, CALIFORNIA STATE PRISON AT SAN QUENTIN, 1969.

good. And sometimes they have pork ribs, maybe chicken, spareribs. It varies. Usually about three entrees. Costs eighty-five cents to a dollar usually.

CALIFORNIA STATE PRISON AT FOLSOM
GARCIA PEREZ, INMATE

Oh, about ten-thirty, then it's lunch time. They start lining up on the yard about that time. You can hear the whistles blowing. I go to lunch most of the time. The lines are longer when there's somethin that's considered a choice lunch, like maybe bacon and cheese sandwiches. This is the hot lunch meal, the best one compared to maybe some of the others. Yesterday, oh, lemme see, soup, vegetable soup, cold cuts. Some unspectacular thing. Usually it's macaroni or baked beans and corn bread—jus things. You don't really remember—they all blend in.

Takes, I'd say, about half an hour. I do a little more talkin durin lunch, sit with different guys. Most of the times we have things in common that we maybe cut up there. It's not that hard to sit with who you want to sit with. It's no problem there. There's no set time to go back to work so long as it's before twelve. In my case, if I have a lotta work I try to get back as quick as I can. If not, I just maybe walk the yard, exercise a little. Talk. Kinda just stretch out for half an hour, an hour sometimes, dependin on the conversation—if I'm on a real heavy trip, you know.

CALIFORNIA INSTITUTION FOR MEN
SANCHO SUAREZ, INMATE

Lunch is served here about eleven-thirty and it's over at twelve. Outta the month I go maybe once to eat there. I eat mostly underhand things. I stay away from sweets. We have other little underground movements or I get visits and sometimes get some fruits or some cake. Or usually I'll have that or else kick back and drink me a cup of coffee.

Since they don't shut the print shop, I'm there durin the noon hour runnin what you call my underground paper. It consists of nothing but facts, the truth, the way the Department of Correction does treat the inmates throughout the penal system in the State of California, not because it's a breakdown of black or white, it's just because we're convicts—that is the basic discrimination here with the majority of the correctional officers. It goes out to the outside. Right now I'm workin on my next issue. I write it myself and some of the other brothers here, and contributors from the outside. We call it La

Raza and Pinta Habla Aslam. Aslam is the Southwest. Pinta is convict. And Habla is to speak. We run about six or seven hundred copies. It's actually almost into a booklet form. It's not one of those regular newsletters that they have over the Department of Corrections over in CIM. Because first of all there's only one newsletter they allow here, which is the Pardoner's News, that is handlin nothin but publicity the administration has in there. The truth does not come out, and all they want to hear is what the administration wants to say. So with this we have to let the public know what is actually happenin inside the joint, not what they hear on the news. Sure, you know, you'll hear that there's a stabbin. But why? They only say there was a stabbin, but they don't tell you why.

It takes me a little over a month to get out my full edition, because I have to do it in chapters—got to hide the plates and everything. Basically I have durin the noon hour forty-three minutes and thirty seconds exactly. If I run, let's say for example, I'll use a small figure, let's say five hundred copies, I'll be able to run about maybe two thousand pages, but which consists of four pages, maybe a little less. Sometimes I have a little problem with the machine. Once I have it typed, then it's takin it to the photo so a positive can be made outta it. Then durin the coffee breaks when The Man's gone, I get my plates together and my negatives, strip it then, burn my plates, develop it, and have it ready.

I work on it myself since I don't go eat chow at noon. And since this is what I call a hot item here. If I get caught with it, I get busted, my date taken away. Cool, you know. But there will be another brother that will continue the struggle.

ARKANSAS STATE PENITENTIARY
SAMUEL LEXINGTON, INMATE GUARD

Load em on the truck, they go in an eat their dinner, take em back to work. Everybody eats together. All the freeworld people, state troopers, police, come in with their guns, check in their guns—they got inmate guard out there that receives your guns; when you get ready to leave, he hands it back to you.

They got a freeworld man at the gate and an inmate at the gate. Inmate on each tower, twelve-hour shifts—there's one for a day shift, and one for a night shift, all inmates. And down here in the hall they got inmates guardin the hall and help the freeworld people keep the count, keep order. Then you got your gun cages on the end,

106.

guns and clubs and tear gas in case they have any trouble, like a riot or somethin. They gotta man that guards that.

They give you a well balanced diet: meat and you get vegetables, cake and fruit cocktail; you get milk, tea, orange juice. Kool-Aid or somethin. You gotta woman up there—she's a dietician—she writes out the menu. And then they got supervisors to prepare, and they got inmates to cook. You get fed pretty fair. It's not what you get downtown. Better'n nothin. I haven't lost any weight in six months.

CALIFORNIA STATE PRISON AT SAN QUENTIN
LOUIS S. NELSON, WARDEN

Lunch yesterday I had tuna fish sandwich and a piece of blackberry pie. I ate in the employee snack bar. If I eat here on the grounds, I eat in the employee snack bar. Today I'm going to be in Palo Alto speaking to the Los Altos Kiwanis Club, so I'll have lunch down there today, but generally at least four days a week I eat here on the institution grounds. I try to get away for lunch with some friends or with local law-enforcement officials, I generally try to get away one day a week and have lunch off the grounds to do some sort of community relations.

INDIANA STATE PRISON
WILLIAM SIMMONS, INMATE

Beans, lunch meat. Once in a while they have hamburger, pork steak. I'd say on average I eat one meal a day, lunch or supper. Well, I think they have the ingredients. I believe it's in the preparation. I know it's difficult to cook for a large number of men but it seems like it could be done better—seasoning and taking a little more care in how they do it. It's prepared by cons, and they don't have a great amount of interest in what they're doing, I imagine, and they're not very careful.

I look at the menu, what they have, and take my choice. They have a commissary, so fortunately I can get a few things off the commissary to kind of make up for the lost meal. Well, they have, just like a grocery store, they have crackers, ah, bread, peanut butter, canned goods, they have a pretty good variety. It's pretty high, high price: can of peaches, thirty-five cents a small can; loaf of bread, thirty-three cents; Ritz crackers, forty cents a box; cigarettes, twenty-nine cents a pack. I usually buy bread every week and rolls, peanut butter, different types of cookies. Course all this is—I wouldn't be able to eat it if I didn't get money from home. So, ah, like I said, I'm pretty fortunate.

107.

MESS HALL, CALIFORNIA STATE PRISON AT SAN QUENTIN, 1966.

This institution has changed since the last so-called riot. I see minor changes on the food line. The tea is a little sweeter. They have Kool-Aid on the line. Stupid changes. Nothin really beneficial.

INDIANA STATE PRISON
EARL GRADY, INMATE

Garbage, garbage. You know by garbage I mean you got a basic diet of mashed potatoes and gravy and beans. This is the basic diet. Lunch meat. Baloney, piece of baloney. Couple hot dogs sometimes. They just change the shape of it, you know, it's the same thing, just got a different form to it. They recognize Sunday as a great day: on Sunday you might get a piece of chicken, a piece of beef, pork steak or something like this. And they alternate, you know, from one Sunday to another. So down there every Sunday at noon, damn near every guy goes to chow. Those other six days, man, it's kind of pitiful, you know. It's the whole thing, survival bit, in the sense of eatin. I've been here so long now that eatin doesn't mean anything. You just eat to live, you know.

Ah, if you're a big eater, you can end up in the hole for takin too much. Because, you see, on most items like meat and dessert, the items that everybody's concerned about, the server on line passes it out. Now the inmate can only have two weiners, he can only have one piece of steak, he can only have one piece of chicken. Now the nature of incarceration is such that you want more, you know that cook can't give it to you. If officer sees him give you two pieces of chicken, they write him up and he'll lose his job. So what he'll do is tell you, "Get it yourself." Now if you reach and get two pieces of chicken and nobody sees you, that's perfectly all right. But if you get caught, you gonna go to the lockup. He may write you up, and they may not lock you up, but more than likely you'll get several days in your cell, locked up. If there's any sort of pressure, if there's any sort of argument about it, you get locked up in seclusion. It happens quite often here.

DISTRICT OF COLUMBIA JAIL
CECIL MASTERTON, INMATE

Livin in the jail here, you get three meals a day. I would say the meals are good. And some of the meals are badly cooked. In other words, you have pork, it's gotta be cooked real done. Sometimes it's not actually done. You blame that on the stewards for rushin, not havin time to get it done. They shoulda take time. Otherwise, the meals, you couldn't ask for no better jail to be fed or no better camp that you get in. You eat good here.

You go to court, you carry a sandwich—ham sandwich, cheese. You get two of those sandwiches. You can't beat it. That's a good meal for goin to jail, goin to court, cause chain gang Virginia, you get six sandwiches at dinner time, and they're peanut butter and jelly. And you're still hungry when you get through that. Cause I've been on Virginia chain gang and I know. You eat good here in this jail.

Food you get on a chain gang—was at lunch time. They did start bringin beans out and stuff like that in a pot, you know, and have em like that they stay hot. Bring em to you if you hadda work the rock pit. In the State of Virginia, in the rock pit, they'll bring you hot meals out, beans and some sandwiches and stuff like that. And you have hot coffee, you make it yourself. That's in the State of Virginia. That's not here at this jail.

CALIFORNIA INSTITUTION FOR MEN
JAMES M. CURTEY, INMATE

I eat on the diet line. Always get milk, and if they have chili con carne on the line, we get cheese and macaroni or hamburger or boiled beef stew. It's better and tastier than what they have on the menu. We get puddins and Jello, yogurt and ice cream. I think the food is pretty good for an institution. It gets old because it's practically the same, week in and week out. Havin been other places, you can't complain about the food here.

CALIFORNIA INSTITUTION FOR MEN
COMRADE SIMBA, INMATE

Personally I don't eat swine, you know. They have a diet line here, where people with ulcers or some kinda weakness about their body, it's pretty obvious that they don't feed em any swine, because it is bad for the body. On the main line, where you don't have a diet card, they have swine on the menu, and at times I won't go to chow, cause I check out the menu.

I never been in the Black Muslims, I'm not a member of the Black Muslims. I recognize common sense. I notice this diet line. At night we might have hot dogs; on the diet line they may have liver. One brother, he got into a masochist bag or somethin—he wanted to like do somethin harm to himself. So he got his diet line, he got his liver, and

110.

he gave his liver to me, and I gave him some hot dogs, I wasn't gonna eat em. Ate the hot dog and he was spittin up blood for a week.

ARKANSAS STATE PENITENTIARY
JAMES JESSE JONES, INMATE

Keep me sick. Maybe my stomach—have a bad stomach anyway, but it's all starchy food, you know. Like you have chicken, you have such stuff as that sometime. Sometimes the chicken be tainted, all the meats don't be cooked exactly right, you know.

Some of em get sick. Most of em don't because they used to it, you know, from bein in here so long. Quite a few of em do.

CALIFORNIA INSTITUTION FOR MEN
DONALD E. BAILEY, SURGEON 2

Actually the food here is quite good. They complain less here than they do in the Army, I know. Course they always complain. Another thing is the amount of food. Ever watch them eat? You and I would eat an ordinary plate of food—two or three big helpings would be fine. Their idea of a helping is about this much and four or five slices of bread. Probably a nervous habit, but they tend to overeat.

DISTRICT OF COLUMBIA CORRECTIONAL COMPLEX
LOWELL MILLER, INMATE

Life here seems like it's one continuous meal. They just seem to flow into one another. And the meals are pretty lousy, so that it doesn't help my attitude. It puts me up tight, the food here. If they had palatable and attractive food, I think my head would be in a better place. But the food's so lousy. There's no sense of any kinda sanitation. So I'll eat this disgusting lunch and maybe my colitis will ache a bit and I'll have a loose bowel movement, because maybe I'm not getting the proper diet that doctors recommend for me. And every time you try'n find out why you're not getting what, they give you the Lorton shuffle—they run you around.

CALIFORNIA INSTITUTION FOR MEN
COMRADE SIMBA, INMATE

They have the inmates cookin, so naturally the food is at times pretty fucked up. We now and then will get a cook in—a real cook from the streets. They'll usually snatch up somebody like that and put em in the personnel kitchen.

111.

FIELD WORKERS, ARKANSAS STATE PENITENTIARY, CUMMINS PRISON FARM, 1935.

# AFTERNOON.

CALIFORNIA INSTITUTION FOR MEN
MICHAEL COONEY, CHAPLAIN

On Tuesday and Friday afternoon I'm regularly scheduled to go over to the reception guidance center and see the new fellas comin in. You can't keep em very long, just a few minutes, just tellin em what program you have available to em. Some people think just givin that few minutes is a waste of time. Why don't I call em all in, whole bunch of em in a room together, and say, "Listen, fellas, here I say Mass over here every Wednesday and Sunday, and then I'm here other times. If you want to see me, fine." But I find even two or three minutes to meet a fella, shake hands, ask him couple more questions, give him the opportunity then if he wants me to do somethin or other.

Actually I much prefer if I would work full time over there at the guidance center, because they're more receptive at that particular time—it's a terrible experience for em, first term of comin in there. He's comin into this awful place—"What's gonna happen? Will I ever get out?" If they have a term of five years to life, does that mean they're gonna be around for life? Then with the switch from the county jail up here, they haven't heard from the wife or the mother or somethin like that. There are things like that that mean little to us, but big ones to them. So we get through with those.

113.

You can never let the opportunity of talkin go by. I go down into the receivin room, where the poor devils are comin in, talk to them then, goin through that demeanin process there—come in with the irons on, strip down, clothes are gone, they're issued their blues and weighed and measured and take a shower, they're fingerprinted and mugged, the whole bit. Oh, Lord. They become a nobody, they become a number.

So a little word at that time—nothin very much, just casual conversation. No use in sayin it's not bad at all. It's as bad as it can be for em at that particular moment. I just say, "If there's anything I can do for you, don't hesitate to shout." Course you can meet some of the old characters goin back for postgraduate course. That's rough all right. Some of em, you know, this is more or less their home. They've been out for so long, bout time they came back again.

CALIFORNIA STATE PRISON AT FOLSOM
EARL STRAUB, CORRECTIONAL OFFICER

You'd be called in to meet the new arrivals with a body shake and a clothing shake, then escort them up to a quarantine row or wherever they happen to be assigned.

Well, I don't think I feel any stranger than the inmate himself going through the shake. Except for the new men, they've gone through it so many times, and I've gone through it so many times, become just a routine, standard procedure. I have no special feeling whatsoever. I'm not embarrassed and the individual's not embarrassed, going through the shake. You see all kinds. You see clean ones, you see dirty ones, you see filthy ones, don't have any hygiene whatsoever. All we do is assign them, usually, after we body-shake them, assign them to a cell, take them to a cell and give them clean sheets and bedding and what not and that's it.

CALIFORNIA STATE PRISON AT SAN QUENTIN
HAROLD W. BROWN, SERGEANT, CORRECTIONAL FORCE

One thing you find in searching large numbers of inmates—the physical frisking of their persons—the different modes or lifestyles of their cleanliness. Some inmates, you just have to hold your nose, cause their body smells so bad. Other inmates are clean, of course, and it's a pleasure—if you can call it a pleasure—to search them. Of course, when a man gets a little too dirty, then the officer will take it upon himself to get him cleaned up if possible.

To skin-search a man is not a desirable part of the job by any means. It's absolutely necessary. It's very very disagreeable to

114.

strip a man down and to look at his body cavities, and to handle his dirty clothes. When you're searching a man's undershorts and have to go through every double layer of cloth, all the seams and stuff, is very disagreeable. But it's a necessity. The inmates will play upon the disagreeable part in order to try to beat you, try to outwit you. If in the crotch of a man's shorts, in the seam, there's three or four bindles of heroin, and he is got what we call chicken tracks in his shorts, be very easy to not touch that part. And the inmate's playing upon it as a course. So therefore if you skip that part, you're going to miss two or three bindles of heroin maybe. And he beat you. But if you feel you can always wash your hands when you get done, then you're gonna beat him.

ARKANSAS STATE PENITENTIARY
CLARENCE JAMES LEE, CORRECTIONAL OFFICER 1

All I know is jus everybody comes in new has all their hair cut off. In my opinion, when they have all their hair cut off, you can tell which ones of em should have privileges that's been here, and the people that aren't really been here. Cause you may go in the barracks and want somebody go out on a detail or somethin, and you don't know who these shorthairs are from people that's already assigned to a job already, so by havin their hair cut low you can jus about tell who these shorthairs are.

ARKANSAS STATE PENITENTIARY
WAYNE E. MIFLIN, INMATE TRUSTY

The first thirty or sixty days, you're in the Dark Ages, plowin the ground with ole mules. One of the things that got me, the sheriff brought me down here and said, "This place is under federal rule." He made it a point that this place—this was in sixty-nine—was modern and everythin. There was none of that brutality or anythin. We pulled off the highway and he undid the handcuffs and said, "You don't have to worry about nothin."

I thought it must be kinda a nice place or he wouldn't be that confident. We drove down the road about half a mile before we got here, looked off to the side, and here was some old trusties. And I've done a paintin at home—I wanna keep it—there was an ole trusty guard. He was the ugliest man I ever seen in my life. It was cold and he had his coat pulled up. He was jus lookin. Scowled at the car when it went by. Had his ole shotgun over his arm. He was out there beside an ole chuck wagon, it looked to me. They were steamin coffee. And the inmates were out there takin turnips and cleanin em off with their hands

115.

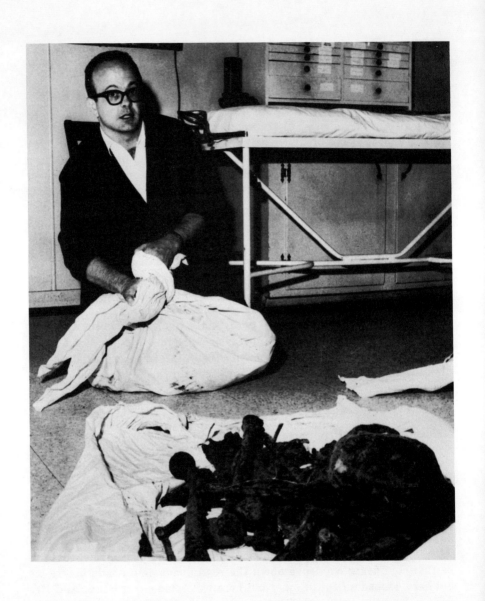

HUMAN SKELETONS FROM "GRAVESITES" AT ARKANSAS STATE PENITENTIARY, 1968.

and puttin em in little sacks. Modern prison, huh? Pulled up, and I seen the ole pieces of metal, rusty and stuff. You can find horseshoes and muleshoes that look like they musta been bent outta regular cast iron fifty years ago. The ole is just hangin on here. It's jus a ghost hangin over this place.

It's so famous for all those killins. All the new inmates here wants to go over and see where those guys got killed, buried. Kinda like a museum. You catch yourself usin their slang words, callin inmates "ole things." They still use that—"Come here ole thing."

The first thirty or sixty days you can't believe all the stuff that's goin on. The rest of the time is jus monotonous, and you can't wait to get away from here. What you do get, you jus got to get on your own. They got a real good gym, but workin out—the coach, he's only here about half the time, and no regular schedule. Some basketball games. But that's only for the West End. You get those big ole rooms down there—they're big, but still, when you pack two hundred guys in, they're jus crawlin all over the place like animals. And sooner or later tempers are gonna flare. That's where your trouble starts.

ARKANSAS STATE PENITENTIARY
MICHAEL JOHNSON HAWKE, FIELD MAJOR

If I have any new arrivals that aren't assigned to a squad, I'll interview em and talk to em and try'n fit em in a whole squad where they will probly get along better with the top inmate. I think different field majors do it different ways. Some do it by escape records. Some do it by penitentiary records. Some do it by height and weight, you know. And I particularly myself like to do it by age and, ah, medical ability and, ah, jus physical make-up and attitude.

I have a squad of young inmates out there that have good attitudes; have a squad of young inmates that don't have good attitudes; I've got two squads of older men out there that are jus old and are jus, ah—I really—all I want em to do is jus go out there every day and jus do what they—the individual inmate—thinks he is able to do. The officers that carry this squad, they know jus about what each inmate can do, and they don't try to push him into doin anythin more than what they figure he's medically capable to do.

DISTRICT OF COLUMBIA JAIL
CECIL MASTERTON, INMATE

When you come to this jail you go by the control center. There's a little place to bring one hundred men or seventy men at one time off of the bus. They're all crowded up into a little space, which is not room to have the men at one time. They're close together. They're all handcuffed together. Two marshals try'n take the handcuffs off, wigglin around through these men. Then the officer that's in the control center will open the door and say, "Answer to your name. If you're a new man, say, New Man. If you're a returnee from this jail this mornin, say, Returnee."

There's another door. It's locked. Until they get every one of these men in, you stay there. After he has em all in and the marshals leave, a convoy officer takes you to the R and D. And R and D you have three telephones. If you have a dime, you can make a call. If you don't have a dime, you can't make a call. You can have your people's phone number but you still can't call em cause you don't have a dime. You can also wait for your name to be called again, and you answer. The Man calls you, change clothes, takes you down, search you, then put you in another cage. "You go to CB-Three." "Come on, you go to CB-Two. Come on." Each officer will then take the men to his blocks where they live in jail.

CALIFORNIA STATE PRISON AT FOLSOM
CHARLES AMITY, INMATE

The convict comes to prison expectin prison to be something else—expects it to be a place of punishment, place like you see out in the movies, drab and so forth. The minute when he begin to lose his fear, he goes to try and see what it really is. He begin to see what it is; he begin to see what it's not. It's not a rehabilitation place.

He begin this orientation in the county jails when he sees all the fellas crowded in there with him, listening to them, "Well, I've got my lawyer's gonna do this for me." "If I can get at this amount of money, my lawyer said he can straighten this out."

A very, very small percentage of the fellas who commit crimes even make it to prison from the county jail, not because they're not guilty or anything, but many of em make deals, many of em turn on other guys, many of em are able to pay off some money or cop out to lesser pleas or something like that, probation and so forth. So I think the average guy, he gets in prison, he starts thinkin, too. And he has more time to think about one thing more than anyone else, and this is prison: prison facilities, prison life, prison environment. And he thinks about it more than anything else. It's his life.

Then he listens to the statements that are made by the executives, and he begin to watch things. Like the court handed down a decision recently that fellas in the adjustment center, which we call

118.

Four-A—this is the disciplinary unit over here—are not to be held in this place over ten days. The attorney general advised the department of correction that they could comply with the court order by releasin the fellas after ten days, and then put em back in there, right after they take em out. This is what makes prison a game.

So when he first comes in, it's a place of horror. Then once he gets here, he sees it's a shuck and he takes advantage and he goes along with it, gets the breaks out of it he can. He'll wet his hair and snivel.

ARKANSAS STATE PENITENTIARY
DEWIE E. WILLIAMS, CHAPLAIN

We do our best to help em adjust. We have right now three counselin groups. I run them as a sort of encounter group, really. It's more just a sharin group. All three are different levels, very different from each other. But basically it's a matter of sharin—to get a man to trust others. Then we begin to move in from that turmoil, strife, beatin each other, the conflicts. We let them express themselves to move them into more constructive acts of will: "What's wrong with me? How can I correct this so that I can live in society and live right?"

Take the women's group. The women little more paranoid, little less likely to trust each other, maybe with reason, I don't know. They do not make as good progress because of this lack of trust. So you've got a group there, where we deal more with lettin them just verbalize some of their feelins and get out some of their hostility against the ministration, the food.

The men's groups, they're similar to the women in this lack of ability to trust, and they are not to that point where they want to understand what goes on in their lives. They're not near as ready to try to interpret "Why do I do this? How can I correct it?" They're still in this verbal sparring.

The third group is a men's group. They've already gone on out there, and they can really confront each other. They've already gotten to the point where they can confront each other with why a man does this. For example, one man was talkin about the crime that he'd committed, and he said he did it while he was drunk. Another inmate said, "No, you're lyin to yourself. You didn't commit it while you was drunk. You drunk that whisky so you'd have the courage to go do what you wanted to do in the first place." This kind of open confrontation.

I had private counselin session this afternoon with one particular girl. Some weeks ago I had two or three sessions with her, and they were jus more exploratory and supportive. Then I ask our psychologist up in rehab if he would give me an evaluation on the girl. So he ministered some tests, then gave me an evaluation. So I studied that yesterday and some today, then went down and had a session with her, and explained to her that we would be workin as a team to try to help her, try to help her understand herself. And then we began to explore some. She began to talk and verbalize some of her feelins. And then I simply tried to interpret those feelins and help her to understand what caused some antisocial behavior on her part.

She's the oldest of three children. Her next youngest sister is five years younger than she is. She had all that she wanted, all the attention, all the love that parents could give for five years. Suddenly, she is replaced in her feelins. She is replaced, and this caused a feelin of rejection. And then whenever she was around thirteen, she began to act this feelin of rejection and this feelin of anger or hatred toward her parents. And the more she acted out, the more trouble she got into, and so the greater separation. Her parents did not understand this, obviously. Neither did the girl understand it. So she continued to act out. And I helped her understand that these things that she had done were simply her acting out her—I didn't use those terms—that she was acting out this hostility toward her parents. She grasped it readily. She is an intelligent girl and she grasped it right away.

INDIANA STATE PRISON
WILLIAM SIMMONS, INMATE

In here, the local psychiatrist has interviewed me several times. And he's got an open-door policy. If he hasn't got a real busy schedule, I can go in any time I want. And several times, I've really been up tight and I went and talked to him, and it helped tremendously. Plus I think I have matured more in the last five years than I had in my whole life. I've grown up. I know what life is now. Before I was so mixed up and things weren't in order. But now I believe that—I'm not saying that everything is one-hundred-per-cent okay. I'm not saying that. I'm saying I'm sorry for what I did. I wish I could change it, but I can't. I believe that from the time that I committed the crime to the present time, I'm a different person. I believe that I can make it now. Back then I had very little chance of making it, cause I was very immature and too many tensions, pressures. But now I believe that with the help that I'm getting I have a real good chance. If I'm given the opportunity I'm sure that I can make it.

120.

I believe that because of, ah, my past background, I had built up certain tensions inside. I've always held things within, and I think that all the pressure and everything just got the best of me. I can't explain why it came out in the form that it did, but I just reached the point where I assaulted a woman and subsequently killed her. There was absolutely no reason for it. I didn't know her. Just happened.

I entered her automobile, forced her to drive out in the country, where the crime took place.

I got caught because I tried to commit suicide, and while I was in the hospital, I confessed. Couldn't take it.

On advice of my lawyer I pled guilty and accepted first-degree murder. He was court appointed, bargained with me. In fact, I think he told me that I would be better off in prison than I would in a mental hospital.

Well, I've always felt I shoulda had a jury trial. He made me go before the judge—a bench trial. I've always questioned that. He was only outta law school two years. It was his first capital case. I think the prosecutor just scared him to death. And I'm pretty sure that with this new attorney, we'll have very good grounds for a retrial.

I'm not an expert. I don't know what constitutes insanity. Just like premeditation, I don't know the time element, how long you'd have to premeditate, you know, to prove it. You'd have to prove premeditation. I don't believe that's true in my case. I had assault on my mind. I didn't have on my mind to kill anybody. The doctors told me in jail, determined that—one of them did—said that after the assault she said something to me that set me off where I lost control. Well, she said—she asked me a question: if I was trying to prove I was a man. And the psychiatrist that examined me said that this pulled the veil down in my mind where I lost control and I became enraged and there wasn't any way I could stop myself.

And like he determined that I have always been— well, he was convinced I was trying to destroy myself. And I never had faith in myself or confidence. In other words, I put myself down. And, ah, he made me realize that's the wrong outlook, and through several conversations, I think gradually I'm building myself up where I can feel confident about things. He mostly listens unless I ask him for a comment or ask him what he thinks. Well most of the time he says, "How do you feel about it?" you know, "What's your opinion?" I guess he wants you to do most of the talking.

The judge that sentenced me put a special stipulation on my packet that I never be paroled. So right now, I'm dead. I mean, I have no future, so my only hope is to go back to court. Even if I get another murder charge, another first degree, at least that stipulation won't be on there. It'd be removed.

As long as it has an end, you know, it makes a big difference. When you can't see the end, it's forever.

If there wasn't somebody outside, that I knew that cared, it'd be pretty rough. Like I get mail maybe three or four times a month, which helps. And I write every night. Without the outside contact there, pshew, I don't see how some guys do it.

I celled with this person up until about three months ago, and he knew that I didn't get many visits and letters. So he asked me one time if I would like to correspond with somebody, and I said yes. So it was arranged to have this individual come up and see me. And she was approved to correspond and visit. And since our meeting, things have gone very well. If I ever get released, I think we'll be married.

ARKANSAS STATE PENITENTIARY
SAMUEL LEXINGTON, INMATE GUARD

For me now everybody in the penitentiary is a little nuts. I believe they're a little psycho, and there's been several guys here that's went ape-shit, went off the handle. But for me, a man keeps hisself in shape, gets the proper sleep, work, keep that freeworld off your mind.

FEDERAL DETENTION HEADQUARTERS
GABRIEL POTTER, INMATE

They have an officer working here that is charged by the State of New York for illegal use of a weapon and oral sodomy. He took his weapon, which he's allowed to bring back and forth to work, picked up a girl on the street, held it to her head, and made her suck his dick. The police caught him. He's working here.

ARKANSAS STATE PENITENTIARY
A. L. LOCKHART, SUPERINTENDENT

I ride out in the fields, afternoons, where they're workin, get out and talk to the field supervisor and see how things are goin out there—if he needs anything, any suggestion, could give him ways to improve the particlar areas that he's workin in, any problems I can help him with. If they're cleanin up, pickin areas that have priority in cleanliness, tell em what to do with the junk, stuff to be moved.

Everything on the farm is my responsibility—figurin

what to do with the cotton—it's not solely my responsibility. Have people responsible for little particular areas, and if a problem arise with that area, they will confront me with it, and we'll work it out as a group. I don't ride out and say, "You all take all this and put it over there" on every detail. I jus ride out and say, "This particlar area'll be cleaned up. This has priority over this here," you know. And they do away with it.

ARKANSAS STATE PENITENTIARY
ROBERT TALBOT, INMATE

Like we're in the cotton field: if one-spot be ahead of two-spot and two-spot be ahead of three-spot and three-spot be ahead of four-spot, the spot that's behind, they don't want you to talk, want you to catch up with the other spot, all stay together, which is impossible, cause some dudes can't pick cotton, and some can. Ones that can pick, they jus run up'n leave the others, draw heat on the ones that's behind. So when you see two or three guys talkin, you go over'n tell em "Be quiet and catch up," things like that. Inmate guards act jus like real guards. They'll be askin you to be workin.

The line I'm in, that's a pretty good line. But this line they call the hot line, that's mostly young dudes or dudes that don't wanna work. They put em in the hot line. They run you with the horses and things, try to make you walk fast. They usually walk to work all the time, and they try to hurry em to the field, hurry em back outta the field, hurry em to the dinin room, hurry em back outta the dinin room, back to the field, back to the buildin. And they be walkin and the guards, they be on their horses. If you don't keep up they'll jus ride on over you, knock you down, make you get back in line, keep up, maybe you be outta breath maybe. And they jus do you like that.

They kick at you. I don't think they have any sticks, but they close to one, they probly would pick it up'n hit you. They mostly say, "All right, ole thing, get in that line," or, "You better catch up before I put a foot in your behind," or somethin like that. They would mostly shoot up over your heads or shoot down by your feet. It happened to me once, when I first came here the first time. I was at the tail end of the line, and we was walkin to work. We were walkin about five miles to a cotton field. And the guys been in a long time, well, they'll pull in the line, walkin fast. The guys that jus came, they couldn't keep up. They'll be at the tail end of the line, and the guards be walkin behind em or maybe on a horse behind em. They say, "Catch up," and they will shoot down by your heels with shotguns. Sometimes maybe buckshots will hit you in the leg. Might have a buckshot in you all day long and evenin. Well, you complain to the doctor, and they'll take their time bout takin it out or somethin like that.

You get along better with the inmate guards because they try to look out for theirselves, cause they know they gonna get breaked one of these days and be in here with you. And so they try to take care of business, you know, treat a man right. The freeworld guards, well, they know they haven't gotta sleep with you and be with you and so on. So I guess it jus don't matter how they treat you.

ARKANSAS STATE PENITENTIARY
WAYNE E. MIFLIN, INMATE TRUSTY

You have a security line out in the field, and if a inmate gets too close to that, you fire a warnin shot, keep him from gettin close, cause if he does get past that, your order then was to shoot him down or disable him where he couldn't move—fire a couple of warnin shots then drop him. They didn't have the freeworld people here to control. They put you in a position where if you didn't, you'd actually be worse off than the one that got away, so to speak. They jus bust you and put you back in the line. And then if a trusty got busted and put back in the line and put back in the barracks, he was jus dead—they jus stab him and kill him, because you'd been a gun guard. The past superintendents here were real smart in gettin inmates to use themselves against other inmates. Actually it was a benefit to them cause they didn't have any money or anything. They could move into some money, move into a sellin job, supervisory-type job. But when I come in, it was jus on the way out. They jus let bigger inmates or stronger inmates or ones that knew how to handle firearms to be there as a threat. Jus before I came here some freeworld people shot twenty-three people—that's with birdshot. As far as shootin down inmates, I know I never seen an inmate jus shot down.

It's a little better now. Inmates are not usin inmates like they did before, jus makin slaves outta them. Like then when they would let em have furloughs—go home, spend five days in town as pay, inmates worked harder and harder. That's what led to a lotta the brutality—jus rewardin em. I get along with rank men and trusties, too. They've used me for different kinda riot situations. When I first came here, they had a barracks where all the troublemakers—people that killed other inmates or people that stabbed other inmates—were all in one barracks. They put me in there supervisin em. But they were all real belligerent. I jus finally had a talk with em and told em I was jus there to do a job. They stabbed a guy right after I left—the guy who

124.

took my job. They killed him, they stabbed him right off the bat. But I made sure they all ate good meals, clean clothes, they sorta halfway respect me. But they'll push trusties off in jobs that nobody else would have—they couldn't hire a free man to do it.

ARKANSAS STATE PENITENTIARY
SAMUEL LEXINGTON, INMATE GUARD

Freeworld people take care of all the troublemakers now. The more freeworld people they got out here, the better this place'll be. If they ever take all the guns, it'll be better for everybody. It'll be better for me. Ain't nobody likes to have another convict guard another convict. But I'd rather guard and try'n benefit myself than go out there on the line and work like a dog. I've done it before, three or four years in the long line. Then it took three, four years to get a break here.

Over in our line, we don't mistreat nobody. Convicts try to take care of another convict, jus like he wants you to take care of him. Now we're out there, we gotta job to do, we're not gonna let a man run off. We ain't gonna mistreat him—walk up to a man, knock him in the head. If a man tries to run off, we're not gonna run up, beat him with a club half to death.

When I get in the barracks, I don't ever have to worry bout anybody stickin me with a knife. When a freeworld man comes, they say, "They're criminals down there. They're vicious and treat em like dirt if you want to. They got to respect you cause they're inmates. If they don't, well, jus beat the hell out of em." They indoctrinate every freeworld man. The inmates resent em. There are certain freeworld people they hate real bad.

Freeworld guards and the inmate guards don't associate too good together. They look down on us cause, see, we're convicts. Jus cause we're a guard, that don't make us any special privilege character or anythin. To them, we're jus another inmate here. Once we put that gun up there and go to our buildin, we jus an ordinary convict. When you put that gun up, you're a sorry son-of-a-bitch.

One day they had three guys try to escape from our line. So we had to go back, get all the men outta the field. They took these three, instead of callin to the buildin and sayin, "Send me a truck," they put em in front of that car like a deer, and they made em sit up on the car like that with their hands like that. And they said, "If you fall off we're gonna run this car over you and shoot you."

So naturally they're scared and they pulled aroun to the front of the car. This one dude, he gets out there and he starts

125.

FIELD WORKERS, CALIFORNIA INSTITUTION FOR MEN, CHINO, 1967.

wavin. I guess he's about half dingy anyway. He waved and said, "Hi, y'all."

They stopped the car and said, "What's wrong with that crazy ole thing?" Then they tell him, "If you fall off this car, we're gonna run over you."

And so they take em all the way to the maximum security. So when they got em into the buildin there, you see, they put em in maximum security after they gave em a little head work—little correction—clubs, blackjacks.

Had em in there in the cell. They throwed some ammonia on em. You know ammonia's strong bout to take all your breath away from you. They jus poured it all over em. So we filed writ in federal court on it—they did. And when they got up there in federal court to answer these charges, they denied em, said it didn't happen. And out there in maximum security, they can regulate that temperature out there—get it real hot or get it real cold. And it's soundproof. It's bulletproof. It's scapeproof. It's a new buildin, automatic locks on the door an everythin. And it bein a soundproof buildin, they can do anythin they want out there. Nobody gonna hear you or see you or nothin. Lotta things goes on back there behind that buildin nobody knows anythin about.

ARKANSAS STATE PENITENTIARY
WAYNE E. MIFLIN, INMATE TRUSTY

The kid who died last week—I don't know—they were bein kinda careful in a way. I really believe they might've been guilty of scarin him to death. But he was too little, and everybody had called him on the fact that he was too small—they jus got a kick outta him, he was so small. Lot of em really regretted it. It amazed em, cause what a time for somethin like that to happen, with court investigations goin on. They're smart enough. . . .

And if they were as crazy as many people think they were, they surely wouldn'ta made a mistake like that and killed somebody. I think he probably worked real hard. I've never even heard of any kinda system at all that was half as good to work em and really work em hard. Seemed like a freak accident.

ARKANSAS STATE PENITENTIARY
SAMUEL LEXINGTON, INMATE GUARD

Like that kid that died, they brought him down here to the main gate, and they run him through the buildin. I wasn't here to see it, but it's described that way through the grapevine, inmate grape-

127.

vine, jus like a telephone. They say this here sheriff brought him in. They run him from the gate all the way to the armory. This freeworld man takes a shot at him down by his feet, and then they got him there and harassed him, scare him. Jus a kid. Anythin they could do to scare him—holler at him real loud. And they said he had sickle-cell blood, some kinda disease. Most inmates feel they harassed him too much, scared him to death, cause a lotta these shorthairs—we used—they'd shoot at em, terrify em. They jus bust caps all around the head, beat em, slap em aroun, make em drink ole dirty water, take em down, make em walk in dirty water up to here—snakes, glass, mud slung all over em—give em an ole piece of dried toast, scared em. They don't know what to think. Don't know whether they're gonna be killed or what's gonna happen to em. Probly what killed him was fright.

The one in charge was Major Hawke.

ARKANSAS STATE PENITENTIARY
WAYNE E. MIFLIN, INMATE TRUSTY

Major Hawke, he's a professional correctional officer. He wouldn't make a mistake like that in the first place. If he did—I can't picture him ridin a horse over anybody. He's bossed some real tough inmates. He's ridin over all the long lines. He probly harassed him, cussed him, but I know here in the buildin when he comes in, he's more lenient with em than the people that are in the buildin: the inmates kiddin him and jokin him, teasin him, you hardly ever see him raise his voice. But he does expect work and he tells em what they have to do. He works em hard. But he ain't runnin a horse over. Specially while the federal court investigation—the day before he's sposed to appear as a witness. They make em do push-ups and jus ridiculous kinds of exercise and stuff like that. Completely keep em exhausted.

ARKANSAS STATE PENITENTIARY
MICHAEL JOHNSON HAWKE, FIELD MAJOR

I jus wanna get the work done—the most amount of work done we can with the least amount of trouble. Anybody wants to get out there and work, I say, "Leave him alone and let him work."

This is a good thought: to tell a guy when he's doin good, and also you've got to tell him when he's doin wrong.

As far as bein under the gun, shouldn't bother em. The better inmates, after a while havin worked, don't even realize they're under a gun. I mean, that's somethin in the back of their mind. They're not thinkin about it. All they wanna do is jus do the work, do what's right.

But still there are people who were raised hard, and I appreciate it. I appreciate it now, the fact that I was raised hard, because I got a firsthand look at the world, you know, from havin to earn it. And it's not really that bad. It's not that bad bein hungry, cause when you do get somethin to eat, you appreciate it.

I mean, I have always been this way: my granmother told me, "You hire on to dig a ditch for fifty cents an hour, dig it like you're diggin it for your life, cause you wanted the job, you asked for it. If you don't want it, don't ask for it. Quit and leave." That's the attitude that I wake up with every mornin. I asked to come up here. Mr. Lockhart and them were gracious enough to give me the job. I took it. If I can't make it, why, I'll leave. If I feel like they're doin the wrong things, I'll leave.

The young black that died, this is the first inmate that I ever had die on me—that I ever had any contact with. I spent the entire day with that boy, myself. That boy was not mistreated—not like what was printed in the newspapers. I don't see anybody get hurt. If a man cuts his finger, I could tell him "Tie it up with a rag and go back to work." But I refer him to this infirmary. This has always been my stand. I don't like to work when I'm sick. I do—in my seven years of corrections I've had two sick days. There's not many people in the outside world that's got that kinda record. But I'm a high-tension, nervous person that likes his job. I didn't say need his job. I like it for what it is.

There are things that happened in the past that I don't agree with. I think this business of the strap* and this telephone† business that I heard about when I come up here, I mean, that's ridiculous. But also, too, might I add, that any time one of my children don't say "yes, ma'am" and "no, ma'am" to their mother, I will tear their rear end up. And the same to me, "yes, sir" and "no, sir," and if you walk into my house, they'll call you "yes, sir" and "no, sir." Now I was raised this way. I don't know, maybe I was raised wrong, I don't know. But I was raised this way. I gained by bein polite to people—the authority or anybody else. And I don't think it's wrong for those inmates back there to show that kinda respect for the officers. Now I'm not talkin about bowin and scrapin. I'm talkin just about a simple "yes, sir" and "no, sir."

---

* The bullhide strap, intended for use on animals, sometimes used on prisoners.
† The Tucker Telephone, named after Tucker Prison Farm, division of the Arkansas State Penitentiary, consisted of an old-fashioned, wind-up telephone, the lead and ground wires attached to an inmate's testicles and toe, so that when the handle was cranked an electrical charge would go through the victim.

129.

The less I have to do as far as punishment to an inmate to get him to understan what I want him to understan, the better I like it. If it's, "Hey look out, man, don't do it," you know, that's all I want.

As far as brutality since I've been here, and in all honesty, I haven't seen any inmate—I have some cases of officers strikin an inmate after the inmate hit him in the mouth with a pair of hand-cuffs, but now I think this is a reaction. I mean, you can't lay up in the corner with your mouth bleedin and say, "Oh, I've been hit." I don't think anybody would expect you to.

Lemme say, since I have been here, there have been some shots fired over there to get fights to break up, to let me know maybe that they need me down on the other end from where we're at, you know. But not over an inmate's head. There's a difference. It's straight up, that's over his head all right, but is that over his head or is that over his head?

I've got count of every shot that's been fired in my field since I've been here in September. I runnin a count. I told my officers when I first came here, it sounded like a small war, when I first came here. I told em, "Only time I want you to pull your gun out is when you're being attacked or when an inmate's tryin to escape. And that's it." And that's what they did. Cause if they do it otherwise, I don't need em anymore.

ARKANSAS STATE PENITENTIARY
JAMES JESSE JONES, INMATE

The las boy I saw get shot at was a one-day wonder, before this boy died. I seen em make him kiss a mule and put—ah, go out and take stuff on out of a ditch—this, ah, well, we call it a nasty name—I don't guess—the sanitary—shit ditch, what we call it. They made him dig all his pocket and put all the stuff in his pocket and put somethin in his mouth and kiss a mule and made him run up and down the thing with brakes in his hands, you know, like you do in service, run up and down there and puttin wood out in his hand. Made him call hisself a punk. Told him he was a punk in the street. And lotta stuff such as that. They do shorthairs like that, and make em get off in the ditch. They used to. I don't know but the one they make him get off in the ditch and work in those. Mud, you know, was aroun their waist. And be really too fast for a man to go all day. If you come in here one day, you never know—jus scare you to death. That's what happened to these las two.

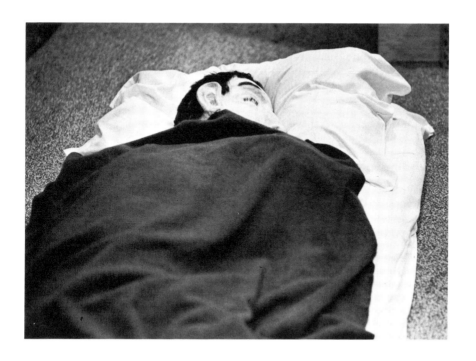

DUMMY HEAD USED IN ESCAPE ATTEMPT, ALCATRAZ, CALIFORNIA, 1962.

We don't tolerate brutality. We don't—we can't live with brutality. And our officers, they're not brutalists. I'm not gonna keep an employee on payroll that, ah, uncalled-for come in contact with an inmate. And they been instructed how to handle themselves. Ah, but if you and I got to fightin, you went out and told somebody, your story's gonna be different from mine. And lotta time, we only hear one side of the story. And it's usually the inmate's side in a lotta cases. And, ah, it kinda gets distorted a lotta times.

Afternoon, this might be a routine day, you just take a tier, you know, you open up the tier. And there may be inmate in the cell or there may not, but you just start at the first cell door and work your way on down, looking for contraband.

Well, you're looking for any type of weapon or iron that could be made into weapons—rods or steel or sharp pieces of plastic. In the contraband of course there's a lotta masking tape or wire or ropes of every kind.

You can make many things out of masking tape. Ah, they can make ropes outta it, steal sheets and make ropes out of it. And also they could plaster up a dummy head, paint over it and make it into a face—make a dummy. And because it's a good restraining material, if they wanna tie you up, they could put masking tape around your hands. You'd be pretty well secured.

I've never found a weapon myself. I've been with people who've discovered weapons, pulling down a clothes hanger rack that would be screwed to the wall—dismantle it and behind the thing would be a homemade knife. And another one was a cross: a man had a cross over the head of his bed; dismantle it and there was a knife behind it.

There's always ongoing searches for weapons—zip guns, stabbing instruments, these type of things. And quite a quantity is picked up each month. It's by no means one or two articles or weapons per month, but many weapons per month. If you would consider San Quentin as being a whole complete city with a wall around it, some twenty-four acres, if I recall, with everything here that a normal city would have outside with the exception of women walking down the streets—and of course we have our counterparts—you can readily see that weapons can be manufactured. They can be made from most anything—from a toothbrush handle ground down, which is a very effective stabbing instrument, to the more elaborate daggers or steel blades.

Lately the zip guns we've been picking up are the muzzleload type, made out of pipe: explosive part would be part of matchheads, a projectile can be anything from broken glass to nails to little stones or pieces of concrete. Extremely dangerous and very, very deadly. And they shoot beautifully. These are the things the officers have to keep their eyes open for. If you don't know what you're looking at, you can get yourself killed. If you don't recognize sounds, you get yourself killed or hurt. This is part of the game though.

BUCKS COUNTY PRISON (WESTERN PENITENTIARY)
RAYMOND WARD BURNS, INMATE

It's not like it used to be—guys'd stand up and fight with their hands. They're gonna fight with a weapon now. And they're gonna try'n hurt you—just knife through you over any little thing.

I had a knife. I've never been caught with it. But you know, I don't carry it, I don't use it, unless I really have to. And then I use it. I will use it. Cause I'm not gonna get killed over something stupid.

And the guards know that they have them, but they won't stop them. Everybody. You practically have to have some sort of a weapon in there now. Your blacks are coming in and they're starting a lot of this homosexual thing. They're attacking younger white boys. They're also attacking younger black ones, too. But it's mostly the blacks. There're a few whites that do this, but not like they do. You know, they put a knife on a young kid and sexually molest him. And if the kid kill them, I couldn't blame him. I couldn't blame the kid. And they shouldn't even take him to court for it. Those animals should be taken care of some kinda way. If the institution's not gonna do it—they encourage it. God-damn place shouldn't be an environment like that. I mean, they're encouraging them. Anyplace all these men together, what else they supposed to do? I can see where something has to be done, but that's not the answer—encouraging them to commit homosexual acts, especially with new men, you know, young kids that don't know what it's all about. I don't approve of that. And if a kid should—I think every

133.

CONFISCATED HOMEMADE WEAPONS, KANSAS STATE PENITENTIARY, LANSING, 1960.

young kid that comes in prison should be given a knife, and they should make him use it.

INDIANA STATE PRISON
HENRY WALTERS, INMATE

We've had several rumors of major riots between the races. Ah, las summer anything could have set it off. God, one of the fellas got burnt up here. The trial is presently goin on in Michigan City. I was hopin they'd bring him through here while you were here. A fella poured gas on one of the blacks and set him on fire. Burnt him to a crisp. He is bein tried downtown now. They handled that. Mike Laden. They handled the hell outta him.

Some of the blacks got very emotional because they seen the guy walkin down the range with the meat droppin offa him, you know, that black guy. He tried to get up and walk to the ambulance, you know, and as he was walkin, every time he took a step, they said big blocks of meat just fell off on the floor. He was dead before they got him to Indianapolis. And they saw that, some of the younger blacks, and they got very emotional, very upset, you know, A-Cellhouse. And like I don't know what kind of bag these people here come out of, but they were angry because the blacks were upset. They thought that they should welcome that sort of scene, you know, like, "So what. God damn it, don't get excited just cause he got burnt up. We still gotta run this institution here."

Now I admit that their anger couldn't have brought him back to life. However, I think their anger was a natural thing, and it could have been handled differently. As it was, several of em got the shit beat out of em. They brought the state police in here, and they had another field day, the riot squad. And they like that, you know. Any chance to bring down the riot squad and the state police, they're always ready for that. It's a real gas, man. And all it's doin is buildin up the resentment, so that you're not really dealin with men, you're dealin with people that are so up tight, full of hatred, so much hate, that they don't even act like people, you know. And there's this weird thing like, "Okay, do your own thing now, cause I'm gonna do mine first chance I get."

The system in here has been worked to perfection by the staff, by these old-timers. They divide and conquer. They divide the whites from the black, and they use em against each other. They go tell the white inmates that we're gettin the better jobs because of the big press for civil rights. So they have to keep us in line. It works. You'd be surprised how well it works.

135.

INMATES' GRIEVANCE SIGNS, MADE FROM BEDSHEETS, HUNG OUT AT NEW JERSEY
STATE PRISON, RAHWAY, 1952.

If they see a black doin anything that they consider out of order, about sixty per cent of these whites'll mention it to one of the white officers. He doesn't consider that snitchin. He's just keepin them niggers in line, keepin em from gettin out of place. Because they've been made to believe if they don't do that, then we'll overrun the administration and take the penitentiary.

Some of the white inmates have indicated to me that they have been told by white officers that, ah, "Blacks're takin over this joint." And, you know, "We all white men. We gotta keep these niggers in their place."

Now believe it or not, I didn't believe that until I heard one of the leadin staff members around here with my own ears three years ago tell a inmate that was in here doin one to ten for theft—this was his third conviction, so you could consider him a criminal—I heard a man that was in a very responsible position say to this inmate goin out the door of the vocational buildin, and he's a bigshot, said "You know," said, "you're an inmate. We're all white men now. And we've gotta stick together."

And the old inmate shook his head and said, "Yes, sir."

And it cracked me up, you know, for a man in his position to be talkin to an inmate that way.

Well I started askin questions, and some of the gray dudes tell you that this is common. Any time they wanna know somethin real bad or they want somethin done, they play off this racial climate. Now they'll get together with a group of blacks, and they'll indicate that they think white boys got a lot of hostility against us for certain things. That is very bad. It keeps the blacks upset and suspicious, keeps the whites upset and suspicious. And you have a situation like that for very long, somethin's bound to happen.

ARKANSAS STATE PENITENTIARY
SAMUEL LEXINGTON, INMATE GUARD

We had a race riot not too long ago. Brought the state troopers in. And they kicked ass, whipped heads. And the inmates here, they claim that the colored couldn't live with the whites, white couldn't live with the colored. And majority of the white people here, they don't like Negroes, cause like this one boy, he said, "There's two types a people here in this penitentiary—there's people'n there's animals." He said, "I'm a people. I'm not a animal."

They classify the colored as animals. They don't have

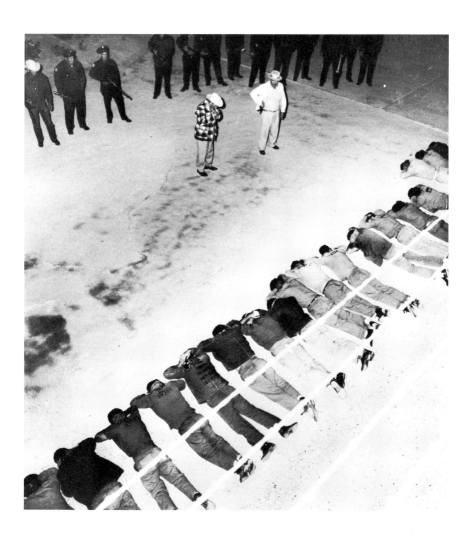

SUBDUED PRISONERS (PHOTOGRAPHED THROUGH BARBED WIRE FROM PRISON
WALL) AFTER A RIOT, ARIZONA STATE PRISON, FLORENCE, 1958.

no consideration for em. They got what ya call Black Moslems here and Black Panthers take over the penitentiary, see. They jus step on you and everythin else. There's people here that couldn't get along, that's fightin each other—have knife fights and stabbins and bare-knuckle fights—it was gettin outta hand. The superintendent that was here called the state police and the national guard. They brought the state troopers in. They whipped the motherfuckers until they decided they could live together.

This one trooper told this white man and this colored man—they had a cotton sack—said, "Get in that cotton sack."

They said, "It's too little, We can't get in that cotton sack."

"I said get in there," and knocked the hell out of em. They got in the sack.

They tear-gassed em, beat em up, and run em aroun naked out there, no clothes, jus runnin aroun'n aroun. Make em do push-ups. And when they come here, all the freeworld people don't have no say so. Told the freeworld people, "You leave. We have charge now. We don't recognize nothin but blue." Slappin the freeworld people aroun. They disarmed all inmate trusty guards, put em in the barracks. And now everybody's integrated. All the barracks are integrated. They got colored freeworld guards and white freeworld guards; they got colored trusty guards and white trusty guards. Everybody gets along cause they have to. Don't want no trouble from the state troopers. They don't wanna see em back. All the hatred and vengeance, they take it all out on us.

ARKANSAS STATE PENITENTIARY
WAYNE E. MIFLIN, INMATE TRUSTY

Course I wasn't here when the big change came—when they integrated. And there was a lotta trouble then—fights. The colored inmate here, I'd say sixty to seventy-five per cent of em at least are outta the topnotch colored people in the street. They've had a better life'n most of em, and they're a little better adjusted than normal colored people, if you're in Arkansas, that you sociate with. They're not that hard to get along with, and they keep their place clean. They shower, clean theirselves regularly. There's prejudice on both sides, but there's not any trouble in this end. And on the other end they use both sides as a force and a power. It seems like they'd be squabblin among themselves. But I've seen instances where they'd be a colored guy on the other end start an argument, and we'd have to go in and take

140.

somebody outta the barracks, and some other colored guys would come and stop him from creatin any trouble. Cause they don't really want any trouble. They know if they do start any racial trouble, probly bring state troopers in, get all banged up again. This is close livin quarters. Didn't take them too long to get to know each other better.

ARKANSAS STATE PENITENTIARY
JAMES JESSE JONES, INMATE

They call you nigger and black'n all that, but you be stayin here, you get used to it. Black guards, they badder than the whites. I guess they meaner, been down here so long, all the convicts. Yeah, they always goin to The Man, you know. I don't know what kinda letter they give him, but The Man'll accept anythin that the trusties say, even though it's wrong. And if a warden, he come in and get you, wanna give you a disciplinary even if it's wrong. And when it come up you got a disciplinary, you get a set-off on the board. The board don't understan what it be about, so when you come up, you jus can't win.

When they call me out for shorthair, if I have to go three or four times a day, and I know the next man haven't been, I'm ready to hit the warden in the head cause he continue to do that. You're ready to kill him. There's this dude got burned up in Little Rock yesterday mornin. They said they found him on his bed, dead, burned up in the house. But he was a trusty here, and so many peoples wanted to kill him. You can't tell how he died. I know him was messin with lotsa peoples.

When he was here, he got lots of em whipped, put lots of em in the hole. You put me in the hole and I'm ready to go home, when I get out, I'm gonna kill you, cause I can't go home no way. I hafta least do my time. I know what I'd do, hard as I'm scufflin now tryin to go home: like if you put me in the hole, I'd kill you when I got out; if you write a disciplinary on me for nothin, I'd kill you.

One guy, Percy Jones, he's in maximum. He came in with five years. He got out in the hole with this young white boy. He was gonna turn him homosexual. And boy told him they'd have to kill him to do it. So they kilt him. So they got life now. If they'd let him go on home the first time when he did good to make the parole instead of givin him a disciplinary and sendin him in the hole, he'd a been at home now most likely. He's out there with life. And the other boy's dead.

Say, like I'm black and you white. If you white and you sit in my chair, I'm sure gonna kill you, because the white scared of the blacks and the blacks scared of the whites, of killin each other, cause

141.

nobody like each other. And when you get down here, you sure don't like each other. If I hit you and you white, and you go back there, I won't know you from the rest of em. You might come back and stick me while I'm sleepin. So I'd have to try to kill you.

Boy took a quarter of mine, and I broke all his ribs when I's here the first time, with a iron pipe, see. Before I came down here I never did have any intention of hittin anybody. Only thing saved him, when I hit em, my shoes slipped and I fell, and he fell down on top of me. Now I learn how to control myself better since I been out and wanna go back.

BUCKS COUNTY PRISON (EASTERN PENITENTIARY)
RAYMOND WARD BURNS, INMATE

They had a riot down'n Eastern. Nineteen sixty-one. Actually what it started out as was an escape attempt. Five or six guys wanted to escape. So when they got one out, the other five go out. No one else was sposed to get out. They had keys that they had made, and they got outta their cells. They grabbed the guard. They were gonna try'n go out with the guard. That didn't work. So they went and un- locked every cell in there—guys that wanted to come out. Then they broke into the hospital and they stold all the tranquilizers and drugs. They took the tranquilizers. Then they broke into this one particular block, segregated block where the homosexuals were, and they grabbed a few of them. And the place just went wild until the troopers come in. Everybody that was out was getting banged up. Cops just come in and started swinging. Whish. They shot so many bullets. They had six or seven guys outside. There was snow out there. They stripped them down nude, you know, beating them on back of their heads and everything else. They beat them right down into the snow. And guys on one block were yelling, you know, "Leave them alone." They just turned the guns loose at the whole block. Everyone had to jump to it quick. Then they came on the blocks. If the door was unlocked, guy was in trouble.

I was fortunate. I jumped in and told the guy to hit the lock. Guy with the key hit it, locked himself in, threw the key away, cause if he'd a got caught with the key, he'd a really been in trouble. He got it from one of the guys that wanted to escape. He didn't wanna escape himself. He just wanted to have a key to be a bigshot. So he got the key. We got locked back in. We were lucky.

They allowed you to buy like shoes if you had trouble wearing the state shoes, which a lotta people had trouble wearing them state shoes. They allowed you to buy shoes, such as Jarmans and so

GUARDS TEAR-GAS RIOTING INMATES, NEBRASKA PENAL AND CORRECTIONAL COM-
PLEX, LINCOLN, 1955.

forth, cost up to twenty-five dollars, something like that. And you had books, law books, legal work that you handle yourself. And the troopers come in, and they cleaned your cell out looking for all kinds of contraband—knives, whatever—and they threw everything out. Whish. All your personal stuff, your commissary, everything you actually paid for. They went out. You started all over again—new clothes, new issue of everything. But they didn't repay you for what they threw out, that you spent your money on. So you lose out there from a riot. And if you're out, you're gonna lose out on that, too, cause you're gonna get your head caved in. And if you say anything when they come in, you got more trouble, cause he's gonna beat on me again, really bad.

ATTICA CORRECTIONAL FACILITY
HERBERT E. PERONE, INMATE

I did have forty law books, but after the riot they were destroyed by the administration along with my seven years of legal work—my entire file destroyed by the administration. They didn't tell me why, but I do know how it happened. A-Block, in which I locked prior to the riot—when they returned the men from the T-Block riot area after the riot, they removed all of the belongings that were in the cells of the inmates of A-Block, and they stacked these belongings next to the wall outside the cell. And they placed these inmates inside the cell in A-Block, and the following day and for two or three days after, they dumped the personal belongings of all the inmates who resided in A-Block into barrels. They transported them to the back of C-Block, and dumped them in the back of C-Block. And a payloader dumped them into a dump truck, and they took them for land fill in the town of Attica, and dumped these personal belongings into this land fill. I lost everything that I had in my cell—my photographs of my family, my wedding band, my clothing, everything.

When the riot started, I was working in the powerhouse, and the powerhouse is isolated from the prison. And there was no rioting in the powerhouse. And all of the inmates that were there, including myself, throughout the entire day when the riot took place, the initial part of the riot, we caused no trouble whatsoever. We left the powerhouse peacefully, and we were taken to E-Block and locked in cells down in Fifty Company in the E-Block. Now prior to leaving the powerhouse, chief engineer in the powerhouse, Mr. Houston, and a lieutenant, they gave us a signed statement in which they declared that none of the inmates in the powerhouse caused any trouble whatsoever. This was on a Thursday we were locked in E-Block, and there was no

HELICOPTER DROPS TEAR GAS ON RIOTING INMATES, ATTICA CORRECTIONAL FA-
CILITY, NEW YORK, 1971.

water in the cells, cause the water main had been broken. And we hadn't received any water, any food. And on Friday I asked an officer to provide us with water, something to eat. And he said to me, he says, "You cocksucker, when we get through with your buddies in B-Block, we're gonna come over here and kill you."

I broke down the wall in the cell, and I went out on the gallery. And towards the end of the gallery there was a locked gate, and another officer, Officer Jones, had an M-Sixteen rifle, and he told me he was gonna gut-shoot me. He said, "I'd be doing people a favor outside." Said, "Beg for your life." And he couldn't understand that I'd rather be dead than beg to him for my life.

Meantime, the rest of the inmates, seeing what's happening, were creating a disturbance. The other officer ran over. He told Officer Jones, "Kill the cocksucker. Kill him. If you won't do it, I will." And he snatched the rifle from Officer Jones. Third officer, Officer Brown, struggled with the second officer to take the rifle away from him. He shrugged Officer Brown off, pointed the gun at me, said, "Get down on your hands and knees and beg like a dog or I'm gonna kill you." I told him the same thing I told Officer Jones.

In the meantime, due to the disturbance of the other inmates, several state troopers came running, tore off the bars at the end of the gallery. And the Sergeant Goddel—with the approach of the trooper, Sergeant Goddel, the officer, put the gun down. And he wasn't pointing it at me anymore. And I cut my hands when I broke out of the cell. And Sergeant Goddel with three or four other officers took me to the hospital and got my hand fixed. And from there I was taken to C-Block, Twenty-six Company, One-Cell. And after the prison was retaken by the troopers, I was taken to One-Company, Six-Cell in A-Block. And subsequently institutional charges were brought against me by Officer Jones, which he said that I broke a cement-block wall down and let myself out, and that I went out into the galleries and made derogatory remarks toward him, and that I made a demand to be taken to the riot area in B-Block. The making the demand to be taken to the riot area is false. I did break out of the cell, as I told you. I dismantled the bed and I used the back of the bed.

See, there was a great deal of brutality after the retaking of the prison. Inmates were run through gauntlets who were being transferred to other prisons. I observed them being beaten with pick handles, ran naked through the halls. And most of the inmates who are still here were beaten. And naturally there was a great deal of hostility on both sides, although I do believe the emotional height of it has reached its peak and it is now receding.

CAMERAMAN AND REBELLING PRISONERS, ATTICA CORRECTIONAL FACILITY, NEW YORK, 1971.

Now, any issue here is generally decided in a violent fashion. And naturally most of the inmates would seek to protect themselves and to have a weapon available, a knife or even a pipe or a lead pipe or some type of weapon like that. And there always was a possibility that a riot could erupt of a racial contact. I mean, this could happen, although most of the inmates wouldn't want that. But during an eruption, people aren't thinking—they're merely acting out their ingrained prejudices. And the white inmates are well aware of this, who I associated with, and the blacks I associated with were aware of this. And this was a problem that was a possibility. There's no doubt about it.

And inside this prison, I mean, there are some emotionally disturbed people in here. And the way the setup is, you are going to place protection upon yourself, and you're gonna prevent somebody from hurting you. And also most of the inmates wanna get out of here, and they don't want the resulting disciplinary report, so they project a vicious inmate in hopes that this will prevent inmates from thinking them soft and perhaps making a play on them or to try and take advantage of them some way or another. And that is why they would have weapons available. They would like to give the impression that they're ready to hurt somebody at the drop of a hat. And I know quite a few inmates who are able to go through the period of incarceration at Attica by projecting this image, and yet they never had any serious trouble, because nobody called their hand.

BUCKS COUNTY PRISON
PRESLEY MIDDLETON, CAPTAIN OF OPERATIONS AND
SECURITY

Some inmates provoke incidents, but there's some officers provoke incidents, too. Depends on what officer's involved, how he takes it. All sposed to be a cool-cat officer, but you got some guys in there, they're too young and so forth, and they don't know how to react when that situation arises.

You can't physically handle an inmate. And that is necessary. Spose it's a disciplinary matter, where you tell a man—let's say he did somethin wrong, you suspect he did somethin wrong. Let's say we had a man break into the maintenance. He was one of our suspects. So normally we lock him into a cell, then we normally collect the redlocks, then he go before a disciplinary board and they decide whether he's guilty or innocent. But sometimes when you try to move a man, tell him to do this, he'll rebel. So our only alternative is, we must

148.

use a little more force to make him comply with our orders. So sometimes the guys—you have to go as far as to grab your club and your mace and everything else to—just by a show of force, sometimes you can get the guy, convince him that it's best for him to go into lock rather than get a club side of head or somethin like that. But it's rare we come in contact with an inmate, physical contact.

I think since I been here, I seen a club used once in this jail, one time. I wasn't involved in it. I think it was three other officers involved tryin to put a man in solitaire and the guy was puttin a good fight. I think one officer by accident used his—he meant to hit him on the shoulder, I guess, and it so happened that durin the tussle, the guy moved his head and the officer mighta hit him on side of the head with the club. Guy involved, his head has a little scar there. That's about it.

But it's very rare that we actually use force. Very rare. But we always have the show of force here. Couple of times, let's say in the last past week, where we had to arm ourself with the club and the mace and the shield and all this and convince the guy he's gonna go away—either he's gonna move or we're gonna use this stuff to move him now. But it's rare that we come in actual contact with a man.

INDIANA STATE PRISON
EARL GRADY, INMATE

We had a riot here once. It wasn't a riot. Seven guys were drunk, and they called it a riot, and locked us up for two or three months, three weeks, you know, something like that. But of all the riots I've ever heard about, the only dudes that get killed are the cons. Basically. So unless a man's ready to die, don't go in that riot bag. You know, you can talk this way, "Look, Jack, come on. I'm with you, but I'm gonna be behind you. You get killed first." That usually breaks it up, you know.

DISTRICT OF COLUMBIA JAIL
JOHN A. KNIGHT, INMATE

Had it definitely been for a cause—no, I wouldn't even rebel for a cause that I know I couldn't win, cause I know ain't nobody gonna hear you. Those people in the streets are not gonna hear you, jus like Rockefeller wouldn't hear those guys in Attica, you know, somebody that really mean somethin, you know. If you rebel, ain't nobody gonna hear you scream. You can scream top of your voice, ain't nobody gonna hear you scream.

149.

In a place like this, we have plans. I guess every place has different plans and different setups for what you do in certain situations. For in a place of this sort, what happens if anything does happen, it's gonna blow. And it's a spontaneous thing. So all your plans that you have may not apply at all. If it blew up in the school and I'd be by myself, what am I gonna do? The first thing I'm gonna do is try to get out. But we have plans here where we should move to a certain area, do this, do that. It never works out that way, cause you're dealing with people, and people are unpredictable.

DISTRICT OF COLUMBIA CORRECTIONAL COMPLEX
GEORGE F. X. LINCOLN, INMATE

When prison was establish by the Quakers, it was called a penal colony, cause penal meant to repent. An all they did was place a man in there for the purpose of repentin for the crime he had committed against society. They took care of him. Now when it was discovered by the economy that this was a large reservoir of free labor that wasn't bein used and how they could utilize this to work for the state, it was no longer a penal colony—become a penitentiary. And from that day it was big business.

CALIFORNIA STATE PRISON AT FOLSOM
DOUGLAS A. BORSIN, INMATE

Only thing is, to get the work out once it's necessary. We're not under pressure like a lot of other places are. In the laundry, for instance, they've got certain days that certain buildings turn in laundry, and they've got to have it back either that afternoon or followin mornin, so the men can distribute it. We don't have this kind of pressure up there. So we're pretty much free to our own devices.

We have quarterly notifications that go out to various departments within support by such and such a date, which is usually the middle of the current quarter, to put their local requisitions in to us, so we have time to research em, to check contracts, check prices. And if we don't have contracts with prices, have to send out letters of request for prices and get this information back in, so that by about the fifteenth of the third month within the current quarter, our supplies for the next quarter will be comin in. There for about five, six weeks, you're pretty damn busy about once every three months. But the rest of the time, it's normal routine. You have, oh, requisitions that come in from time to time that people wanna buy some merchandise for the institution or purchase orders authorizin repairs to be made, and of course, your correspondence and everything. But let's say about six weeks outta every year, we're pushed.

Over'n the tag plant, where all the metal fab, as they prefer to call it, where your license plates and everything are made, guys bust their ass for twelve and a half cents an hour. The state feels generous cause it gives em eighteen to twenty-five bucks a month. Outta this eighteen to twenty-five, a guy smokes, if he drinks coffee or he wants to brush his teeth—course they furnish tooth powder, but hell that's nothin—and he wants to buy soap or any creature comfort at all, so the prices eat him up on that, and he can't save anything to take out with him, you know. And a lot of these poor bastards have already got themselves booked for it, too, when they do get out. So these are points of contention. They should pay these guys better'n they do.

BUCKS COUNTY PRISON
RAYMOND WARD BURNS, INMATE

Vocational training is no good, because just take for instance machinists. Some of the machines they work are so outdated that when you go out and try to work a new machine, it's a new thing to you—might not even be able to understand what the machine's all about. It's like learning all over again. You haven't learned anything. Carpentry, the old tools that they use—hand planes and so forth. Clerical work, the typewriters—one we got down there must be, ah, fifty years old. Well, the typing, the experience is good, I guess. Learn on an old typewriter and you can still type on a new one—it's the same keyboard. And the clerical work, the filing and so forth, they still have the same systems out there—the Dewey decimal system, you know. Nursing, it'd all be new. They're always learnin something new about nursing, so there's something to learn there. Machine work, they're gonna have to come up with new machines, cause they're gonna teach them with old machines, they still can't run the new ones. It's entirely different, you know.

They got to keep up-to-date practices in the institutions, and it costs money. So I can see their point, too. It does cost money. And you're only funded so much. But they ought to come off with some of that money that they're putting in their pocket. They're making money on the license plates. They're making money. They claim they're not making money on the—they make filing cabinets up Western, they claim they don't make money on that, but they do. They have

151.

leathercraft shops there. They pay the inmate so much. He does all the work. They sell the leathercraft. They have shoe shops. So many shoes go out to different places, you know. They say it's institutions. There's no money for that, cause it's all institutions, all one thing, state funded, the whole bit. But they're making money on that. They're making money on almost everything they do in the institution, that the inmate does. They pay them, the inmate, certain wages, and if he did this type of work in the street, he would have to get at least minimum wage. And they couldn't afford that.

Yes, they could. They could afford that if they weren't pocketing the money themselves. The money they make should be turned back to the inmates plus back to new materials. And they're still gonna come out ahead.

DISTRICT OF COLUMBIA JAIL
CECIL MASTERTON, INMATE

The barbers that work in barbershop, they get sixty cents for a haircut. They get twenty-four cents of that sixty cents. The rest goes back into a fund to buy supplies—towels, clippers, and tools to work with. That's the percentage the barber makes—twenty-four cents out of sixty cents. It's sixty cents a shave, sixty cents a haircut, sixty cents shampoo. Everything is sixty cents that you get in the barbershop.

ARKANSAS STATE PENITENTIARY
SAMUEL LEXINGTON, INMATE GUARD

They gotta school down here for learnin trades. They got upholstery, pay you here. You go to school, they give you ten dollars a week. You can learn mechanics, upholstery, you can learn agriculture and stuff like that. You learn that kinda trades here. And you're obligated to go to school for a year, and you can't quit. You're under contract, and they guarantee you a parole and a job. You gotta have enough time when you get this here schoolin finished to be able to go on the board for parole. They'll guarantee you a good job when you get your diploma out here at the school. Then they gotta school for high-school education, high-school dropouts, you wanna earn your high-school diploma. And then guys can't read and write, it's a good thing for em. But not everybody's eligible to get in on that. Jus certain people.

CALIFORNIA STATE PRISON AT FOLSOM
DOUGLAS A. BORSIN, INMATE

They've got program or two that I could take advantage of out there, but nobody's gonna hire a forty-year-old clerk. Let's face it. I'd like to get into computer programmin, data processin.

152.

They've gotta pretty damn good school down in Chino. I'd like to go into that. But will they let me do it? This I don't know.

I investigated last year, first part of this year, in fact. I went to the parole board in July, and so they told me, "Well we're thinkin about a six-month to twelve-month date. Now what can you give us in vocational trainin?"

Well, I told em, I say, "In six months, I can't give you a damn thing more than what I have but work report, because there's no school that's that short within the system." So I say, "I might blow this six-month to twelve-month date, but if I can have a nine- to twelve-month date, I can go to Chino, they'll accept me in school. And when I get out, I got a job with the company that's trainin me. This is the key I need."

They say, "Beautiful. You really sincere about it?"

I say, "Definitely."

"We've talked to your counselor. We know you are." This is a right answer. "We'll let you know."

So my results come back, there's no date involved. It's a nine-month denial. And they say, "Well, give us this vocational trainin in the next nine months." But hell, they won't take me in the school unless I've got the date. So all they're doin there is sayin, "Here's the key, but we ain't gonna let you have it. You've gotta come out and just snatch it from us." But hell, you can't snatch it from em, cause like you say, they've got the power. They put that chicken-weight key in their pocket and this is the end of it. There isn't a way in hell you can get to it. So in Folsom, they give a guy nothin whatsoever, no incentive, no initiative to prepare yourself for gettin out there, even if you're sincere about gettin out there and stayin outta these damn places. And without the keys, what the hell can you do?

BEDFORD HILLS CORRECTIONAL FACILITY
DIANE LARET, INMATE

I work in IBM, so that's the only thing that keeps me goin. That's somethin I enjoy. I've only been there five months. I've been advancin myself as hard as I can. So I was a key-puncher, now I'm a verifier. I haven't been certified yet. I'm supposed to take the test some time this week or next week.

The verifiers are the ones that corrects the key-punchers' work. In other words, they have to key punch a certain way, and any little error, if we let it go, it might cost another company money, you know, large amount of money. Like what we let go, it has to be computed. Once it go in the computer and the card is wrong, it can mess up the computer. So we have to make sure that what we correct—it is correct. All we do is, once we run across a mistake, we give it back to the girl who keyed it, and then she corrects it, and we go back and notch it, you know, notch it correct. Then go on to the next card.

It's for the county of Westchester. And she told us the other day, the people we're really workin for is the transportation of the state. But we get our pay from the prison. And every so often, if we rate a raise, we'll get one. She'll put us in for a raise. And right now, makin fifty-five cents a day. When I got there, was makin a quarter.

CALIFORNIA STATE PRISON AT FOLSOM<br>WALTER E. CRAVEN, WARDEN

We have been able to progress in the development of our system to the point where there's more comfort, more liberal programs, and the opportunities are there when the individual wants to change. But the means of moving him in accelerated fashion in direction of this change is another matter.

We have been successful in providing what I call fortification programs. Once he's decided to change, the training programs, whether it be academic or vocational, and all of the other programs are gonna develop in him the self-confidence that's necessary to be successful as a citizen over there. It's just getting him somehow stimulated to participate in them. That is our real problem.

Well, actually, there's less opportunity at Folsom than any of the other institutions in our department. I'm saying that in general our department provides this kinda opportunity. And less here because our prison's more restricted by our classification of being maximum security and by the fact that we have older inmates, and they don't change. But nevertheless, there is opportunity here. Any man who wants to involve himself in self-improvement programs that will equip him to better function in society has that opportunity. It's an empirical fact. We're educating people, they're receiving degrees, we are providing them with the training that's necessary, that allows them to acquire journeyman status and go out and earn a livelihood. We are providing them with programs of self-improvement wherein they develop the confidence to communicate better with each other. And so these are there, and there at each of the institutions in varying degrees, and in a greater degree than is provided at Folsom. So it's just a fact that they are there. Now the degree to which the man participates in them and takes advantage of them is another matter.

154.

DISTRICT OF COLUMBIA CORRECTIONAL COMPLEX
GEORGE L. WHITE, INMATE

This is a slave camp. Actually all the man makes is three dollars a month. I read an article in the paper one time, where it says that newspaper boys make more money than that a month. I think they make about a hundred'n twenty-five dollars a month. All we get is three dollars a month. Only shops that make sixty to seventy dollars is the furniture repair, tailor shop, maybe the print shop. You hafta be there maybe six to ten months before you can get this type a money. They got jobs around here, man, where some guys don't even get no money.

There's nothin here that I can see that can actually help a man when he go back into the community. This is what the committee that I'm workin on is tryin to do. We tryin to set up a trainin program where a man can go on the job trainin, computer assembly, computer parts.

BUCKS COUNTY PRISON
RAYMOND WARD BURNS, INMATE

What they need is more work release and rehab centers. In other words, put you out to work in the community. Your money that you make will be put toward your upkeep at the rehabilitation center, plus restitution to the people that you've robbed. That would be more in the line of rehabilitation, because this way you'd be working, you'd realize, have more realization of what this money means to you. Most burglars, they don't care about these things til they're put in the position of having to earn it.

If punishment is needed, restitution is much of the punishment, you know. Pay them back. I'd be in trouble if I had to pay back all the money I stold, but I have twelve years in prison, too. I think I've paid more'n enough back. What I could be able to earn during those twelve years woulda more than of paid it back.

DISTRICT OF COLUMBIA CORRECTIONAL COMPLEX
JOHN O. BOONE, SUPERINTENDENT OF ADULT SERVICES

We will never be able to pay for the kind of skills men need to compete in the community. Who thinks that they gonna provide for a high-class vocational trainin system in prison? So I say, as soon as these men can be trusted, we need to let em go into the community and participate in some of these things. We gotta let em out, because if we keep em in prison, they learn more skills about how to do crime, more bitter and hateful and all of that.

155.

Thanksgivin of last year, I established classification system Thanksgivin, where I classify men maximum-close, medium, and minimum. Of the more than fifteen hundred prisoners, I let three hundred and twenty that in our opinion could be trusted—well, we didn't have three-twenty in November. In the beginning we had a hundred'n seventy. Thanksgivin Day we sent a hundred'n seventy men home just as a trial, and I told em they were participatin in an innovative program that could have great impact on the corrections of the future and all of that and what we visualize, and that they should take this into consideration.

Hundred and seventy men went home. Hundred and seventy men came back. It shocked the staff. Staff said they had pools, layouts that twenty would not return, ten would not return, and you could bet on that. So they were shocked. And the men didn't come back drunk. We didn't detect any dirty—we gave them urinalysis to determine whether durin this trip out in the community they took some heroin or somethin like that. Nothin close.

So Christmas came about. I had two hundred fifty classified men home. I sent two-fifty out, two forty-nine came back. One stayed away. Caught him in two weeks. So we had the inmates, staff'n all workin on this furlough program. And we sent men out. We sent four hundred—almost five hundred men out. Outta that number, six did not come back. Ninety per cent successful. Vastly successful.

However. Soon after that, some law-enforcement people and some judicial people said, "It's illegal." It was ridiculous. They weren't worried that we couldn't find the three hundred and twenty men out of fifteen hundred that could be trusted. They said, "It's illegal." Says, "This is philosophy." And I don't blame em. Cause they don't understan that we have failed in the past. We've got to come up with somethin new.

BUCKS COUNTY PRISON
PRESLEY MIDDLETON, CAPTAIN OF OPERATIONS AND
SECURITY

The program is nice here. The ideas are nice. But unless you got the manpower to institute or back up or supervise these programs then, ah, you'd be pissin up a creek. Let's put it that way. That's the way I see it. That's all it is: pissin up a creek. We jus goin forwards, but we're not accomplishin nothin, the way I see it.

We had a sergeant today, one of my best sergeants on security, he made a comment that all this constant hassle, this eight-to-four shifts today, he'd jus as soon throw his keys in, he said. He went so far as to say if there was another job opportunity, another job open up tonight, he'd a thrown his keys in and walked out.

CALIFORNIA STATE PRISON AT FOLSOM
ARCHIE DALE MACDONALD, CORRECTIONAL OFFICER

The mail and visiting room, where the free people come in and check in—they'll come in and say, "I'd like to see inmate so and so." And that officer out there will check and see if they're on the inmate's visiting list. And if they are and they're authorized visitors, then he will call the custody office and say that so and so has a visit. Well, we record it by number and name. Then it's our responsibility to get the inmate over to the custody office, get him his visiting pass, and get him up to the visiting room.

INDIANA STATE PRISON
EARL GRADY, INMATE

You can get a visit every day, but your visitor can visit every two weeks. But you can have a different visitor every day. You can do your whole bit in the visitin room if you got enough different visitors.

CALIFORNIA INSTITUTION FOR MEN
JAMES M. CURTEY, INMATE

We go out here on the big visitin ground. We usually have a picnic lunch, talk'n discuss things, mostly concerned about the institution, make plans for the future.

You see a lotta young couples sittin round embracin, kissin. Sometimes when the officer thinks they're gettin a little carried away, he catches their eye or jus taps em on the shoulder. They're very lenient here.

ARKANSAS STATE PENITENTIARY
WAYNE E. MIFLIN, INMATE TRUSTY

I've got a real good relationship with ma wife. I think I liked her a whole lot before I got here, but I don't know if I really, really love her. We learnt how to talk to each other. I don't have some problems a lotta people here have. And we can sit here on Sundays, and she can tell me about different things that happened to her at work. Really, some of the people, some of the girls at work have a lot worse problems than she does. Same thing here. We hate bein separated—the aloneness and everythin. We got the future to look forward to.

They used to have an ole joke when I first came here that said, "God wasn't allowed in the front gate because he couldn't qualify for a pass." The ones that did come in here then would jus jump in here on Sunday and jump back. They jus didn't like bein here.

ATTICA CORRECTIONAL FACILITY
HERBERT E. PERONE, INMATE

I was receiving visits mostly every week from my wife, and she was indicted in the Bronx two years ago on a murder case, and while I'm out on bail, she absconded from bail. But prior to that, Superintendent Mancusi forbid her from visiting me in view of the fact that she had been indicted. He felt that this indictment was indicative of her guilt, and he would not permit her to visit me anymore.

BUCKS COUNTY PRISON
JOHN D. CASE, SUPERINTENDENT

I've never really taken a stand on conjugal visitin. I've never really made up my mind. I basically feel that I'd rather see people goin home on weekends. Ah, I happen to feel that the sex act should not be cheapened. And I think when you bring a woman into an institution—they do in Mississippi and some of the other states—and you know there's a little red house, a room in it, you go in there and there's a bed, you're just there for one reason, that's to get laid. That kind of makes a cheap relationship. I'd rather see the situation where you let the guy go out, go home for a weekend.

CALIFORNIA STATE PRISON AT FOLSOM
DOUGLAS A. BORSIN, INMATE

Now one of the administration came over yesterday and sposed to check up on a trailer, two-bedroom job, to bring out here for so-called family-type visitin, like conjugal visitin, family type— parents or something. Hell. Most of the guys'd want their wives to come up and be able to spend a couple days here. Of course they stuck em right out there underneath Three-Guntower, right there together, so you'd have to have your blinds pulled all the time.

CALIFORNIA STATE PRISON AT FOLSOM
CHARLES AMITY, INMATE

I was called up on my job: "Hey, the warden's office wants you," and I answered the phone. "Hey, Ray, this is Johnny Moore"—and Moore and I, ourself and Craven all come through Quentin. "Look here, I got a guy in here, gentleman's from New York, who's interviewing some people—three free people and three prisoners. He

158.

CONJUGAL VISIT, CALIFORNIA CORRECTIONAL INSTITUTION, TEHACHAPI, 1968.

wanna interview a colored guy, a white guy, and a chicano. And somehow or other your name came up. Would you be interested?"

And I said, "Well, interviewing em about what?" you know, and then curiosity set in as to why. Another is I'm goin to the board in eighteen months, and fella in the next office over there is the one who instigated the procedure for puttin me up eighteen months before I was supposed to go. And I thought I'd better not make any waves—he's really strainin the system for me—I ought to go check it anyway. If it's not anything that would put me on either side—see, like I've spoke of the things that society sees first—rehabilitation and things like this. I can't come out on that side. Yet, in the meantime, something that's gonna be published and my name's gonna be used, I can't come out against the fellas on the yard either, I hafta live with. So I said, "Let's see what it's about."

Then my friend is editor of the paper here. He was wondering—mostly he handles these things of this nature. I was tellin him about it. They called me yesterday to tell me, you know, bout the interview for today; and I told him last night about it. And he was tellin me about how a buffer has been placed between him and outside contacts. And he is—I like him. He is a concerned fella—concerned with the prison problems. I stopped in and told him I was comin in here to see you, and he says—I explained to him, I told the other editor about you and that I was surprised that neither one of them were contacted. So it couldn't be the fact that he's a black militant. Because there's another editor who is an awfully good black. You couldn't have him either. And if he was a black militant, what difference would that have against your interviewing him if you were tryin to get the points, the people involved, period?

CALIFORNIA STATE PRISON AT SAN QUENTIN
JOEY WILLIAMS, INMATE

I wish the people in the freeworld would wake up to what's really happenin in these institutions, you know. That's what's wrong, you know. You really don't know what's happenin in this place, you know. I can't really sit here and tell you about it on this tape, you know, because if you really knew what was happenin in here, man, anyone, I don't think society would go for it. You have to be a part of this world to know what's really happenin in here. And when I say a part of it, I don't mean a convict or inmate, you know—whichever you choose to call it, you know—it's somethin that—you have to be able to sit and speak freely without any sweat.

160.

Well, what's gonna happen to me after I get through talkin? Boom. This guy, really what he says? You know, this guy really gonna do what he says he's gonna do? Is this guy puttin me on or are they bringin someone in to find out what's happenin, you know—"Let's get this person here to see if he will talk or give us up what's right that's happenin with the institution." Ah. Wow. "I don't believe this is happenin," you know, "He's rationalizin all these topics," you know. "Well this isn't what's happenin."

You're gonna get a guy who's gonna be reluctant to say anythin, because he don't know what's gonna happen to him after you leave. There're good things I could say about this institution, and there're bad things I could say about this institution. But I'm only one person, you know. Even bein this one person, what is the administration staff gonna do to me? I sweat these things. I'm not gonna lie to you, say I don't. Am I gonna go to the hole as soon as this guy get through talkin to me? Or what, you know. Or will there be some kind of repercussions further down the future? Say, for instance, I get down and down and down and then what? Damn. "This guy was workin such and such a place. Read this book. He was one of those wise-asses," you know.

ATTICA CORRECTIONAL FACILITY
MATTHEW BAKER, INMATE

I dread going back there with the information I have given out, because I still have to make parole from there yet. And it'd be a real hassle. A lot of things I said, I'm sure they wouldn't be happy with. They'd throw me right in the hole just for telling it like it is.

ARKANSAS STATE PENITENTIARY
SAMUEL LEXINGTON, INMATE GUARD

Up there in the visitin room, they got freeworld people up there, they watch you while you get a visit. And you can't bring nothin back with you. No money. You're allowed one dollar in freeworld change bring back with you. And they watch you, and you can't be intimate with your family, nothin else. Can't go huggin and kissin. They don't go for that. And they give you a visit crammed in there with all them other people—crammed together. And you might get two hours off for a visit, then out the door you go. They restrict on visits. Used to be the trusties go out there'n visit their families on the yard, out there in summertime. And, ah, they would get all day long to visit and bring a big old box of groceries in. And the rank man would get a pretty good visit, too. Now it's everybody—they're scared you're gonna bring dope in—there are people gonna bring you some dope or

161.

METAL DETECTOR USED TO SCREEN VISITORS, CALIFORNIA STATE PRISON AT SAN QUENTIN, 1947.

some whisky or some contraband—knife or a gun or somethin—maybe you're gonna get somethin in. So they real strick about the visit.

FEDERAL DETENTION HEADQUARTERS
GABRIEL POTTER, INMATE

They have contact visits here. The way you get a contact visit, you submit what is commonly known as a cop-out. It's a piece of paper that you write in and request this visit and tell them who it's with. They have a group of officers here that approves this contact visit. There're certain requirements to get it. You have to be in the institution six months, and has to be an immediate family or girlfriend. Before you go in this room for this contact visit, you strip-search— that's taking everything off. You open your eyes, raise your arms, spread your cheeks. They look up our asshole and everything. Before you go in and when you come out, you do the same thing. They're limited to one hour. The visits you get here which is telephonic are limited to only twenty minutes. If it's crowded, less than that at times. If it's not crowded, longer'n that. It varies. It depends on the man who watch you and how well he can run his job. Some men can make this room run smooth. The others, they just can't do it.

DISTRICT OF COLUMBIA CORRECTIONAL COMPLEX
ANONYMOUS CORRECTIONAL OFFICER

We do not search visitors per se. Naturally they are not permitted to bring in umbrellas and large packages, this sort of thing. They are not permitted to bring packages at all. They may bring in packages which are permitted on certain holidays.

And we do from time to time oversee the visiting procedures. We're in the process of changing some of our visiting procedures because of sort of infiltration into the institution of contraband. And this is a growing problem. This is something we constantly have to be aware of and check day to day. I do not believe that anyone will ever stop the flow of drugs or contraband. But I think you can keep it to a very minimum.

And as far as narcotics are concerned, there are many, many ways that this can come in. We know that visitors are able to. Our present visiting procedures are that the residents are permitted to embrace. And we know that in doing so, it is possible to pass a balloon in mouth-to-mouth contact. A balloon can hold naturally two or three spoons of heroin. If it's strong enough, it may be cut and distributed throughout the population. And we'll have to constantly be aware of this when we do have information that the residents or the visitors do

163.

breach security by taking advantage of the type of visiting privileges that we have. Then we're able to monitor this and naturally take this man out and even remove the visitors from the visit.

We don't know generally if visitor has brought something in. But if an inmate is suspected of having some narcotics or he is witnessed by an officer, he is taken to a hospital. We have the facilities at the hospital of x ray that we're able to use, although we are concerned and don't want to subject an individual constantly to x ray every time he has a visit. If he's having three visits a week, three x rays a week—I think this would be overextending it. Rather, we would either screen the visitors and screen him or place him in a particular situation where he would be under a certain type of control where he wouldn't have this type of visit.

BUCKS COUNTY PRISON
PRESLEY MIDDLETON, CAPTAIN OF OPERATIONS AND
SECURITY

I think it was the past Saturday we got authorization to make spot checks on the visitors comin in. And so I jus picked this kid out to make a shakedown. I brought him into this office. I asked him whether or not he knew that it was illegal to bring drugs into the institution.

He said, "Yes."

I said, "Well, you don't mind me checkin you out?"

So he consented. He put all his stuff on this desk over here. I went through all his personal effects, went through a pack of Tiajuana Smalls, cigar box, there's a little, small container of marijuana. He was bringin it in for one of his buddies.

This is county property. Once you get on county property you're under my jurisdiction. And once you come through our front gate, we don't have to let you out unless we want to. We got the authorization to check anyone out who comes through that front door.

So this kid, I made a complaint to the Doylestown Borough Police. I made the first arrest, and I called em, and they came up and, I guess, sort of took him out to the JP and he arraigned him. Bail was set at five thousand. According to—bringin drugs into the institution, you can get five years, two thousand dollars' fine.

CALIFORNIA STATE PRISON AT FOLSOM
WALTER E. CRAVEN, WARDEN

Well, drugs, big is a relative term, a big problem as compared to what? We do have some drugs in our facility, and we've accepted the risk of having these by establishing a liberal visiting

164.

program. We feel that the benefits to be reaped from having this liberal program offset whatever problem is created by having drugs come into the institution. It's reasonably easy for an outside person visiting under our system to smuggle drugs in. We understand that, and as I say, we've accepted that risk. We've had a few instances where inmates under the influence of drugs become problems, and we've had a couple situations where inmates in their smuggling of drugs have died—they've swallowed containers that have contained concentrations of drugs and for one reason or another these containers broke open and killed them. An overdose. But I feel that the value of having liberalized open visiting with loved ones offsets the problems we've encountered.

CALIFORNIA STATE PRISON AT SAN QUENTIN
HAROLD W. BROWN, SERGEANT, CORRECTIONAL FORCE

We recognize the fact that there's a drug problem in a prison. In this state, ah, far as inmate an visitors coming in, we have contact visiting. That means they can embrace. And you can't stop balloons transferring from one mouth to another and being swallowed. This is one of the ways a lotta stuff comes in. We know that we can't grab these fellows and put them under a fluoroscope and pump their stomachs out and everything else. You can't do it. Nor can you really put up a big bulletproof glass and have them talk over a telephone to each other. This isn't really humane either. Society really doesn't want this.

We're on constant guard, constant vigilance at all times, every officer is, as a team, to constantly search, constantly take this stuff up. You're outnumbered ten to one. You can't watch them all—it's impossible. So the avenues of contraband coming in that we know, we do our best to seal these off as we can. But when you seal off these avenues, new appears. And then with the large number of employees that we have here and nonemployees—volunteers that come in here, it's safe, I would assume, to say that at any given time you could have one or two dishonest volunteers or dishonest employees, and this again is another avenue to bring in narcotics or other contraband.

INDIANA STATE PRISON
EARL GRADY, INMATE

I don't think we have as many dope addicts as people make out. Lotta dudes sociate themselves with dope in order to glamorize. They don't really want no dope, you know what I mean. A man who really wants dope is gonna make it available to get it in some kind of way. But basically you don't have this situation here. You always got a few, but basically there're not too many dope addicts in here. You know, we got a lotta dudes that talk dope, for sake of conversation, you know. "Two-hundred-dollar-a-day habits," and this is common talk. But when you get down to the nitty-gritty, it's just talk.

I've seen dudes in here get their first shot in here, you know, their first form of dope in any kind in here. Get one shot, and then he's been on dope, man, for two hundred years. They still make it attractive, as though it's a great thing to be a junkie or be on dope. I think that's fifty per cent of the problem all over the country with dope. The dudes on pot, you know, they make it attractive. Most people that use it, they make it attractive. "Man, it's a gas," you know. But whether a dude smokes it or not if he's in here, element is smokin in here— "Yeah, man, I smoke pot," whether he does or not.

CALIFORNIA STATE PRISON AT SAN QUENTIN
RAFAEL HERNANDEZ, INMATE

The first time I heard about acid, you know, I was in here. First time I took it was when I was in here.

FEDERAL DETENTION HEADQUARTERS
GABRIEL POTTER, INMATE

I had a drug habit and I kicked it. Sixty-seven. And I haven't used any since then. If I was associated with that scene, I'd probably be in it, but I'm not, you know. I just don't want in. I started with an amphetamine habit and ended up with a horse habit, a bad one, three thousand dollars a month. I still got tracks that'll never leave me, you know. Most guys have them here, and I see you lookin already. Mine is in my groin. In sixty-nine I still had spots—you could lay cigarettes in my groin, where the veins were so sunken in. And that's one way I kept it down from the police. They always thought I was addicted but they could never see it here, so. And I never got that hard up where I shot it in my arms, because I was shootin good stuff and I could afford it.

CALIFORNIA STATE PRISON AT SAN QUENTIN
HAROLD W. BROWN, SERGEANT, CORRECTIONAL FORCE

Head kits are constantly being found—everything from the sophisticated-type normal syringe and needle to maybe a Prell tube with a needle on it. If a man has got narcotics and he needs them, he feels he needs them, he'll go to any extreme to induce them into his body—to the point of even taking a razor blade and cutting a gash in his arm and putting the powdered heroin in the gash and holding it there until it's absorbed by the body.

Last time we found dope it was in a plastic container talcum powder come in, which they sell up in the commissary. And, ah, the top screws off. It's kind of a big nut top on it. And we took that off. Usually what you do with something like that, you wouldn't spill it out, but stick a pencil or a pen and kinda feel around in there with it, come up with a small glassine package, some form of narcotic, white powder. They never determined exactly what it was. I don't know if it was heroin or some of this methadone. And a homemade syringe, and a needle, which was probably got out of the hospital some way during sick call, cause there's only one MTA in there at a time, and sometimes you have fifty, sixty men going to sick call. So it'd be easy for one man to try'n slip behind and pick one up, you know.

Usually you find it on a man, on his person, or in his personal property. So nine out of ten times, you know exactly who it is. And some of these fellas have been narcotics users in the street. And they admit, you know—they're on this methadone program, but maybe sometimes that's not enough for them or they just can't take it fast enough, so they'll admit that they're trying to do something else. Out of the ones we've found, the men admitted that it did belong to them. There was fresh needle marks on one man's arm. The other man was still bleeding from it.

They have these methadone pills that they give these fellas. When they go into the sick-call line to get this, a lotta times they won't swallow it, they'll put it in their mouths, take a drink a water and really don't swallow it. And they'll save three or four or five of them. And they'll all get together. They crush them up some kinda way, and they'll mix it with water and shoot it like they would heroin in the street.

We tried the methadone here, and it worked out great. In this institution, on the level that it's workin now, it started on March twenty-second. And we have close to eleven thousand people gone through methadone detoxification program. On March twenty-second we opened up an area where all newly admitted drug addicts are offered the methadone detoxification program. If they refused they were brought to this floor, and after they calmed down and relaxed they were again asked if they wanted it. You have a situation where you have many

167.

people refusin medication because it would mean admittin that they're a drug addict and it may go against their case. Which of course is not true. Strictly interested in the medical point of view.

I doubt if you can get a drug addict on the outside and talk him into programs unless he's gone through a traumatic experience where he seeks it. Here, the guy is captured, he's in an institution, and he's admitted to be a drug addict or medically noted to be a drug addict. Now you could sit down with him and talk to him about the available programs on the outside. Right now it's gonna be extended with the courts, and the judge may consider the man's case if he's gonna seek treatment on the outside. All of this is in the embryo stage right now.

CALIFORNIA STATE PRISON AT FOLSOM
CHARLES AMITY, INMATE

Around three-ten, cut the machine off, wipe it down. Come down at three-twenty, run to my cell, get my grammar book, go to school for an hour and a half. College level. I got my high-school diploma in prison. I quit formal school on the streets at ninth grade. Then I got a high-school diploma in San Quentin nineteen fifty-two, I think it was.

This is the only course I'm takin now. Yes, it's very good—very, very good. We have an instructor, Mr. McElroy, who's a very conscientious person. And I really don't think he's an exception. He's a concerned-type person. However, the book is more of a self-teaching nature. It's exercise after exercise of paragraph composition and imagination, creativity. It's really repetitious exercises, examples and more exercises.

CALIFORNIA STATE PRISON AT FOLSOM
DOUGLAS A. BORSIN, INMATE

The only thing that the academic education's lookin for is a good record so they can get these federal and state funds. Guys who can actually use an education upgradin, some have been told, well, you know, "Sorry, we can't use you. You can't go in the program."

They approached me to go in the program. I got my high-school certificate through the Army GED while I was in Korea. Department of Education gave me a certificate of high-school equivalency. These people down here, they approached me and say, "You haven't got a high-school diploma. We don't recognize this." Well, damn near every state recognizes the GED test. So they wanted me to go over and take a check—U.S. history, U.S. government, California history and California government, for twenty points, I think they said I needed to get my high-school diploma here in California. I don't need this education.

Poor guy out here's got a third-, fourth-, fifth-grade level, they say, "Well, you're too damn dumb to go to school." Oh, they do take a few show cases. This poor guy's got second-grade education, out in the newspaper they say, "Hey look at us, givin this guy high-school diploma from second-year grade school." It makes em look good. But in reality it's not gonna complish anything.

INDIANA STATE PRISON
EARL GRADY, INMATE

I got a high-school diploma here. But I didn't earn it. See, I was teachin—I taught English, I taught math. And, ah, when I got sick and went to the hospital, they brought me a diploma, cause I had never graduated from high school. But gettin one of those diplomas just a matter of sittin there x number of hours, you know. They changed over to **GED**. We don't have any formal education anymore, in the sense of classrooms—we have **GED** program, adult basic education program. This is what we have in the sense of college courses for people who are just interested: correspondence courses. Buck a course. We stopped the regular education about six months ago. Just normal routine, you know.

But that field is so funny, man. They set it up as normal education, sposed to be apply in the streets, you know. And we have unique situations in here. Majority of em is dropouts from school and society as well, but the curriculum didn't fit us on the street, so why would it fit us in here? How anyone's interested in science and biology and all this jazz, and they place emphasis on this and try to teach it. I said, "Take it out of your curriculum," you know.

"Oh, we can't. Wouldn't be standard. Wouldn't win a diploma."

You know, one of them things. What we need is vocation, more vocation. Give a man a skill, you know, along with psychological trainin. Dude have problems in here and no where to go—counselor's good for nothin, you know.

ATTICA CORRECTIONAL FACILITY
ANONYMOUS CORRECTIONAL COUNSELOR

We have program here where if these people do test below the sixth grade, it is mandatory that they go to school. After that, in a lot of cases, they're not interested in education. It's kinda tough to

169.

CLASSROOM, OSSINING CORRECTIONAL FACILITY, NEW YORK, 1969.

tell a thirty-year-old man that if you can really, you know, even get a high-school equivalency diploma while you're here, your chances of getting a job with a high-school equivalency diploma as compared with your chances of getting a job without any diploma at all are much better. But you know, "Well I got as far as I did for thirty years, then I can still get along." You know, that's very frustrating, because you know a thirty-year-old man has got another forty years to live on the average.

BUCKS COUNTY PRISON
RAYMOND WARD BURNS, INMATE

They used to say—it's an old saying that it's a school of crime. Well, it is a school of crime when you have nothing to do but sit around with four or five cell partners or in a group in the yard, talk about crimes that were committed, how they did them and everything else, you know. And you hear of all kinds of crimes. You hear the sex crimes, you hear the burglaries, the armed robberies, the murders, the perversions—you hear everything. And once you're exposed to all that, pshew!

DISTRICT OF COLUMBIA WOMEN'S DETENTION CENTER
JANE MASON, INMATE

To me jail has never stopped a person from doin nothin that they wanna do. An anythin that I can see, it's made people go out and do more wrong, you know. Whereas you take a prisoner ain't know how to do nothin but steal when they came in here, so they got busted for petty larceny or grand larceny or what have you, and he gonna come in here, and he got five or six robberies sittin in here, bank robberies charges, an couple of possession of narcotics, heroin—you got a zillion people in here for that—you got four or five people for possession of works, they gonna learn from these people that're in here. They're gonna learn how to go out and sell dope. If they don't know who to get it from, they'll learn when they get in here. If they ain't know nothin bout stickin up no bank, they gonna learn it when they get in here. If they ain't know nothin bout housebreakin, they gonna learn that when they get in here. If they ain't know nothin bout stickin a gun in somebody's face'n jumpin across them bank-tellers' cages, they gonna learn how to do all that when they get in here, you know, because this is all the people talk about in here, is they charges and how they got em and what they gonna do when they get out. An I've got my first time yet to hear one say, "I'm goin outta here and get me a job an try'n better myself." But it would take more fingers and toes than I have to tell you how many of em say, "I can't wait for my reinstate so I can go out and get myself a nice shot of heroin." Or, "I can go out there'n get high." Or, "I'm gonna have the dope man waitin for me," or, "When I get out I'm goin directly to the dope man." There's more of em in here that say that than there is officers in here all the shifts. Believe me.

ATTICA CORRECTIONAL FACILITY
MATTHEW BAKER, INMATE

Like you get out of the shop about three-oh-two in the afternoon, and you come back to the company, and you get there at approximately three-oh-five. And, ah, you know, you want to change clothes or change your shoes or get your coat and hat or something, you know. Well, if you have a nasty guard on, he's gonna start clickin your doors, you know. They're electrically or hydraulically operated. And it's very annoying. An this guy'll just sit up there and start clickin the doors, you know.

Ah, out in the yard, they have weightlifting, they have a heavy bag, heavy punching bag. Ah, you could run around the block. They have baseball when it is in season and football when it is in season, basketball, handball, and that's about the extent of it. So you either go out or stay in your cell for an hour or so.

BUCKS COUNTY PRISON (EASTERN PENITENTIARY)
RAYMOND WARD BURNS, INMATE

A guy come up, accosted me in the yard one afternoon. I was by myself. A little alley down in Eastern. And he made some kind of a smart remark. Then he pulled out a knife on me. And I tried to take the knife off of him. Well, I missed when I grabbed for him, and he stabbed me. But I turned around, I ran into my cell. I had to lay in my cell for two days, two and a half days actually, just holding the wound closed.

If I go into the hospital, what would happen then is that the officials would of questioned me. And I would of had to tell them or else I would have got locked up cause I wouldn't have told them. So then what really happened: when I stayed there the two and a half days after the wound had healed, I had a knife taped outside my window, and I went over to the block where he was in. Well, he had got transferred, so I never could get back at him. But for the first few years after that, if I'd a seen him, I'd a tried to hurt him bad. He's still in prison, but I don't know which one.

172.

Well, the yard was running and coming in from upper yard in the evening about three-thirty for lockup, and we pulled a drunk outta the line. He was very intoxicated, and we pulled him over to the side, another sergeant and myself. And we asked him for his identity, his identity card and privilege card, and he said, "Well, if you want it, you're gonna have to take it."

So the sergeant started to reach in and get his card out of his pocket, and man took a swing at him, and we jumped in and hadda restrain the man and got his card. And we set the man down over in a seat while sergeant went over to get an assignment where we're gonna put this man. When the sergeant left to go down and get the assignment, the cell assignment, this man jumped up and attacked me. He swung at me. And he started to wrestle. Then the tower across the yard fired a shot. At that time the inmate stopped a minute, and he just looked up the tower, and he says, "Go ahead, shoot me now if you wanna." And by that time inmate come back and start wrestling. Well, I subdued the guy down and got him down by the time the sergeant and the extra personnel, hearing the second shot, come running to my assistance. And we just forcefully took the man over to the adjustment center, put him in a quiet cell.

I wasn't frightened. I was more frightened at the man in the tower, cause I didn't know what he was shooting. And here I was grappling with the inmate, wrestling around on the ground and what not, and course as inmates are, they like a show like that, and they all started yelling and hollering and screaming. Then when they hear a rifle go off, they're all attracted to that area. And I was more concerned with the rifle, man who was pointing the rifle. I was hoping he wasn't trying to shoot at us or shoot the individual. But later on he said no, he was shooting it in the ground. But it didn't slow the man down at all. Like I said, he stood up on the first shot and said, "Go ahead and shoot me."

They have a number of what they call unlocks. This'd be for a general population come in off the yard. They all proceed off the yards and go to their cells and their tier and to their cell. And it takes an officer to go up, unlock the bar on the tier, pull the bar, so they can go into their cells. And it's a regular routine. And they have these just about once an hour. Those people would be coming in from the yard or they may be workers coming in after they've gone to the canteen and picked up their purchases on their way back to the cells.

At three o'clock you prepare for the four o'clock count. At that time, you pull the wires and let anyone that has to count outside the building, that's gonna count elsewhere other than the building, they come out at three o'clock and go to area where they have to count. And then at three-thirty, general lockup. The yard, they all come in to lock up in their cells. And then the workers come down from industries up in the lower yard. And everybody's locked in. And when they all get in off the yard, approximately ten minutes to four, they sound a double whistle. The institution starts to count on that double whistle. And it might be ten to four. It might be four o'clock. Then it takes approximately twenty minutes, fifteen minutes to count the entire institution.

CALIFORNIA STATE PRISON AT SAN QUENTIN
RAFAEL HERNANDEZ, INMATE

One time I was sittin down in the block. It was about quarter to four, and I still had fifteen minutes til lockup. So I'm watchin the guys comin into the block from the yard. So this fella stop and talk to me. So I'm rappin to him right then, and this bull tells me, "I'm gonna lock up."

Told him, "Lockup ain't until four o'clock, man. I still got fifteen minutes."

So he told me three more times, but every time he was tellin me, he was really started gettin a little more harsher. So I jus jumped up, I was gonna hit him, but I held myself back.

I told him, "Get that lockup and shove it up your ass as far as I'm concerned," you know.

So when I jumped up, he jumped back, and I guess he thought I was gonna swing on him.

Nothin happened. He threatened to write me up, but he never did.

INDIANA STATE PRISON
DANIEL ENGLAND, CORRECTIONAL OFFICER 2

The inmates don't seem to feel I'm bein weird by turnin the key or anything. They don't care because they know somebody has to do it. I felt a little funny when I first started, but after I seen the procedure, and everybody looks at it the same way, you know, I figured what's the difference? It's not my job to help the inmates with anything, and I don't. If anybody is gonna help the inmates, it's gonna be their counselors or someone else. I just let em in the doors, and I do my job. It's a job. Make a livin at it, you know. If I don't do it somebody else will, you know. I'm gettin paid to do the job, and I do it.

174.

### BUCKS COUNTY PRISON
### PRESLEY MIDDLETON, CAPTAIN OF OPERATIONS AND SECURITY

I told a couple a guys, couple a the inmates, rappin with a couple a guys when I stay over late, "You know, it hurts me more'n it hurts you to lock you in." Especially when you get to know the guy. Might be my clerk. And say for the las three months, he was my clerk, and he sort of told me a lot of things about himself, you know. You get to sort of size a man up. And then when I have to go in that block at night, lock him in, and the guy might say, "See you later then, Cap," it makes you wonder, you know.

I drive home twenty-five miles and I think about that, back of my mind—this guy said like, "Hey, good night," or, "Good mornin," and it bothers me.

Somebody has to do it. Somebody has to clean out the cesspools. Somebody has to do it. You have to have lawyers. And you have to have—you know, you name it. You have to have police. I jus happen to be the bad guy with the key who locks these bad guys in. Let's put it that way. Somebody has to do it.

### BUCKS COUNTY PRISON
### RAYMOND WARD BURNS, INMATE

Jars all through you when the door shuts. You just feel all pent up like an animal.

### ATTICA CORRECTIONAL FACILITY
### MATTHEW BAKER, INMATE

Four o'clock was the big hour, you know. It's when all of the people are really sort of tightening on, you know, the security really starts tightening up. There's also a shift change right then. They lock up and count.

### FEDERAL DETENTION HEADQUARTERS
### ANONYMOUS CORRECTIONAL OFFICER

This is hectic. This is one of the crazier jobs. You've got to get ready for the four o'clock count, which is the most important count of the day. We count bodies, so to speak, at the four o'clock count, whereas during the rest of the day, all they do is count heads. And this makes it more important, cause you should be able to locate the fella, where he is at this four o'clock count. Four and seven.

Four o'clock man, myself, ah, he's responsible from the four o'clock count up to the next morning's count, six o'clock a.m., the next morning. So if one's fouled up between then, the whole count the whole night and the next morning can be fouled up. That's why this here's a little more important than the day count.

First of all, you have to make sure all the men are pulled from court—everybody that's supposed to go to court is marked out to court; everybody's returned, they're back into the log, so they're accounted for either in or out of court. This's the very first thing. Second thing, you see a bus shipment going out which is late, so you have to make sure all the men are pulled out of a Quarters Book we have. And, ah, make sure they're all out. If they're not out, of course, you have one man or several men over in your count. So that's the very first thing you do when you come in is check the book to make sure all the men are pulled out of the books that's supposedly out in the institution.

You have a master list that's made up the night before of men going out to court. What we have is what we call a Quarters Book. Each men are assigned quarters, so many men per quarter. Everything in these books is the official count of the institution. All the men that you have in here is in that book. If he's not in the institution, he should not be in that book. If for some reason the man has not been pulled out of this book, he's assumed still here. And if he's appearing in here and you're counting him here, of course, your count's messed up, so you've got to make sure the man is pulled out if he is not here.

CALIFORNIA INSTITUTION FOR MEN
JOSEPH A. MCCARGAR, CORRECTIONAL OFFICER

Four-thirty count, the other officer counts the north side, I count the south side. As we go through each grill, we lock that grill behind us. And when we come out the other end, we lock that grill. And this way, in case that the count doesn't clear readily, if the guys get impatient, you know, then they can't go from one section to another section—at least they can't go upstairs or the ones upstairs can't go downstairs. Now we get upstairs to count and that's the dormitory style, and it's kinda divided into quarters. And neither of us can count until we meet between the two latrines. And one officer stands there while I count one of my sections, and he stands there while I count my other section. And then I stand in that spot while he counts his two sections. The reason bein: if we didn't wait for each other, then conceivably I could count a man, and the minute my back is turned he could slip into another section and cover for somebody who isn't there, and we'd never know the difference. Because with so many men and the rapid turnover

176.

that we have, you jus don't know when you look in the bed, maybe you don't know who that man is.

We use a count board with blank sheets of paper on it. We take a positive count and at the same time we scribble down every empty bed, and then when we count each section we can tally our positive, plus the number of the empty beds and see whether that section is okay or not.

Control calls us and asks us for count, and if it agrees with us—you see a lotta men will be out-counted at work and different places—if he agrees with us, then he'll tell us the count is clear. If he doesn't agree, then we have to hang onto the phone, and when he finishes the rest of the institution, he'll come back and he'll say, "What do you show bed two-eighteen, positive or negative?" And we tell him. And maybe he'll have a couple more beds he'll ask us about, and if it appears there's enough of a discrepancy, he'll instruct us to recount the whole unit. On the other hand, he may jus say, "Read me your negatives." And this way, if we iron it out this way, then we don't have to recount the unit.

FEDERAL DETENTION HEADQUARTERS
GABRIEL POTTER, INMATE

Mail call's held here at four o'clock count. I'm in the boiler room, so when I get back up to the tank, the mail is either in the tank that I live in or they pass it out to one of my friends, some guy that knows me.

INDIANA STATE PRISON
WILLIAM SIMMONS, INMATE

I pick up my mail in the cellhouse about four o'clock, and most of the time that's when I write my letters, outgoing letters, read my incoming letters. As far as the correspondence lists, well, they're pretty lenient in this respect: anybody can be submitted for approval or disapproval. Now I don't know exactly what procedure or what scale they use out front to determine, you know, whether a person is turned down or approved. But I have quite a few, I have—ah, unfortunately I don't hear from too many of them, but I have quite a few of them on my mailing list—thirty-five. Person has to be approved by the warden's office. We're allowed to write five letters a week. You can have as many as you get in the incoming mail, but writing out you're only allowed five a week.

Well, you buy your envelopes through the commissary department, and figured into the cost of the envelope is the cost for

177.

the stamp. You pay a total of nine cents for the envelope and stamp. Pay for the envelope.

They have a box in each living quarters, and you drop it into this box, and the night officer, the twelve-gate shift officer, takes to the mail room when his shift is over at eight o'clock in the morning. You can't seal it. The only you can seal are to lawyers, judges, Department of Corrections.

CALIFORNIA INSTITUTION FOR MEN
COMRADE SIMBA, INMATE

You can't write from penitentiary to penitentiary— it's part of the parole stipulation that you can't even relate to another parolee—it's a violation of parole, unless it's immediate family, and you have to get approval from superintendent of both pens, plus they censor the mail in that case. They say there's no censorship but it depend on the individual—what kinda classification they got this individual on. If he's a revolutionary, they're gonna censor his mail. When you get the mail in a letter it's opened. Now they say they're checkin for contraband —they won't let contraband go out or in—that's bullshit. Some people, they first don't read the letters, some people they read the letters, but they say there's no censorship. If the letter is sayin somethin in terms of revolution, they take a photocopy of it, put it on his jacket.

DISTRICT OF COLUMBIA CORRECTIONAL COMPLEX
JOSEPH SAKALAUKAS, SERGEANT, CORRECTIONAL FORCE

I have been approached occasionally to mail a letter for one or two of em. But I've never done—fly a kite, as they say. But this was when I was new and I was young, just came to this job. I've never done anything like that. But I have been approached to do something on the outside—illegal in other words. That term "fly a kite" means to take a letter and send it outside the gate through illegal channels—some way besides legally, other words, the mail or somewhere.

The only thing, they've been hiring a lot of people here from the District, and this has been the last few years. And only thing I notice is that there's a lot more familiarity between the new officers and the inmates, because a lot of em went to school with the inmates or they lived close by, they're neighbors. They knew each other's family, things like this. And when I came to work, this was—you wouldn't consider it. You wouldn't be working here if you was that familiar, cause one thing they didn't want you to do was get too familiar with inmates. But since then they've changed over. They try to get you more involved with them.

178.

The officer himself, he's gonna have to decide whether he's gonna go along with the inmate on some of the requests. Like I say, they're neighbors, it's really easy for one inmate to tell some officer, "Say hello to my mother," or, "Tell June I'll come down this weekend." Or any kind of a mess like that. Where with us, don't live in their community with them or have that contact with em, you'd have to really go out of your way to do it for a guy. We just don't do it.

BEDFORD HILLS CORRECTIONAL FACILITY
BERTHA WATERS, INMATE

I guess you could send out as much as you want if they're on your writin list. They have to be on your proved writin list. And it has to be what they call immediate family, and then they break— every now and then you can have a friend write to you. They have to screen em, and I don't think they're allowed to have a record. They have someone go to interview. They have to write back a letter sayin why they want to write you and how long they've known you. I don't know about boy friends. Like if you had a kid by a fella, he's allowed to write you because that's the child's father.

The books hafta come from the publishin companies. Can't come from—no one can mail to you. They screen that. If they feel you shouldn't read it, then that stays your property until you go home.

FEDERAL DETENTION HEADQUARTERS
GABRIEL POTTER, INMATE

The way you get a novel here is ordering direct from the publisher. It has to be mailed direct from the publisher. There is one other way: an attorney can bring the books himself and leave them in parole office to be searched. This is because they claim, about four months ago, they found a blade in one, hacksaw blade.

For books, every book has to come through the parole office and be searched. Bound novels are searched. They open it up, and where it's bound in the back, they stick a fingernail file through it, search and so forth to see if it's got any contraband.

CALIFORNIA STATE PRISON AT SAN QUENTIN
LOUIS S. NELSON, WARDEN

We're allowed to restrict under the law those publications that preach racial supremacy, incite to violence, and are clearly obscene. That's the only thing we can restrict. Now we can restrict any particular number, any particular edition, of any paper if they fit in any of those criteria. We have restricted some on a general basis because they have persistently incite to violence or preach racial—for instance the Black Panther newspaper, which consistently preaches black supremacy, and they used to be—I don't know whether they stopped or not—at the end of every column, they had "off the pigs." Well, when people read that that are short-tempered and raw moods and so forth, we don't need that kind of inciting of our people to kill the pigs, kill the personnel. We don't need that. So there is that sort of restriction. Generally that's all the restriction.

### INDIANA STATE PRISON
### EARL GRADY, INMATE

Man, they stopped Negro Digest. They changed the name of it from Negro Digest to Black World, and I had a subscription, and oh, it was about halfway through the subscription, they changed the name to Black World, and they stopped it. So you know, you can see how stupid it is. Yeah, Ebony's all right. But those are all the people that's got it made—none of the violent, the angry people, the mad people—you know what I mean—mad at the particulars that got him in this condition.

You know, any time you stop a national magazine because it happened to be black, that's pretty sick. No book's gonna make you do anything.

Hey, man, the same ideas that are anywhere else are already in here. Revolution. Kill the screw. Tear the joint up. They're all here. They don't have to come from anyplace else. It's here already. They think that everybody brings you an idea. Everything is here already.

### CALIFORNIA INSTITUTION FOR MEN
### JOSEPH A. McCARGAR, CORRECTIONAL OFFICER

When the count is clear, then one officer rings the unit bell jus one time. That release em from their beds. And the other officer runs around and unlocks all the grills that he has locked. Then we wait to be notified for chow release. Usually about five minutes to five. Half of the institution goes early each day, then the other half of the institution goes early, so release for chow can be within ten minutes or within forty minutes. An they get real impatient waitin to go on.

We have to keep the men waitin inside the grills. They're all packed in there, and if you were to have an incident, it would be a real unlucky thing. So we keep em back behind the grills, then we ring three bells and away they go.

If every inmate went to dinner, that would be fine, and if they were all gone forty-five minutes. But such is not the case. Many of em don't go. They have things they buy in the canteen, foodstuffs they brought in from the visit. You have burglaries goin on, footlockers bein broken into and pried open.

Usually it's not one individual. It's usually two individuals. One of the individuals will do the work on a locker, the other one's what you call a point. Maybe he'll stand over here where he can watch the office, not doin anything, jus standin here smokin a cigarette, while his buddy down there goin into the cell is dependin on him. Soon as the officer gets up and leaves the cell, he'll cough, maybe he'll just stomp the cigarette real hard with his foot. In my experience I have never caught anybody goin through a locker, but I have complaints while I'm on duty that guys are doin it while they were gone to chow.

CALIFORNIA STATE PRISON AT FOLSOM
DOUGLAS A. BORSIN, INMATE

If you lay somethin down, you know, not everybody's an honest crook. There's some guys in here'll walk—they've swung with radios, they've swung with watches, everything else they can lay their hands on.

It's a bad deal when you've got guys inside that steal from each other, but hell, let's face it, they do the same thing outside. There's a few of us got a little bit of morals about us, won't steal from a fellow convict.

But hell, I've been ripped about four or five different times. Not anything major, mostly canteen—ten or fifteen bucks are shot, because I'm out all day. Now they've got what we call an outcount, but our normal count is about three-thirty in the afternoon, and I work out there in the office until five minutes past four, when they clear the main count. Then I come on in, go to chow, and go to my cell. I'm out all day. And some of these guys got aware of it, and there for a while, man, it's pretty heavy in my bill.

Cells are supposed to stay locked, and the building sergeant's supposed to maintain control of the keys both for the bar itself, which locks all the cells, and the spike to unlock the individual cell. We used to have a sergeant over there—what the hell, anybody could walk up and say, "I live in such and such cell, I'd like to have the key." So guy'd give him the key to the bar and spike to the door, and hell, that someone could walk up and take your everything. Didn't necessarily mean that he lived in that cell.

181.

If you have quite a bit of clothes, understuff, razors, combs, deodorant, lotta cosmetics and things, well, if you don't have anything to put this in, you have to get yourself a box. Dudes'll come by when you go for chow, if you jus lay down for a little nap, after you go to sleep, they gonna pull your box. Lotta dudes, they have two or three boxes with locks on em. Well, they would sell em to dudes that jus come in. Maybe they will sell it for four, five dollars, box worth maybe dollar and a half. Dude'll buy the box, cause he got a big ole bag with a lotta stuff he wanna keep, you know. Lotta ways a dude make money husslin aroun. Dudes come in and they say, "I'll let you keep your stuff in my box til you get your box. I'll charge you a dollar a week," or somethin like that. Give him a dollar a week, when you come back, get ready to get your stuff out, half the stuff is gone.

And of course, chow is an ideal time for homosexual activities, because the majority of the people are gone. So you jus supervise the buildin the best you can.

They had a bad incident at San Quentin about eight months before I got up there. These two inmates were engaged in homosexual activity in the library and one officer jus wandered in to check the place'n he caught em in this homosexual activity, and the result was they killed him jus like that. There come a second officer after a couple of minutes, lookin for the first one. They killed three and chopped up the fourth one pretty bad, but he pulled through. So it's not a good thing.

It isn't a question of you don't look, but I would have to say they have more finesse than to be pretty flagrant about it. And then again, if they really want to get somethin on, they can always give a third man a couple packs to watch for The Man, too. This is one of the big operations in prison is the point man.

Over in South Dorm, I've had a couple of em that are so awkward. They still will give the alarm all right, but they were so clumsy about it that I actually called em down to the office and told em, "Well, if I wanted to do somethin, I'd look for another point besides you. I never saw anyone as clumsy as you are." Then I ask him point-blank, "Is that two packs or five packs?" I tell him, "If you want to go on bein a point, you better practice and get a little finesse to the operation."

The reason that you know he's a point is that he gives himself away. Like if I come around this corner here and here's a guy readin a magazine and, "Ahem." Then it's all over. Now there's nothin I can say to this man cause all he did was clear his throat supposedly. There's nothin to find.

BEDFORD HILLS CORRECTIONAL FACILITY
MICHELE PEREZ, INMATE

You could do what you wanna do right on the corridor, and we have somebody watchin out. Take a minute, you know, somebody be in your room but a minute. You be in another room, and you be doin and drinkin. You do what you got to do, you know, as far as sex is concerned. The other person in the other room will see down the corridor, so before they get to the girl that they gotta pass, you know, you already know, and you sit up in the bed and be rappin. They say, "You said I could borrow your sneakers or your desert boots. Could I have em?" You know. Then they call your name. You know when they ask you for somethin, you know that the police is comin. And they haven't got hip to that one yet.

CALIFORNIA INSTITUTION FOR MEN
GUFF A. ROREX, CORRECTIONAL OFFICER

Usually head home more or less accordin to if I have some errands to do on the way home. Go on home, maybe work around the yard. We still have our ridin horses. We have em on a piece of leased ground. Feed those on the way home or after I get home I go up there. It's about two miles from home. We have four. Usually ride on my days off, at least one of my days off. Have em up next to the foothills so we have a nice place to ride. I guess that's my favorite hobby year round. My wife and I have a camper, and we like to get away in the summertime, go up in the mountains, Montana. One year we went down south as far as Gulfport and circled around. Last year we were up in Montana for most of the three weeks.

When I leave that gate, soon as I leave that mail at the post office, I get my mind on my interests and I don't let this bother me.

When I get home some days, if I don't feel good, maybe I'll go in and lie down for half an hour. My wife teaches, so sometimes if she's late comin home, maybe I'll have some dinner cookin when she gets home.

PRISONERS WHO MISSED MEALS BECAUSE OF A DEMONSTRATION USE COAT HANG-
ERS TO PASS INSTANT COFFEE FROM CELL TO CELL. TENNESSEE STATE PRISON,
NASHVILLE, 1924.

# DINNER.

CALIFORNIA STATE PRISON AT SAN QUENTIN
HAROLD W. BROWN, SERGEANT, CORRECTIONAL FORCE

Now there's one portion of the segregation unit that does eat in the mess hall, but for the most part the greatest portion of the segregated unit or segregation unit, these men being in isolation, protective custody, administrative segregation, they do eat in their cells. And the night officers would supervise the filling of their trays and the passing of trays out and the coffee and beverages to the cell and supervise picking up of the trays, make sure they get them all back, cause once in a while if a tray is kept they can be broken down, turned into weapons, sharpened-type instruments.

CALIFORNIA, STATE PRISON AT SAN QUENTIN
JOEY WILLIAMS, INMATE

Dinner in the hole, they might have cold beef, creamed potato, corn, cake or pie or coconut somethin. Coffee. Jus main menu, regular menu. It's cold. By the time you dish it up and pass it out to all the guys, it's cold. It never take me over five minues to eat, cause I don't get everythin on my tray. You know, like a whole lot of crap, cause it be cold, it jus wouldn't taste too good. Jus dump it down your shitter.

185.

Basically everything here's operated on a whistle and a bell. If you're in a cell house, ah, the bell rings twice, get in your cell. It rings once, it means come out. You come out to eat maybe four-thirty, five o'clock.

Very little is automatic in this joint. Everything works by hand. And if I don't close my cell door, they can't close it unless they come way down the range and close it. So we have to close it ourselves. And then they got a bar that they got enough automation that they can roll the bar and close the door. They got a bar that in essence, it moves and closes all the doors where a man cannot get out, but the final lock is by key. Dude has got to turn the key. And the less they can turn the key, the better they are. Now, no inmate has this key to the doors. All officers. And as much as they can get away with not openin it, they leave it open, so they don't have to get up and unlock it and sit back down. So they don't really lock these doors until after you eat.

They roll the bar—inmates roll this bar, you see—bar opens and you just come out. Depends on what officer's on, how he feels, sometimes just walk on out, sometimes you have to wait or some of the officers attempt to make you line up. Nothing's constant in the sense of, if a officer has the discretion to make up his mind, whatever he has to make up his mind about is not a constant factor—it's something that could change with the officer.

Two minutes' walk to mess hall. Walk down side of that line and you got just enough space to line up, and two men line up, and you know, shoulder to shoulder.

I take a position in what we call a cell-block rotunda. I direct all the inmate traffic into and out of the South Mess Hall. This is a feeding time. This is immediately after the institution count is cleared. And everybody has to eat then. I kind of direct all the traffic of all the inmates, plus I insure the fact that my officers are performing their duties—that is, locking, unlocking, the proper bars, getting the proper inmates out the proper sequence for feeding. This has to be done so the inmates of various housing units don't mix together to a great degree. This is to control their movement, their whereabouts, and to maintain the security of the area. And normally we have new or young officers there who don't look at this with too much of a great depth except what they have to do for their own job. So I have to oversee this part and make sure it's done. Every man has to have the opportunity to eat. And it gets to be a large job after a while, specially when you're working with several hundred people at a time.

These men are released one tier at a time. This causes a constant flow into the mess hall. It might be interesting to find out that on our steam tables there's an officer supervising each steam table, not only to see that food isn't stolen and wasted, but also to ensure the fact that every inmate gets his full issue, his full ration. There are inmates serving the food, and so this opens up a point where one inmate might not serve another inmate, and this can't be allowed. It happens, sure. You can't watch everything all the time. But when it comes to a man's food, his mail, his privilege, we closely supervise, make sure he gets everything he's got coming.

Unlike James Cagney and the portrayal of how a prison operates, the men come in through the chow line, pick up a tray, much like they serve in the military. Their tray is filled on a serving table, and they find themselves a seat to sit down. We guide what area of the mess hall he's gonna sit in, but we don't tell him what table he must sit at. There's none of this standing at a table until a table's filled and none of this by-the-numbers bit. It's very relaxed. Only thing that is not relaxed is maybe smoking during the meal. And this is for the officers as well as the inmates.

CALIFORNIA STATE PRISON AT SAN QUENTIN
PRESTON S. SMYTHE, INMATE

Tonight it's either gonna be—let's see—we have beef stew, Salisbury steak, ah, pork steak. Sometimes you have chop suey, spaghetti and meatballs. Tomorrow night we got a Mexican meal, be tamales and burritos, which I can't eat. I forgot what we got tonight. Got somethin pretty good, too. It's not bad. It's better'n the Army, let's put it that way. It's better'n when I was in the Army anyway. The food on the whole, it runs to starch and carbohydrates. You have to watch yourself like a hawk, otherwise you blow up like a balloon.

This is one of the biggest bones of contention in here as far as the mess hall's concerned: dirt, It's the inmates not carin about their jobs, staff because they won't make the inmates do their job. And the inmates that are doin that job generally the worst element. In other words, these are the tough boys that can't work anyplace else, so they put em in food service. Trays always dirty. I've gone through half

187.

CHOW, ONE-MAN DUNGEON, CHATTANOOGA, TENNESSEE, 1937.

dozen before I found one that didn't have somethin from last meal on it. Cups same way. When you can get em. You're always waitin for em. Lines starts and stops, starts and stops. Silverware? Las night they had nothin but spoons on the line. The night before they had nothin but forks on the line. It's a problem.

You ever try to eat puddin or ice cream with a fork? You know, I mean, Jesus, man, it gets to be a hassle. It's like they'll have somethin like that. Maybe they'll have soup in the afternoon, you can't find anything but forks. Well, you just don't eat any soup, unless you wanna slurp it out of a bowl. They haven't got em quite that far yet.

INDIANA STATE PRISON
EARL GRADY, INMATE

Got a rack there with trays on em. You get your tray, grab the first one. It might or might not be clean. Sometimes they're greasy and all this jazz. Raise hell and complain.

"Well, hell we don't have no hot water."

So. That's the situation, sometimes, you know, sometimes. Everything here is antiquated, so it breaks down. You've got to expect it. Sometimes there's no hot water.

We get our trays, then there's a guy on servin line that serves you. You don't serve yourself. They'll probably have some beets and corn and string beans and potatoes and gravy and a piece of lunch meat. That's it. Normal meal.

Same at supper. Or cheese sandwich, grilled cheese sandwich, something like this. Nothing varies about the food. I don't really kick it too much because I have got used to it, you know. After six and a half years, you see, it doesn't really change much, you just have to accept it. Why bitch about it, you know, it's not gonna improve any.

Long tables, long and narrow, and they really don't have enough room to do anything. You don't have enough room to eat. Three men sit at a table, and you can blow your breath real hard, the guy in front of you'll feel it on his back. You don't face anyone. It's pretty antiquated. And then you sit and you eat. When you finish eatin you take your tray and silverware and put it in the recepticle there, give another guy your tray and walk out. You can rap. Takes twenty minutes, I imagine.

I dig people. I watch people all the time. I might just be watchin you or another dude, and dude that I eat with basically all the time, we would be rappin about that, you see. We got one dude, he sits up and he takes all the heart outta a piece of bread, and the brown crusts he don't eat. And you know, we watch this and this kinda adds a little somthing to it, you know—forget about what you're really eatin. He'll sit there, he'll probably be the last man out of the chow hall. Quite a few guys'll watch him. He's kinda a gas, you know. He's what we call an oddball, you know. No one sociates with him. He doesn't sociate with anyone. And he might have ten slices of bread. He'll do all of em like this. And he's real slow about it, you know. He's in no hurry. Kinda weird. So we watch this. We have to have something to laugh at, too.

ARKANSAS STATE PENITENTIARY
WAYNE E. MIFLIN, INMATE TRUSTY

Here it seems like it's the worst meal of the day. Some days I eat breakfast jus to skip dinner. Mostly vegetables. They're switchin aroun now. They've got better food. Food supervisor—now they've got three or four; they used to jus have one, and he would only work mornin or he could come in afternoon if he wanted. Whenever he wasn't here, the food wasn't up to par. But now they got a freeworld supervisor over the whole thing at different times, and it's picked up a little bit. Fish usually on Fridays or Saturdays. Hamburgers. All the bread you want. You can get more of that than anythin else. But mainly they go roun beans, fresh vegetables, stuff raised here in the garden and stuff. Greens. Salads and meats.

CALIFORNIA INSTITUTION FOR MEN
DONALD E. BAILEY, SURGEON 2

You see at home it would be different than it would be here. At home I have my boys—one, eighteen; one, fifteen—and they're both vegetarians—they won't eat meat. My wife very rarely does. So we have a vegetarian meal of some sort. All the meals at home are that way.

If you're eating out, it's very difficult to get a vegetarian meal, but it's also to get a vegetarian meal that has any nutrition in it. Most of the vegetables you get are overcooked. The nutrition's out of the stuff. I'm not a strict vegetarian. I would prefer to be.

CALIFORNIA STATE PRISON AT FOLSOM
DOUGLAS A. BORSIN, INMATE

Let's put it this way: when it's the only restaurant in town, you patronize it. There's a lot of that stuff the men just don't like. For instance, a big bitch this last time was Thanksgivin. Rumor was

190.

WAITING FOR CHOW RELEASE, NEW YORK CITY REFORMATORY, RIKERS ISLAND, 1970.

started around it was all canned turkey. Well, it wasn't. It was what they call that boned and rolled turkey—pressed. And that didn't go over good at all. Every other place I've been in, they always managed to buy the bird, and they chopped it up and fed the line that way. The majority of guys see that turkey come out, it wasn't worth a damn.

Your fish isn't a popular meal. Liver, yeah, cause you don't get enough of it—iron. But beef stew and spaghetti and meatballs, hamburger patties, Swedish meatballs, these things aren't worth a damn. They've got some good meals, but I'd say probably sixty per cent of em aren't what a guy'd want, what a guy would really pitch down'n enjoy.

You get everything real cold, cause they're only movin one line through there, and you're feedin in two dining rooms— you're feedin Five-Building, Three-Building, Two-Building. So by the time you can get down there—and plus they gotta bring the chow from the stoves, and ovens and pots and everything's a good ways back in the mess hall, because the kitchen facilities are shared by both One- and Two-Dining Rooms. Sometimes you might be standin there five or ten minutes until they bring some more chow out. They use one of these portable wheeled food carts sposed to keep it hot, but, hell, it don't. They serve margarine sometimes. Margarine should melt on anything that's gonna heat the potatoes up, hot vegetables, things like that. It just sits there. It's a bad situation.

CALIFORNIA INSTITUTION FOR MEN
COMRADE SIMBA, INMATE

There's a variety of things. If they have swine, I don't eat it. They have salad or beef, peas, vegetables, some kinda dessert— pies, cakes, what have you, coffee, water, bread, butter. You may get a steak durin the week. They have a pretty good menu. You may get a pretty good steak, maybe a bad steak, maybe a large steak, maybe a small steak. And sometimes they may have beef on the line, and they got all these cows around here, and this is—I only go by hearsay rumor when I comment on this—that when they say they got some beef on the line and you go there and they got some bullshit that don't look like no beef, don't taste like no beef, so you have to relate to the fact of what's happenin on the menu. They got it on paper, got it on the records, but it's a rumor that they kill off so many cows out here, and they'll sell em—some officer around here makin a buck—they'll kill off some cows, and they justify this on the menu. This is not always the case. They have beef on the menu and they have beef on the line.

192.

One time I was up here, they had some nasty-ass people. There was a period of time—it was like a protest really. Somebody made a move where they weren't havin no beef. They had all these cows around here for a long period of time, didn't have no beef. And they know they suppose to have beef. So this is when the rumor's really strong in terms of them killin off those pigs and them cows and tradin off maybe pigs for the cows. So somebody went out there and killed a cow. I don't think those cows were made for cookin, but they cooked em up and they had beef for five or six days. But it was nasty beef.

CALIFORNIA INSTITUTION FOR MEN
GUFF A. ROREX, CORRECTIONAL OFFICER

I still raise beef, and we still have some from the las butcherin in the freezer. I kill em all different times of the year. Las time it was in the spring. The spring is really the best. In the summertime with the flies, that really does hold em back a little. Fall, winter, spring—if you can fatten em up, they'll do a little better.

Fella from the locker plant comes out, butchers it, and takes it right down to the locker. They hang it and cut it up and freeze it. Take it home to my own freezer. Used to do my own butcherin.

CALIFORNIA STATE PRISON AT SAN QUENTIN
LOUIS S. NELSON, WARDEN

I eat dinner at home. My wife does the cooking. We don't have any inmate houseboys or any inmate cooks that take care of us. We have a relatively simple evening meal. I guess American fare, although my wife's Italian, but generally—like last night, I had a couple of breasts of chicken with some rice and a salad, and I think I had a cup of coffee. We don't generally have dessert every night. We don't live very high on the hog in the sense that—nor do we put on a lotta dog either. Pretty simple. That's why I don't have any houseboy or inmate cook. When I get home at night, if I wanna feel free to take off my shoes and relax from the day, I can do so.

My job with the inmates is down here, not at my house. I try to impress upon my staff, if they can at all do so, keep their institution life and their family life separate. They're not necessarily interchangeable. If I've got something that I think my wife's interested in—but the kind of little annoyances of the day, no. I don't share those with my wife, cause I think it's unfair to her. I'd rather—if I can get them outta my mind, I'm happier. And I don't necessarily get them out by sit and talk about them all the time.

PRISONERS RETURNING TO CELLS AFTER RIOT, WEST VIRGINIA PENITENTIARY,
MOUNDSVILLE, 1951.

# EVENING.

ARKANSAS STATE PENITENTIARY
CLARENCE JAMES LEE, CORRECTIONAL OFFICER 1

I don't talk to my wife about my job here, cause I'd hate for—what you might say, rumors to get out. And my wife lives in the neighborhood where there's—not lotta old ladies, but they couple old ladies that live next door, and they're always askin about what happened, you know. Well I say, "I don't know about that," you know, because if I did go and tell em about somethin like that, it would all end up backwards, you know. And plus, too, the fact anythin that happens here to one of the inmates, they may not want anybody to know about it outside. In here, it's our job to protect their secrets as well as to protect them, too. So anythin that happen here is really no concern outside, unless they go out and tell it theyselve.

BUCKS COUNTY PRISON
PRESLEY MIDDLETON, CAPTAIN OF OPERATIONS AND
SECURITY

Everybody's curious. People down'n Lower End are curious about the jail, cause you could read the papers every day, it says that John Doe was committed to the Bucks County Prison, ten thousand bail. They know I work there, so they will definitely ask me a question, say, "Hey, my next door neighbor, what's he doin, how's he actin up there?"

You know. And I jus can't stick my fingers in my mouth'n say, "Well I don't know." I'll say like, "He's okay," and so forth.

And sometimes you got a habit, maybe talkin to your parents, talkin to your girl friend, tellin her bout the jail, you know. My girl is afraid to come in this place. I was gonna bring her in to show her what it look like, and now she don't want no part of it. I told her like it was nothin, you know, "Jus come on in, and I'll show ya."

"Don't wanna come in." She definitely won't come in.

CALIFORNIA STATE PRISON AT FOLSOM
EARL STRAUB, CORRECTIONAL OFFICER

I never talk about prison, never talk about it whatsoever. My wife wouldn't know anything about prison activities or what my duties are or anything. She doesn't know. She's never expressed any desire to know, like asking questions about it. But, ah, she's not too happy with me working up there. I don't know exactly what her sentiments are. I guess just being a guard associated with inmates is not too much of a complimentary position. We don't discuss this too often, but well, just when I was attempting to get a job or come up here and go to work, she thought there were other fields I should get into. Course it was my decision. But now we don't discuss the job or position or even the hours when I go to work or if there's an escape or something or have to go out on escape for extra hours. There's no discussion whatsoever. Same way with the kids. The boy is thirteen, the girl, nine. They hear things on the radio that happen at Folsom, and they'll ask me about it, but otherwise, they're not interested.

I rather have it that way. I don't try to force anything. I don't come home and say, "I saw this," or "I heard this." I never bring any of my stories home at all.

INDIANA STATE PRISON
EARL GRADY, INMATE

After chow, straight back to you cell, and then you have what we call sick call. If you have any medicine comin, the officer there gives you your medicine.

After sick call, then you go in your cell or you might empty your little bucket and get your little bucket of hot water. Gallon—gallon-size bucket. Maybe three times a night, a guy'll come round with a big bucket and give you cup of hot water or somethin like that.

196.

CALIFORNIA STATE PRISON AT SAN QUENTIN
HAROLD W. BROWN, SERGEANT, CORRECTIONAL FORCE

In an honor unit the man can take a shower any time he wants—the shower's open every evening. In a main-line unit, they're not open every evening. Because of the quantities of men, they alternate showerings—first one tier, then another tier. And during the weekends, which we don't have showers, but we do have the medical showers and of course the haircuts and the procedures that's involved in getting the men out of their cells, to the barbership, getting their hair cut, getting them back in, and keeping track of them. Of course this is starting in the dark hours, and this is when security becomes more of an important factor. I supervise the officers in their duties of doing this, and they make sure it's done and done right, without a break.

CALIFORNIA STATE PRISON AT FOLSOM
DOUGLAS A. BORSIN, INMATE

In our office, we're a little bit fortunate. Used to have guards that slept upstairs in little rooms, so we've got showers up there. If we wanna take a shower there, beautiful, we don't have to hassle that thing down at night. But the majority of guys got to hassle this. Same thing is Five-Building. They just recently built a shower into there, or revamped—they put in tile floors and like this and there's maybe six showerheads there. One-Building and Three-Building are set up about like Two-Building. Got about ten, twelve heads that's all open. You got a wall about eighteen inches high in front to keep water from comin off the floor. The rest of it is all in there open. Guy doesn't buy soap outta the canteen, he's got to depend on the people that put soap out there at night for your showers. And sometimes gotta raise hell about that to get soap put out there. Not very sanitary, and hell, there's no privacy whatsoever.

After a while you get used to it. Some guys, they haven't been in service and things like this, you know, are real self-conscious. They may figure they got a potbelly on, maybe they figure they ain't hung right, something along this line, and they're a little bit self-conscious, I think, in the beginning. But hell, after you've done it fifteen, twenty times. But you got a cop, too, who stand down there in the showers to make sure—whatever he make sure of I don't know what it is. I haven't found that out yet. They figure you been down there too damn long, they say, "Okay everybody out of the showers." They'll run you on back to the buildings, back up to your cell. Unsanitary I'd say for one thing, and a guy does need some privacy.

197.

SHOWER CALL, OSSINING CORRECTIONAL FACILITY, NEW YORK, 1948.

Hell, you haven't got it. Even your toilet bowl in the cell is open to the cell. It's just against the back. Bars all open, you know. And the advisory council here suggested to the administration, "Well, how bout privacy panels for these toilets, at least you get this much privacy." Hell, they're still screwin around with that, haven't made decision one way or the other.

ATTICA CORRECTIONAL FACILITY
MATTHEW BAKER, INMATE

There is no showers, except once a week, but, however, they let you have a five-gallon paint can to put hot water in to clean yourself with. There is a sink, but it only has cold water.

CALIFORNIA STATE PRISON AT FOLSOM
DOUGLAS A. BORSIN, INMATE

They go for shower line, one tier at a time, go down'n shower. You can get a haircut then if you want it. The showers are on the bottom floor of each building. And they're all open. Let's see, in Two-Building, there's about ten or twelve shower heads. It's all open to the cold air. And believe me, it gets cold in the wintertime. Wind whips down through there. You jump in there, you grab a quick shower, and of course you know there're guys waitin to get in, so you can't go in there and spend any time at all to shower, you know. Jump out, dry off. Two-Building especially, they need work done on those drains, cause that water can build up. I've seen build up two or three inches deep in there. And this is scummy, filthy water. Twenty, thirty guys been in shower ahead of you, and you've got four inches of dirty soap water in the bottom, don't very much like to step into it, but you have to if you're gonna stay clean.

Then you can go over, except on holidays and weekends, you can change your towels and socks, but you gotta turn in one for one. You dry your clothes down there. Of course, they go in once a week, and you get em back once a week. Usually Tuesdays and Wednesdays we get our laundry back—our clean clothes—underwear and pants and shirts.

ATTICA CORRECTIONAL FACILITY
MATTHEW BAKER, INMATE

Ah, the laundry is done when you take a shower. Once a week you throw your underwear, socks, and shirt in the laundry. And on Thursdays or Fridays you turn in your pants, which you are allowed to have three sets, three pair. So some of the guys get, you know, pretty

199.

nasty, because they don't wash their own clothes or have somebody wash them for them, cept for this one-a-week thing. And, ah, half the time you don't get your right pants back, you know. Either wear somebody's that are too big for you or the pants are too big for you or small even though they do have your number on them. Lot of time the chances are you wouldn't get your right pants back.

They wash sheets once a week also. Ah, they issue you three sheets. You're allowed to wear—or, use two, I mean. Ah, and you turn one in and use one of the other ones again next week with a clean sheet and a pillowcase. They give you two pillowcases. So that is, you know, pretty disgusting, you know. You have to put up with it. What can you do?

Ah they have a waterman, what they call waterman, out of the cell. He's the only guy out of the cell, and he goes around with a—it looks like an enlarged watering pot, you know, you see people watering flowers with or what they would have at a gas station to fill the radiator with. And he hands out hot water. And the minimum is he can give you half a gallon of water, hot water, a night. And that is all he is required to give you. However, if you are in pretty good with the guy, in tight with him, and you pay in cigarettes or something, you can usually get, well, maybe five gallons of water put in between two buckets. You can go wash in one bucket and wash some of your clothes in another bucket.

CALIFORNIA STATE PRISON AT SAN QUENTIN
HAROLD W. BROWN, SERGEANT, CORRECTIONAL FORCE

Most of these units in the evenings we're involved in physical activity for security. There are searches constantly and continuously by all the officers all the time. And officer gets to—as a mode of life, you do things like when you walk past a padlock, you always note the padlock; that is, you reach up and grab ahold the padlock and pull on it to make sure it's locked. It may look like it, doesn't mean it's snapped or caught. Cell doors have to be checked for cut bars. And they accomplish this with a pick-ax handle. They actually pling those bars—we call pling the bars—to see if there are bars cut. So you get to do this after a while.

FEDERAL DETENTION HEADQUARTERS
GABRIEL POTTER, INMATE

I do a lotta welding here. There's a lotta cut bars you hafta repair. If a man saws a bar and tries to gain it to freedom, when it comes time for them bars to be welded, every inmate in this institution

200.

BARBERSHOP, GREEN HAVEN CORRECTIONAL FACILITY, STORMVILLE, NEW YORK, 1945.

knows the only thing I'm gonna do—it's my job to weld them—but the only thing I'm gonna do is stand there and watch the engineer weld them. I'm not about to pick up a torch to weld a bar back where a normal man's trying to gain his freedom. He's got four to fifty years of his life to spend in prison, I'm not about to try to keep him from getting out. I'm not gonna help him either, I'll say, but I'm not gonna keep him here. I'll do anything I can to make it comfortable for a man, but I won't do anything to keep him from getting out.

INDIANA STATE PRISON
EARL GRADY, INMATE

I escaped. Have three years on that. In the process I cut an officer. He and I talked. He said, "Aw, hell, man. I understand." Says, "I won't even prosecute." But they made him prosecute or lose his job, so he has to prosecute. There ain't no real damage done. He had two stitches, that's what he received, you know.

At that time I was goin through changes. I hadn't really received my divorce, you know, and this whole bit. And I was pretty—mentally, you know, distorted.

Well, I was trusty, man, I was trusty. It was close to about the time it is now, close to the holidays, you know. This guy, this officer—he's a pretty decent guy—and, ah, but he had not known what is inside of me. He did not know what I was feelin. He thought he was doin me a favor by takin me around in town, which is perfectly legal, and showin me all the beautiful Christmas decorations and their beautiful homes and everything. And I just got divorced, you know what I mean. It wasn't just a one-day thing. It built up, you know, more and more and more. Then I decided I just had it. "I'm leavin here," you know. "I don't have any reason to stay here now," you know, "my family's gone." The whole bit. "What am I stayin here for?" you know.

I had a little—some kinda tool. I forget now just exactly what the name of it was. And I put it on his neck, and I said, "Man, lemme outta here. I'm splittin." We were out in the street in a van, a carryall, no cuffs, no nothin.

He said, "Man, don't do this."

I said, "Man, I can't help it. I got to split."

He tried to restrain me, but I had my arm around his neck and, ah, he was pullin away from me. And that's when he got cut really. And, ah, in fact, I didn't know he was cut until after I'd got out of the carryall and I ran a couple blocks and then hid under some bushes. And then I saw blood on my hand. And then I saw it wasn't my blood—that he was cut. But I didn't really know that the dude was cut,

UNSUCCESSFUL ESCAPE ATTEMPT, BELMONT COUNTY JAIL, OHIO, 1952.

you know. The next day, after I came back to institution, he told me, he said I just nicked him. He, when I left there, went to the hospital. They put two stitches in his throat.

I was caught the next mornin. That happened about six o'clock in the evenin. It was just dark. Hid under some bushes all night, and I guess that night I woulda committed suicide if I had anything to commit it with. Whatever I had cut him with, I had thrown it away, so I didn't have anything in my pocket. And I can't move cause police are up and down the street. I can see them but they fortunately didn't spot me. It snowed that night. Man, I was caught in the snow, layin down there. Next mornin I got up and, ah, I don't know what time it was, was early in the mornin, and some guy had cranked his car up, sittin in the driveway to warm up, and that's the car—I took the car and split. Well, I'm goin down the highway and I look up, there's an officer on my tail. So I just pull over, and they brought me back. That was the whole bit.

And I'm payin dearly for it, too, you know. They dropped the car theft. They dealed some kinda way. State troopers, they caught me, so they brought me back. And some state troopers, they came in here in the defense mechanism. Other words, "You tell us what happened, and we'll drop the charge of car theft."

So I told em what happened, and they dropped the car theft. They tried me for assault and battery. They give me a one-to-ten suspended sentence on assault and battery and give me three years for escape.

I don't feel they doin anything wrong in givin me three years for escape, but I think I have paid, you know, I have paid.

CALIFORNIA INSTITUTION FOR MEN
JAMES M. CURTEY, INMATE

When I was an escape clerk I'd go in maybe five o'clock in the evenin when I'm through for the day. The first count goes and clears. The second count, ten-thirty, is usually when the guys are missin. So then they immediately—as soon as they determine a guy's escaped, they call me out. The watch commander gets the central files out, which I'm not allowed to handle. I have a form, he feeds me all the information that I need—FBI number, fingerprint classification, date of birth, race, height, weight—all the complete description, a guy's history on this sheet.

I rush back upstairs and make out a flier, which goes

over to the print shop. Soon as I make that and get the printers to work and the photographers who are printin these things, I rush back upstairs and make a teletype to the director and an all-points bulletin for the police departments and rush em back downstairs. The officer grabs em, puts em on the teletype. Now I have to make a report from the officer in the housin unit. His report goes to the control sergeant. The control sergeant makes one to the lieutenant, then the lieutenant makes the final report to the captain. Now these go on dittos and these are run off as quickly as possible, and then I make my package. Then I wait until the fliers come back, and I attach a flier to each one of these. By now it's two, three o'clock in the mornin. But I go around and put copies of all these reports and the flier on the desk of the associate superintendent, the superintendent, and the deputy, and all the people who are interested. And so when they come in in the mornin, they see this report.

The next mornin at about eight o'clock, I have to be back at work. And then we have to make a big, long report to the director of the Department of Corrections in Sacramento all about this guy, his escape, why he escaped. Then we send out these fliers to all police agencies throughout California, make up folders, make the field jacket for the investigator. Then hafta come back.

Last year we had ninety-seven men escape from here. The biggest percentage of em are caught. They have a lotta men at large, but maybe one outta five'll stay. The majority of the men will catch themselves. And on this job, I have to write the legal documents which certifies the records for the records officer, for the investigator to take to court and get an escape warrant. Then if a man was apprehended, don't make any difference if's the middle of the night, they'll call me out. I write an all-point bulletin, a teletype to the director statin that the man had been apprehended, a report to the captain, a report to the director.

These forms are there. If I don't do em, somebody else is gonna do em. It's a procedure. Don't make any difference who does it. The inmate on the job, he's jus doin the work, that's all. Course I never volunteer nothin. Wouldn't say "Look on his visitin card," maybe he's got some hot visits there that people's interested in, his mail card. It's their job, they have to do it. I didn't volunteer any information.

They've got it down to a pretty good technique. They've got a form so you ask for this information. You've got to have it on there or the lieutenant won't sign it. He'll jus send you back and make you do it.

205.

SUPERINTENDENT MEADOWS CONTEMPLATING ESCAPE OF ALL HIS MOST DANGER-
OUS PRISONERS, IVY BLUFF PRISON, NORTH CAROLINA, 1954.

CALIFORNIA STATE PRISON AT SAN QUENTIN
HAROLD W. BROWN, SERGEANT, CORRECTIONAL FORCE

Security is more difficult during the evening hours. We have men checking out for school, night college, and gym and movies, ah, various religious groups, ah, and of course officers are charged with the responsibility of checking these men out of the unit and then checking them back in. This causes a situation that we know the whereabouts of any particular inmate at any give time or where he should be. If we check him out and he doesn't report to where he's supposed to be, he has to be found, of course.

ARKANSAS STATE PENITENTIARY
JAMES JESSE JONES, INMATE

You can see the chaplain at any time. He will try to help you in any way he can far as I know—anythin I asked him. Any way he can, he'll help us. He gave us Christmas cards to send out to peoples for Christmas and stamps. We have a little group every Tuesday night. They have church on Sundays. They have a AA. They have a rehab comin every day. Talk to the rehab. The ones that need a job, rehab is good. Like the chaplain can check if you don't get any mail, if they hold up your mail or somethin. If you live close by here, get in touch with your people, ask them to write you, kinda keeps you outta trouble. Thas the good thing about it that they used to didn't have. They used to didn't have this black chaplain they have. Had a white chaplain. Now I can't say nothin bout him. I ain't never heard a him helpin nobody. The black one, he does that. I know that for a fact—he help lots a people.

ARKANSAS STATE PENITENTIARY
DEWIE E. WILLIAMS, CHAPLAIN

Evenin religious services are quite varied. Usually the program is presented by freeworld personnel from various parts of the state. It might be a singin group, nothin but singin. Then next Tuesday night it might be a group choir. Sometimes we'll have a regular church-type revival service, say, an Assembly-of-God group from Harrisburg. Maybe the next Tuesday night it'll be—oh, I've shown, one time here a while back, I showed some home movies when I was on a couple of campaigns on the island of Jamaica. And the men and the women both thoroughly enjoyed those things, cause it's somethin different, you see. It transports them outta this prison settin way over yonder. Next Tuesday night an adult choir'll be here, and they'll have a scripture readin, Christmas carols and so forth—Christmas program.

I should mention one other thing about these programs on Tuesday night. It's not only the religious that is important—and that certainly is not to be minimized—but this gives the inmates the opportunity for contact with freeworld people. This is somethin that many inmates do not have very much, and this gives em that person-to-person relationship. Keeps em in touch with that world.

My philosophy is this, and I think I brought it from the New Testament: we speak of bein saved, and we think of salvation. You hear these words, and you read these words in every medium of communication. I think that most of us put the wrong connotation to the word salvation. Accordin to the Bible, the word salvation literally means wholeness—wholeness of the person. So to me, a man does not have a soul, man is soul or spirit. He's a person, he's life. He's a life principle. This is the eternal thing within him, and this exists as mind, body, spirit, and emotions. How can you separate em? To me you don't separate em. The physician that treats the broken arm is treatin more than the broken arm. Any good doctor will tell you that he's treatin the person. The way that arm heals will depend to a degree upon what kinda relationship exists between the physician and the patient. So I don't think you separate them. And to me, salvation is helpin the total person to become a better person. And I see this through the love and the grace of God. I think God who made us knows our physical conditions, our spiritual, emotions, and our mental. And so to me, my ministry is to the total person. Therefore, when a man walks into this office, I see that man's deep need, I try to meet the man where he is and go from there. But I always try to exemplify the love and grace of God —acceptance of the individual in spite of what he's done, in spite of what he feels toward himself. So all of it to me is deeply, basically religious.

CALIFORNIA INSTITUTION FOR MEN
MICHAEL COONEY, CHAPLAIN

Tuesday evenin I have Mass here at six o'clock in the evenin. And after that I have a little so-called choir practice—sing a few things. I don't conduct that. I just hear. I couldn't carry a tune in a bucket.

Sometimes I get off into town, get out then. Once or twice a week anyhow, usually every Sunday evenin, go to one of the priests' houses. And I'm tied up with the American Legion, too. Every second Monday I go to that.

Tuesday evenin we have the choir. Then Friday evenin I have a Mass at six, and after that I have a few of em here in a

CHAPEL, CALIFORNIA STATE PRISON AT SAN QUENTIN, 1966.

kinda religious discussion group. Some of em get a bit of instruction, others are not. And then Saturday mornin, continue with the more formal religious instruction. Then I take off on Thursday. Otherwise, in the evenin I just loaf around here—go over to some of the units, go over to the gym or somethin of that kind, see what they're doin over there.

FEDERAL DETENTION HEADQUARTERS<br>CHAUNCEY O'SULLIVAN, INMATE

Generally on Sundays at night they have Muslim services, but for the last, I say, almost two months, they haven't had any Muslim services. I don't know why. And when they do have it here, it all depends on who's here, you know, the Muslims that are here, who are outspoken, speakin. And if they good, then they draw a crowd up there in that place—they file in.

The reason why they say they couldn't have the services is they have no one to go in there and watch everybody. And that's a lie. I look at it, they have the Catholic services and, um, Science Christian services the mornins on Sundays, and a regular police goes in there, and at times, half the services only had three people in there. But Muslim services they say they have to get somebody from the outside to come in and sit there, when they have the manpower here, if they really wanted to, you know. And to me it's a thing of breakin it up, which they tryin to do.

Like to me it's a resentment. Even though I don't go every Sunday or I might not go for two months, it's a resentment because when I wanna go I want it to be available, you know, not to have to ask the lieutenant why and he tells me, "Well I don't have any manpower."

I said, "Well, you find the manpower for the other services, why not?"

And then he gives you an excuse of—in other words, "Get outta here," and, you know, stops at that.

DISTRICT OF COLUMBIA CORRECTIONAL COMPLEX<br>GABRIEL POTTER, INMATE

We have a good group of Nation-of-Islam people here. In fact, this is one of the first things, groups of inmates, I've ever noticed. When I was in the cell block at the jail, when I was waiting for trial and before I came down here, they were some of the few black men that conducted themselves, as far as I was concerned, as gentlemen. And you know, you don't have to necessarily believe all their rhetoric, but at least they were conducting themselves as a human being. Whereas some

210.

of the other black men, I thought, were just plain-ass sloppy pigs—
plain niggers, as they call themselves.

DISTRICT OF COLUMBIA CORRECTIONAL COMPLEX
JOSEPH SAKALAUKAS, SERGEANT, CORRECTIONAL FORCE

Now we have the Muslims here. And I was here when
the Muslims first started, when they first declared that it was a valid
religion and they could practice their faith in whatever form they do.
An it was kind of hairy here at the time, cause they were talking about
the black man hating the white and all this thing, four-hundred-year
bit. And since then everybody's gotten used to hearing it, and it's
nothing. And the Muslims in here, personally, I think they're the
cleanest, the most well-mannered inmates on the hill. I like em. I'd like
to see more of em join it. They go around with their collars buttoned up
and clean everything. They have their little meetings. We have no
problem with em. Whatever they preach, they can preach anything they
want, that's their business, but they are the better inmates now, I think.

DISTRICT OF COLUMBIA CORRECTIONAL COMPLEX
LOWELL MILLER, INMATE

Guards here have their own special kind of Gestapo-
and threatening-type tactics. They'll bring you into the Captain's office,
and one of them will have the handcuffs ready for you, be five or six of
them around. They'll be this captain, who's about six-ten, this huge
captain named Clodhopper, and he'll say, "Miller, this is your last
chance, kid."

And I'll say, "I'll take it." You know, they'll want me
to shave my beard off.

There're only two other Jews on the compound besides me. And I wanted kosher food and to grow my beard and to
exercise my constitutional right to religious freedom. One of the ad-
ministrators, I wrote him a letter, and he made a comment, he said,
"Miller's got the choice:—he can be an inmate or a Jew," meaning
that if I wanted to be a Jew, I'd be one behind the wall. So I got to see
the superintendent and got into all sorts of hassles. I find that they back
off pretty much if you have people on the outside putting a little pressure on them. So I got in touch with the Jewish Defense League and
some other organizations. I think I might sue the department.

DISTRICT OF COLUMBIA CORRECTIONAL COMPLEX
JOSEPH SAKALAUKAS, SERGEANT, CORRECTIONAL FORCE

Although our job is to try to keep em here, we try to
maintain a little harmony and peace, try to help the guys along that

want help. If they don't want help, they just do their time, that's it. If
they want help, it's available. But here they don't push. A man has to
come and ask for help. Just like this academic school we're in now. It's
available for everybody, but no one makes anyone do anything. A man
has to want it, and he has to come over and enroll himself. He's tested,
and they tell him which area he's weak and strong in. And most of em
want to continue in their strong area. We try to convince them that the
area they should go into is the weaker one, so that to bring it all up to a
certain level and then move it all up together. But the man himself has
to want help, and he has to go out and get it. But it's here if he wants
it.

CALIFORNIA INSTITUTION FOR MEN
COMRADE SIMBA, INMATE

We have night-school programs. You go over there
and you sign in, and they have another count. Sign in at the barracks
were you goin. I'll say there's seventy per cent illiteracy in the pen.
That's a product of the society, and the majority of the people in the pen
are of oppressed nation, come from oppressed environment, so that
means that in the community where the people live, the people are
illiterate. This cat in college, he gotta develop his skills, cause I was like
a teacher's aide. After I got my high-school diploma I became a teacher's
aide, like teachin the brothers to read'n write'n mathematics. And
these brothers, they come in, man, they're keen. If I hadn't been in that
class, I'd never known they did not know how to read or write, cause
they had survived out there in the streets. They knew how to hussle,
they knew how to make a buck, they had a game. Couldn't read or write
but they had survival tactics. It was a trip, man. Conversation, you talk
with em, and they could hold down a conversation and blow on some
deep thoughts; but they can't read or write.

As far as a program, it's to get outta this madness. I
mean, I had to do somethin. If you don't have a high-school diploma,
then they wanna send you to school. So I went to school. I set in the
classes, I protest in the classes, I talked about the teachers. That's what
you do. They teach you wrong, you attack them. If they teach you to
learn somethin within that process, you get some credits whether they
taught you somethin relevant or not. You take so many credits, they
give you a certificate that says you have a high-school diploma, whether
you know somethin or not. Some people take them books and read em

212.

and try'n pick somethin up. A lotta them books ain't sayin nothin. But wasn't no big thing. But they gave it to me. Qualified me to get some college courses. Qualified me to think about goin to college on the streets'n get another certificate.

I'm constantly rebellin, but I got to learn somethin. I pick up what I can and take it down and struggle with it, develop the good in it, you know, and throw away the bad'n start to develop this into another culture, another-type institution, another-type writin. And I think that anybody in the schools, intellectuals, this is what they should be doin. This means they have to leave the environment of the school and go into the community and become part of that community, part of the people, have people's dreams and live their people's dreams and use them skills to help develop the people.

CALIFORNIA STATE PRISON AT SAN QUENTIN<br>JOEY WILLIAMS, INMATE

Wednesday night, go to school. Government. College class. This is the first semester. I jus decided to take the test. I didn't think I could pass it. So guys kept on, "Hey man, come on over here in college. Come on over here in college."

"Ah, to hell with it," you know.

They said, "Go on, man, jus take the test."

I said, "Man, I'm gonna flunk the test," I said. "You know how bad I am in English, man."

He said, "Go take the test."

So I said, "Okay, man." I says, "I flunk this test, and I don't pass it, you and I . . ." you know. So I go, I make hundred and sixty-five. So I passed.

At that time the only class they had open was American Studies. Next semester I plan on takin Biology, Speech Sixteen, and that's about it.

CALIFORNIA INSTITUTION FOR MEN<br>JOSEPH A. MCCAGAR, CORRECTIONAL OFFICER

Five nights a week in the South Dorm we have the upstairs people involved in groups. And nights that I work I conduct one of those groups. And the group lasts for one hour. The one I conduct, I hold it from seven-thirty until eight-thirty, and the reason for this bein that if you start any earlier, then you're gonna have guys up there in the group, and when we have the school release, which is about seven-twenty, and the officer downstairs rings three bells, then everybody wants to go to school. So I found that I wait til after the school release, then hold the group.

We have what you call a **STRU** program over there. The letters stand for Short Term Reconfinement Unit. The **STRU** program is for people who are gettin a little shaky on parole, and they were sent back to the institution by their parole officer. It's supposed to be a break for the person. Instead of bein busted on the street and doin a term and then goin up north and doin another two or three years, he's pulled back in before he does anything too awfully serious. He's in this program for a period of anywhere from four to six months, and then he goes back out again.

It could be that the man refused to hold down a job. It could be that he was—one of the ideal conditions is he went out with a **Five-B** condition, which says he can't drink, and he was found swacked in a bar.

Each man in the **STRU** program has what we call a prescription program, and this is compiled by his outside parole agent on his conduct out there and also based on his past history. And these things read in a pretty derogatory manner, which is actually—that's the way it's intended. The man is sent back here, and he reads his prescription program, and it's supposed to open his eyes so he'll say, "It's pretty stupid the way I conducted myself out there."

To start off the group he must read this prescription program in front of the other inmates. One of the things they haven't been able to break down in prison is the we and they. Now the inmates are together, and the staff is together. It's still them and us, really. And I mention this because as soon as a man starts readin his prescription program, and here he reads this thing that really makes him seem like a dog, now he's gotta couple a buddies in there, they say, "Is this the way it was?"

"Well, no, man, but that's the way he put it down."

"I gotta read it. Who is your parole officer?"

Well, then they run down the parole officer little bit. Now, my job is to try to keep these, what-you-call defense attorneys, from puttin this guy up on a pedestal, and if you can, get all of em, especially the guy readin, to face reality and see that he did have problems out there.

About five or six years ago over the institution here we had what we call compulsory group counselin. Every inmate had to attend group counselin. At that time I was workin in the barracks, and I had a group five nights a week. And that hour every night in the barracks, when it first started, I used to literally wear myself out tryin to get these guys to get somethin down to a serious nature. But what they wanted was to beef about: "Why can't we get more socks, more bath towels, colored TV sets?" "Wasn't that cow in the mess hall terrible tonight?" And then the staff. So I became so frustrated with this type of groupin that I begin to draw up an outline for this. When I had compiled this, I took it into the superintendent here, and he was pretty impressed, and he showed it to the director of corrections in Sacramento. Couple of weeks later I got a very nice letter of commendation, and he gave permission for this to be printed by the institution. Well, as soon as it was printed, I began to group on this.

I started this group in nineteen sixty-six, and I'm still continuin with it, and it meets one night a week in my own time. The nice part about this group, it's voluntary to begin with. Nobody has to get into it. And the second nice feature about it is, I believe, instead of groupin around a man, we group around a problem area in kinda a round-robin thing. As soon as we all get seated, then I appoint a man to be chairman that night. What he does is read the topic, and when he finishes readin it, then I give him a bell and a paper and pencil, and he starts either to his right or his left and calls on each man to express his feelins about this topic.

There are three types of inmates you'll find in a group setting. I consider the A-type a man who is certainly not satisfied with what his life has been, and he would go to any extreme to change his life for the better—he would accept help from any quarter. And then the second man, Type B, who is also quite sincere, he would like to change his life, but not yet—maybe in six months, maybe in another couple a years. We have the third type, and he'll sit in the group, and he'll tell you he can't be helped—that people have tried to help in the past and it never worked; and if you insist that you wanna try to help him, then he'll try to go to work on your case—"Well, if you're so smart'n can help other people, how come you haven't gotta million dollars in the bank?"

CALIFORNIA INSTITUTION FOR MEN
SANCHO SUAREZ, INMATE

Thursdays, like today, my only actual day that I don't have anything to do in the evenin. And Friday we have the Chicano Youth Committee, which basic purpose is to prepare themselves for public speaking, so that when they go out into the community, they'll

215.

be able to relate to youth what is the prison life. They are qualified to speak behind crime, drugs, or whatever subject that organization or school or college would want us to discuss. But basically it's because we want to get involved with the youth. We do not want them to follow the same foot patterns that have brought us behind these bars. Cause it's no fun in here, man. Like three or four chicanos comin down and one of these correctional officers will say, "Here comes the Mexican Mafia." A little shit like that. Or they come up to you and say, "Hey, I'm glad my colleagues have finally got together and they're gonna disband your groups, cause you're nothin but militant individuals. You guys don't belong here."

My reaction to that was, "Fine," I said. "Dissolve the groups. I'm all in favor of it. If you're dissolvin it because of what happened in Soledad, Quentin, Folsom, and just recently at Attica, go ahead and dissolve all the groups, all the chicano and black groups throughout the State of California in the penal system. And I'll tell you—and this is not a threat, it's a promise—what will happen as a result of disbandin these groups here, it will make it look like all that was just a picnic." Which is the truth. Sure, it might sound like a threat, but you know, it's reality. They do not look at it on the convict side. To them you come into a joint, your name is taken away, all you are is a number.

CALIFORNIA STATE PRISON AT SAN QUENTIN
LOUIS S. NELSON, WARDEN

My wife and I, during the evening if we're not going out, we play a few games of dominoes and read a bit, listen to music, watch the television, ah, whatever we do—I guess a couple of old folks. My wife does some knitting. So whatever we do. I do have a hobby of woodworking, but I don't this time of year. It's difficult the winter months, cause I don't get home til it's dark, long after it's dark, so I can't do much in that regard.

I don't read much on corrections. Hell, no. I haven't seen anybody say anything new. I could go back and read the material when I went through the training academy. There's a commentary I saw in the morning's paper where attorney general said they're gonna start academy for training correctional people. And I went through one of those thirty years ago in the federal government, and they abandoned it because it was no use. Now it springs up as a bright new idea on the horizon, as the place for penal reform, part of penal reform. I read books like—this is one, the story of Charles Manson. I just got that far. And at home I'm reading the Bobby Seale, Seize the Time. I recently read some other books that I think will have greater influence on me than the kinds of things that the commissions write about the institutions. I've helped some of these fellows write their textbooks, so I don't really need to read them.

I think it's important to know what the larger community's thinking, particularly about prisons, and I try not to get lulled to sleep by the loud voices of a few people as opposed to the quieter voices of a number of people. Now as far as—if you're talking about politics itself, I don't give one damn for politics. I recognize that up the hierarchy above me where the agency secretary and director—the world in which they move, they must concern themselves with politics. I don't think our director does, but anybody who gets up there, there must be political considerations. For everything that happens in our government, somebody is worried about how it affects em politically. And I can understand that. But on this level, I don't concern myself with political considerations.

But the community itself, sure. Particularly, I am concerned about the militant political movement. That concerns us more than just a normal run of politics in the community. Then I must also— I've got to be aware that on the other side of this militant movement, there's a hell of a movement, too. I get a lot more criticism from people who say, "You're running a country club. When are you gonna start running a prison out there?" A lot more people put it more quietly than the few people who are standing up screaming, "Free all political prisoners," or calling for quote penal reform unquote, and that's all they call for. They don't offer any solutions, and then they call for penal reform. This is as ridiculous as me calling for reform in the treatment of cancer. I don't know what the hell I'm talking about. But if I call loud enough, and enough people will join me, I can make physicians uncomfortable, somehow feeling they're doing wrong in the treatment of cancer. But I don't have the slightest idea what the hell I'm talkin about. And if what I saw in this morning's paper that the attorney general's calling for—it doesn't constitute prison reform. He was calling for the establishment of an academy to train prison people, the establishment of a center for information about education programs in prison. If that's prison reform, deal me out. That doesn't mean anything except we're gonna hire new architects and we're gonna have a new superintendent of schools. And that's all it means.

We're in a ridiculous situation—we're trying to reform the book of administrational justice by rewriting the last chapter, which is treatment of people in prison, and totally disregarding everything that happened before—what happened to the kid in the school superintendent's office, what happened to the kid at home, what happened to the kid in church, what happened to the kid in juvenile authority, what happened to the kid in police department, what happened in the probation department, what happened in the judicial chambers. We're gonna totally disregard all that and say we can change this kid by changing the prison. That is ridiculous. If they rewrite all these other chapters, then by the time they get around to rewriting the last chapter, prison and parole, then they'll find prison people more receptive. But nobody's talking about reforming the convicts, they're just talking about reforming the prisons, without any concern about what part the inmates are gonna play in this reform.

### DISTRICT OF COLUMBIA CORRECTIONAL COMPLEX
### JOHN O. BOONE, SUPERINTENDENT OF ADULT SERVICES

Right now, we are badly overpopulated. We have a normal complement of fourteen hundred eighty-four. At this time, we're movin pretty close to nineteen hundred. We are badly overcrowded as a result of about a thousand new police, ten new judges, court reorganization, and in a great sense no provision for the influx into correctional institutions. This means program and bed space. At this point, we jus behind.

We're financed by the federal government, who provides a large federal assessment plus some revenue items for the entire District government—for schools, hospitals, prisons, and what have you, police department. We have to compete with these other agencies for our funds.

### MANHATTAN HOUSE OF DETENTION FOR MEN
### EDWARD WEINRAUCH, ASSISTANT DEPUTY WARDEN

The count is one thousand four hundred forty-three this morning. It's way above what we should have. I'm against two men in a cell, however we have a situation where we double-bunk cells. When this institution was opened up, there was one man in a cell, single bunks. When I came here in early fifty-four, fifty-three, they was just startin to double the bunks in the cells. Now every cell is double. We don't believe it should be. There's one toilet in there, there's one seat in there. Other than the metal seat protruding from the wall, there's the bed to sit on. We depend a lot on the lock-out system. Adjacent to the cell there's an area for recreation. You don't have a good rapport inside with the inmates, they want more space. They all feel they shouldn't be in jail.

218.

CELL, MINIMUM CUSTODY FACILITY, MORGANTOWN, WEST VIRGINIA, 1971.

And we just carry on the mandates of the law. I'm sure that if an institution like this had only eighty per cent of capacity—all the text-books will tell ya it should be—the other twenty per cent, gives you movement room to walk around, to transfer.

BUCKS COUNTY PRISON
PRESLEY MIDDLETON, CAPTAIN OF OPERATIONS AND SECURITY

This jail was built in eighteen ninety-four. Ah, this place was built for fifty people and right now we got hundred seventy-three. We have four men, sometimes five guys, to a little, small cell here. I haven't got the measurements, but it, you might say, it's inhumane to have five men locked up in a little, small room. They keep talkin bout they're gonna build a new prison, build this. Since I've been here, for the las four years, las five years, they were gonna build a new prison, where they had dormitories stead of cells.

But all they do is talk about it. We have a change of administration, new president come in off this, new commissioners, and they all go into the political field before the elections, they're gonna do this and do that, you know, clean up this and clean up that. For four years I keep on hearin about new prisons, and yet we still got the same old prison. We puttin more and more money into this place when it shoulda been condemned a hundred years ago.

But no. It's easier to keep addin onto this rather than stop and build somethin new, somethin modern, somethin that the guy can go to where he can learn somethin, rather than try to beautify the place here, this old, antique building. This is a museum as far as I care—or a zoo, that's what it is, the way it looks. You can go on the blocks right now—we got one cell-block, you can see—I think one count we had a hundred and twenty-nine guys in about twenty cells. One hundred twenty-nine. And you looked in that one lone block one night, and all you could see—you couldn'ta even walked in it, there were so many people. No room to walk around in. It was jus like big congestion, like walkin down the streets of Philadelphia, where you're tryin to squeeze around the other guy, gettin around him. That's where your morale goes, that's lousy as far as I care. But it seem like the people are always hollerin at us got some excuse why they cannot build a new jail. They will always have prisons. They can better em if they wanted to.

But nobody's takin any action. They always say that's for lack of funds and everything else, but for the United States, we're bein one of the richest nations in the world, and we just can't solve our little, small problems—people bein locked up.

I think the time was yesterday, and we are stumblin

220.

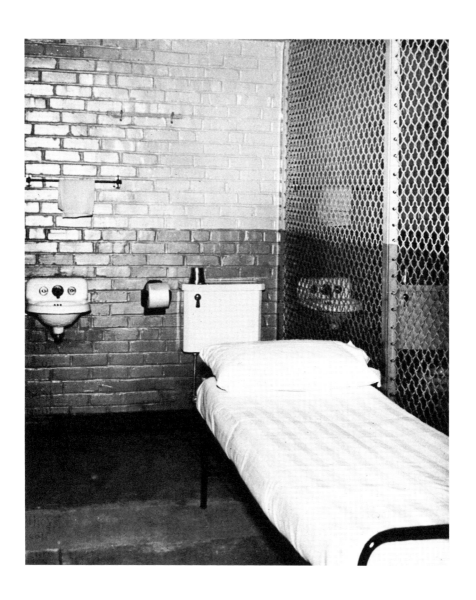

CELL MAXIMUM–SECURITY FACILITY, OHIO STATE PRISON, COLUMBUS, 1938.

through today. And tomorrow we'll say, "Well, we'll pass it off til the next day." But yesterday this stuff shoulda been corrected or attempt shoulda been made yesterday. We always say, "Now is the time," right? Now is the time. But somebody got to start somethin. Somebody gotta start buildin out there new institution. Start it today. But all this paperwork, red tape. You got to please one group, got to please the politicians, got to please the commissioners. And all them people get together and say, "Let's do it." But no. They talk about the money and you gotta go this place, that place, and all over the place. Again they forgot about the jail. And this is where all your problems are at. Problems that they got out in the streets, all they did was jus confine it in one little area, Bucks County Prison. All Bucks County problems are right here in this jail. All the bad guys are locked up in here. And again these bad guys will get out in the streets again one day and be doin the same back all over again. But nobody cares, the way I see it.

ARKANSAS STATE PENITENTIARY
ROBERT TALBOT, INMATE

One thing is like now the barracks are overcrowded an lotta dudes don't have beds to sleep in. They sleep on the floor. They will give em a mattress. They will give em two sheets. They hafta sleep on the floor. We have about thirty dudes in my barracks now sleepin on the floor. They don't have any beds for em. I don't know what the situation's gonna come about that. They sayin they're gonna get some new beds with lockers on em, but I haven't—I heard that ever since I come here in sixty-seven. They haven't gotten em yet.

The las two weeks, I seen bout three or four dudes sell their beds for two, three dollars. Then they had to sleep on the floor. After they sell their bed, they say, well, they shouldn'ta sold their bed. I told quite a few guys, "Why you gonna sell your bed for three dollars? You don't need money that bad. Times aren't that hard like they used to be. The only way you gonna be comfortable, you be in your bed yourself. Ain't nobody makin you do what you don't wanna do. As far as havin money, that's not everythin. You sell your bed jus to get a few packs of cigarettes, that don't make any sense. The floor's cold, wind up with a cold, lay in, keep from goin out in bad weather. Jus not worth it to sell your bed for three dollars."

ARKANSAS STATE PENITENTIARY
JAMES JESSE JONES, INMATE

I have a bed. Twenty-eight without in my barracks. It's too nasty down there. I can tell you that. Cigarette butts and the cans and the paper. Old people chew tobacco, they might spit on the floor, and stuff like that is all round your bed. Bed ain't no good—they irregular, you know. The mattress is tore all up and too nasty, jus be stinkin when you get em, and all such stuff as that.

BUCKS COUNTY PRISON
RAYMOND WARD BURNS, INMATE

The cells, the condition of the cells are pretty bad, cause there's—especially in here, the turnover's so great, you know. They just come in and misuse the furniture, whatever furniture is, which is very little. There's a table, and a few couches. They scrape their initials in the walls, and they leave commissary, like cakes, cookies, laying all over. This attracts roaches and everything else.

Even in a state prison, the guys keep things in their cells so long as it attracts bugs, bedbugs, and so forth. So the conditions there aren't too good. And the lighting, the lighting in most cells is bad. They keep—I don't know what it's for—I guess they keep low amperage or something, save a little money on their electricity.

DISTRICT OF COLUMBIA, WOMEN'S DETENTION CENTER
LUCILLE MCNEAL, CAPTAIN, CORRECTIONAL FORCE

The real capacity is about eighty, and at present you're crowded. They get on each other's nerves, you know. I guess we could house about a hundred twenty-five. We've got one-oh-five now. After that, we probably couldn't take any more inmates at all. It hasn't happened yet. I guess we could put beds in the hallways and take them, because we can hardly refuse a female offender, inasmuch as this is the only female facilities in Washington for women. We used to have to take all the demonstrators, female, and we would crowd them into the basement, into the recreation area down there, or we would take our sick bay or something. But lately we changed superintendents, and we'll just refuse to take them, you know, cause you don't have any place to put them. I mean, if you're already overcrowded and the police department calls you up and say we have arrested fifty women, you just don't have any place to put them.

ARKANSAS STATE PENITENTIARY
CLARENCE JAMES LEE, CORRECTIONAL OFFICER 1

Where else could you put em?

DISTRICT OF COLUMBIA CORRECTIONAL COMPLEX
JOSEPH SAKALAUKAS, SERGEANT, CORRECTIONAL FORCE

The tension, the pressure, this place, I guess, like every place else, is starting to get a little overcrowded. You can feel it. And depending on the man up front, the guy that's running the joint, how he gonna relieve this pressure. A lot of it is gonna determine how my neck is gonna be taken care of when it blow, if it blow. So this is the worst part. Because it's here. It's here with the inmates and it's here with me, with the officers, and everybody that's with em, all the time. Sometimes it gets more intense than at other times.

BUCKS COUNTY PRISON
PRESLEY MIDDLETON, CAPTAIN OF OPERATIONS AND
SECURITY

I think most of our problems happen like on the four-to-twelve shift, when the work stops and the guys upstairs and all the other guys who've been goofin off all day got a lot of power or energy to harass or play around. And these guys'll get annoyed and their temper'll go up again. You'll have a little disturbance.

FEDERAL DETENTION HEADQUARTERS
ANTHONY CORCIONE, CORRECTIONAL OFFICER

The tools they can try'n finagle, either trying to steal when the engineers come up and work, you know, or if they have a connection someplace, you know, bringing it in to them.

FEDERAL DETENTION HEADQUARTERS
GABRIEL POTTER, INMATE

In the riot in April, I was working in the area it took place in. The tools that were used in the riot I was working with. Since then I've been asked many questions about this, and that's as far as I go with anybody. I won't tell you whether a black man or a white man took the tools, and I wouldn't tell you who run from one floor to the other. I would say that I was working with the tools along with two engineers and another inmate. And the tools we were working with were the tools that did all the damage as far as knocking open glass block, ah, with an electric impact hammer—cut the doors, you know, they cut the locks off when they move from one floor to another.

That's as far as I can go. If they knew the people that took these tools, they would press charges.

We was working in the maximum security area on the second floor. They had an officer there named Warner, who in my opinion is an illiterate and a lotta other inmates'll agree with this. I understand he worked in an insane asylum for about ten years before coming here. At the TV room—then they had just the single TV room—they had a discussion between the Spanish people and the black people over the program they was gonna see. And the officer's black. He took the black people side. Walked in and he changed the program. The Spanish

224.

GUARD REUNITED WITH WIFE AFTER BEING HELD HOSTAGE BY RIOTING INMATES,
STATE PRISON OF SOUTHERN MICHIGAN, JACKSON, 1952.

people made a lotta noise—he change the program the Spanish wanted to see—then he changed it back to the program that the black people wanted to see. This was three changes. So one of the black people said something to him. He took a punch at the black man, and then they ripped him off.

He says that they threw him down and took his keys away from him. He lost his keys in the tussle. Five minutes after the trouble started, they offered to pass the keys under the door back to the officer, free, no trouble. Nobody'd been unlocked, anything. They were scared to come to the door to get them, and the door was not unlocked. It can only be unlocked on one side, and that was the opposite side from where the inmates were. They wouldn't come to the door to get them, so the inmates took the keys back and started unlocking the doors.

They unlocked all the doors, everything on the second floor and everything on the third floor. In the paper they claimed they had four hostages. And in my opinion they never had a hostage, because the two engineers that was working with me, they said, "Set down in here, be comfortable, nobody'll bother you." The other two I guess they claimed was the two inmates that was working—we sent around to bring coffee. For about three hours the engineers smoked, drank coffee, and they was never hostage. Nobody was hurt. There was no violence.

The associate warden got on the PA system and asked the inmates to—said he was speaking for the warden—and asked the inmates to return the institution to the staff, and they returned to their quarters, and they all did. It was over with.

DISTRICT OF COLUMBIA CORRECTIONAL COMPLEX
CLYDE E. SETTLE, SERGEANT, CORRECTIONAL FORCE

When disturbance comes up, you know, I might get hurt. Whereas some guy might hit me in the head with a brick and hurt me, you know, kill me, how bout the inmate? It hurts him, too. So when things come up and they hurt this institution, they hurt me and they hurt the guy that's locked up in here. So really, you gotta look at it like that.

Jus like we had—las time we had disturbance here, I was standin out there with a shotgun, you know. It's nighttime, black. I hear somethin hit the blacktop out there, you know. Bump. Bump. Guy was throwin bricks, you know. And I coulda got hit out there with a brick. Well, you get hit with a brick, the guy that threw the brick may be one of the guys you're with every day. You can't see, you know, it's nighttime. You gotta remember it's part of the job. If you can't accept that—like every time we have a disturbance—

226.

WOUNDED GUARD, MISSOURI STATE PENITENTIARY FOR MEN, JEFFERSON CITY,
1954.

I seen a bunch of guys headin for the commissary, you know, officers headin for the commissary, throwin the stuff on the pile, you know, gettin outta here. I think it takes a particular type of guy to work in corrections, to be a correctional officer. It takes a unique kind of person. Like I wouldn't be happy at all sittin in an office somewhere. I'd just go out of my nut, you know. Maybe the little bit of danger involved in my job is what makes it good to me. Because the only kind of work I'd ever want to do would be somethin in enforcement.

When I came to work here they told me, "You get hazardous pay and hazardous retirement for workin here." And you get it for good cause.

DISTRICT OF COLUMBIA CORRECTIONAL COMPLEX
JOHN O. BOONE, SUPERINTENDENT OF ADULT SERVICES

The month after I got up here, this institution was totally blacked out for about an hour durin the electrical storm. And the men decided to take the canteen—a few men, less than fifty. And after that, they wanted to have a little fun, so they decided to burn the buildin. So you heard me referring to the renovation of the burned-out buildins, well, behind that, naturally, it takes you a long period of time to readjust to it. Canteen was burned out. We had to improvise the canteen program. We had to reassure the staff and the inmates that everythin's gonna be all right, because ninety-five per cent of the men had no parts of the disorder at all. In fact, I walked in here and walked around the compound, and of course—I shiver now to think that it coulda been pretty bad—I felt that I had to see what the extent of it was, and I didn't see any real problems.

Of course, when I got back to control, there was shower breaks and some fire bombs in the control center. Now we dropped two cans of tear gas—that's for cover—and got outta the institution. So admittedly, we had to abandon the institution. We felt that we should abandon it. But I came back in the front gate and on the bullhorn invited all of the men that did not want to be marshaled to an area in order to get control of the situation to come over to Gate One. And immediately about eight hundred came over. Some of the men said that they felt that the others did not understan me, and they asked for bullhorns and wanted to come back in and tell them what was happenin. So they got the bullhorns, and the men—most of the others—came over. Now, some was afraid to come. They remembered the last riot, where the newspapers called it a guard riot. There was promiscuous shooting and some residents hurt. So after most of the men came over, I sent a task force in to marshal the men down across the compound to recreation area. And of course, we stood there all night long from about twelve midnight until daylight the next mornin. And we know that as far as the burnin was concerned, less than twenty men did that. But eight officers were hurt, and these eight officers were black, paradoxically.

ARKANSAS STATE PENITENTIARY
BEALLE, INMATE

At night you go back to your barracks, lay down, they might be playin dominoes, playin cards or somethin, write letters. Mos time I be playin cards and poker some. Yeah, I play for change. Yeah, I win Saturday night. I think I win Saturday night. I started about two and a half up, you know, with eleven dollars and some. You allowed to keep fifteen dollars, sir, on you. You got over fifteen dollars, you put it on the book. You get caught with more than fifteen dollars, they put it on the inmate file. I get more'n fifteen dollars, I put it on the book before they catch me with it.

ARKANSAS STATE PENITENTIARY
SAMUEL LEXINGTON, INMATE GUARD

They gamble a lot here, too. They say it's illegal. If you feel up to it, you might win a thousand dollars. They only sposed to have fifteen dollars in their possession, but all those inmates in there, a lotta money picks up. You get in a game with fifteen, twenty dollars, and you get a good streak, you might come out with three, four hundred dollars. Couple a nights you might have a thousand dollars or better.

Dice in there. Seven-card stud—deuce is wild. Some got little games, maybe quarter, half a dollar. Some got big games, dollars'n dollars'n dollars.

For money, well they gotta blood bank here, where you can go. I been goin for the last eight years every week. It don't hurt. It hurts some people—resistance is low and they don't eat proper. So they get sick, catch yella jaudice, hepatitis or somethin. They give you five dollars. I guess they sposed to give you ten. I don't know. They give us five dollars and donate five to the inmate welfare fund. And the welfare fund is what we—the money the inmates put there, they buy TVs and water coolers, ice machine, and they give us a dollar for Christmas.

Now me, I watch the towers for em—he might wanna get the day off, he might wanna pay you to hold his tower for him, might give you a dollar or somethin, go out there and work his shift.

And these pecans—we lug em out of the field, shell em

229.

and sell em for dollar twenty-five a jar. You get a big coffee jar. Buy you cigarettes and candy and Cokes and stuff. Sell em to the other inmates, cause they're not able to get out there and get em. And they'll say, "Don't bring no pecans in. You'll get a disciplinary." Well, it's food and people ain't gonna worry bout no disciplinary. They gonna bring it in anyway, regardless of it's right or wrong.

There's people here that have abnormal sex acts and things like that. They'll sell their bodies for money and favors. There's guys down in the barracks that are that way, you know. They call em a gal-boy or punk or somethin. They'll do it for money or to get a job from the inmate guards. You can't do it to the freeworld people. The free people jus ignore you. They figure you're a little off in the head.

ATTICA CORRECTIONAL FACILITY
MATTHEW BAKER, INMATE *

I used to have fish tanks, you know, aquariums, and, ah, I used to raise tropical fish, and it used to be my thing.

CALIFORNIA STATE PRISON AT FOLSOM
DOUGLAS A. BORSIN, INMATE

Each man's issued headphones that got two channels in a radio. It's captive audience on that. One channel features all your sports activities. Other channel is all music and news. Outside of about three hours each evenin, they have what they call their record-request show. The institution's got turntable, tapes that got a few records on em, and they play this for about three hours. Once in a while we've had news blackouts where, you know, they turn the radio clear off, cause that's been some—like Attica. They snatched the newspapers on Attica. Sunday papers came out, the cop on duty, watch captain, snatched em so nobody'd have em. Warden came back the next day and gave em back to us.

But we figure it's gonna cause em a problem, they're gonna try to censor you down. Let's face it. Now they're bitchin about the so-called revolutions books, publications. You can't get those any more. But they will pacify the boys, lettin em have Playboy, lettin em have Penthouse and all that—these girlie magazines, you know. If they've got a problem, they use a pacifier. Television's a pacifier. Radios that they start committin to buy two years ago's pacifiers. They will not do anything meaningful to help these guys to help themselves to get out there and make it. All they wanna do is, baby start cryin, you stick a pacifier in his mouth. That's what they do here.

230.

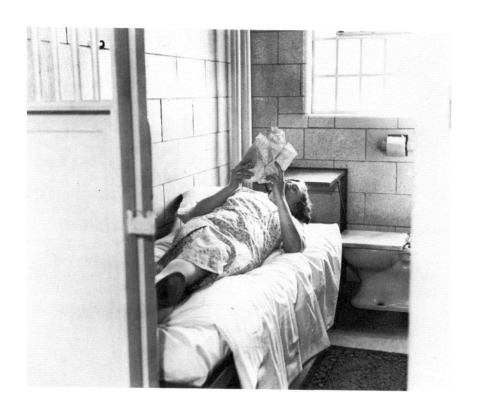

WOMAN READING IN HER CELL, HOUSE OF DETENTION FOR WOMEN, NEW YORK
CITY, 1932.

I'm not boastin, but I read about three hundred pages an hour, fictional work. I've read some pretty good ones—Portnoy's Complaint—so many of em I can't even begin to think about em. I kicked off The Valley of the Dolls, Five Smooth Stones or something like this. About the only things that don't move me too much is like Westerns, cause they call em here shit-kickers.

There're not too many nonfiction to get in here, because one, our library's antiquated, two, there's kind of restrictions on what kinda crap they want us to have here. At one time we probably could have most anything. Like lotta guys read Blueprint for Revolution. They've asked for the Redbook of Mao Tse-tung. They asked for the Soledad Brother. They've asked for a whole slew of em, and the administration says, "No, these are radical books. These are inflammatory. You can't have em." What's inflammatory? For Christ's sake, they used to scream, well, like these girlie magazines, they said, "These aren't good for you, they give you weird thoughts." But Jesus Christ, let's face it, it's the only heterosexual association you can have. Who wants to watch a bunch of kings and queens mate with each other? Not me. Maybe I'm old-fashioned, but I'm hunkier for women. But they scream "This is not the thing for you because it creates problems." But hell, homosexuality is a bigger problem than any damn girlie magazine that come in through here.

And now they feel that this is the same thing for your so-called liberal publishers, your liberal writers. I hate the word radical, cause if a man has a belief in something and he can accomplish some good in life, whether for himself or the majority of people, what's radical about this?

ARKANSAS STATE PENITENTIARY
A. L. LOCKHART, WARDEN

Well, I did read the papers until about three weeks ago, four weeks ago. I stopped readin the papers. I haven't read a paper—well, I'm sorry I did. I read one article that came out in the paper, yesterday's papers, first time since, oh, back in first of November, I guess, middle of November.

Because of the articles that were comin out in the papers about this place, they were so untrue that I jus got disgusted and sick of em. The way that was goin on, I'd say, "I'm jus not gonna let it upset me," cause I knew what was happenin. And I jus didn't care about readin it.

232.

ARKANSAS STATE PENITENTIARY
ROBERT TALBOT, INMATE

They have movies on weekends. Last weekend was—I forget the name of it—it was a war picture. Hundred and eighty-two men at this picture. Three hours I think it was. I only been to two since I been back—El Cid and I forget the one that was on the week before that. It was a pretty good picture. It was about a prison. It was Cool Hand Luke—road gang. I did time like that, six months; and yeah, I believe it was true, because that's the way we worked on the road gang when I was on the county farm. We hadda hot shit like Newman, too. He's here now.

CALIFORNIA STATE PRISON AT FOLSOM
GARCIA PEREZ, INMATE

They have a movie once a week. Some of the movies are—you know, some are movies that have gotten a good review. Last week, oh yeah, One Million B.C., Raquel Welch. Compared to the original One Million B.C., it was a burn. Hadn'ta been for Raquel Welch, it'da been one hundred per cent burn. But she gives you somethin to see, you know, to look at.

ATTICA CORRECTIONAL FACILITY
MATTHEW BAKER, INMATE

I've written three books in Attica, but in order to get a book you've written out of Attica, you have to send it to Albany, and they send it back. Then you can send it to somebody on the street, which takes approximately six months to do. So in keeping with the current thing, you know—what's happening out in the street—well, you're six months late, you know. "Sorry, buddy," you know.

FEDERAL DETENTION HEADQUARTERS
GABRIEL POTTER, INMATE

I'm in the progress of writing a novel, so I spend a lotta time on that.

I spoke to the associate warden. He's aware that I'm writing a novel and so is Mr. Kenny, who's the chief of education and Parole, and some other people. No, they didn't tell me not to write about prison. They told me I could not write about anything that was relative to my crime, about me coming to prison. They didn't tell me that I couldn't write about prison. They said I could write anything about prison I wanted to, as long as I did not use the name of any individual

233.

and so long as it was the truth. Whether it was good or bad, as long as it was the truth.

I understand they say that if you wrote about the crime while you was in prison, it would be a profit-making venture that cause you to come to prison.

INDIANA STATE PRISON
EARL GRADY, INMATE

I like to paint in depth what I see and what I feel. I did one after Attica of a black guy with his hands over his face and a real worried look, surrounded by fire and then bars. And I named it Before and After Attica, because what happened at Attica really will make no changes. Nothin will change, you know. In the limited time that Attica happened up til now in this institution, nothin has changed. They don't hear that message. It's too far away, you know. So that guy is sittin there full of misery and don't even know what's really happenin to himself. Or he might know and there's nothin he can do about it. But he's sittin there, he's burnin up, still behind bars, he's still waitin. Nothin changes.

CALIFORNIA STATE PRISON AT SAN QUENTIN
PRESTON S. SYMTHE, INMATE

I don't read any more. I'm too busy writin. Right now I'm on a sonnet and poetry kick. So that takes my time. But then I'm always in bed nine o'clock. Always. And there's nothin for me to stay up for. The news I don't care about cause I get the paper the next day, and that's all I care about anyway. And I don't wanna stay up til midnight to watch some silly movie, cause then I'm too tired in the mornin. Cause that's somethin you have to watch very carefully in here—you become exhausted very easily. Got to get your rest.

Now you have your boob-tube freaks down there, boy, bad. I mean, they never move except to get a cup of coffee or go to the toilet between counts.

One thing I like around here is the movies. I've generally got my all four feet stuck right into the selection of the damn things, so I do like movies. And escapism, what else? But that's it. It's a circle of days. I mean, you do the same thing day in day out, year in year out. I've had this routine—except for the television when I was over in East Block and they didn't have any—I've had this routine for well, thirty months.

Some people do all dead time. I do all what I call live

INMATES WATCHING TELEVISION, CALIFORNIA STATE PRISON AT SAN QUENTIN, 1966.

time. In other words, doin somethin, keepin your mind busy. If you don't keep your mind busy, you're gone pretty soon—walkin up and down here, and you're not seein anything. The hardest thing in the world around here is to continually be aware, because this is a steel cocoon, and you're in the middle of it, and you don't watch it, thread's going to wrap you all up, and there you are—you're just trapped. You go outside and everything's strange to you.

DISTRICT OF COLUMBIA CORRECTIONAL COMPLEX
LOWELL MILLER, INMATE

People walk around acting out all their neuroses. If you don't watch it, you get into a paranoid bag also. I remember for about two months I was wondering if one night someone was gonna pipe me, stab me, sneak up in the middle of the night and me get piped in the head for some unknown reason. I watch people's behavior that's really psychotic, people who are really dangerous. If they haven't killed someone already and are in jail for that, they could kill someone here. Dealing with people who are what they call abstract, sick. Worrying about not using the shower too long, cause this guy who's doing twenty-to-life might get pissed off'n stab you for some unknown reason. Worrying not to laugh because of a racial issue, something that might be funny, and you're really not being a racist for laughing, but because you're white, a black man might interpret it the wrong way. Getting used to call people "man" instead of "boy." I mean, just the expression "boy" is distasteful to black people. There's a tremendous amount of energy expended to adjust, and it's very painful energy.

DISTRICT OF COLUMBIA WOMEN'S DENTENTION CENTER
JANE MASON, INMATE

The women here, they have so many malices in their heart, you know, it's really hard to get along with em. It's hard to do anythin. Everyone has a clique, you know, everybody hangs out with certain clique. And you have one clique where maybe the girls, they jus like to have a lotta fun. There are no rights and wrongs as far as they're concerned. They're jus good-timin girls. And you gotta clique, you got the shrewd bunch, you know, they into everythin. They know everybody's business, and they—these jailhouse lawyers. And anytime somethin goes down what may cause chaos and confusion, they're right there on the scene. And then you have people that jus stay to theyself, you know. They laugh and talk to a certain set, but they don't get in your business, and you don't get in their business, and everythin runs pretty smooth with them.

Me, I'm a loner. Like to be by myself. On the weekends when I'm off from work, I lock in my room. Or this was up until Thursday—I got a roommate, and it's pretty hard to be locked in your room with a roommate, you know. And if you close your door, the police gonna think you doin somethin illegal.

You get tired of people bein aroun you all the time, constantly askin you, "What's the matter? Why do you feel this way?" or, "Why are you this way?" or, "Why aren't you laughin and talkin?" What the hell is there to laugh and talk about every time you see somebody in Ten-Ten, you know? And this is the way I feel about it. Laughin and talkin and playin all the time—I don't like that—too old for that, you know.

DISTRICT OF COLUMBIA CORRECTIONAL COMPLEX
LOWELL MILLER, INMATE

Where I do gain was living with blacks, number one. It's a black camp. I think it's mostly probably got one of the largest percentage of blacks in the country—I think about ninety-eight-per-cent black population. I never lived with black people before, so that I learned a lot about black people.

I never lived with southern rednecks in my life. I never know what mountain oysters were until I came to jail—they're hog nuts and they eat them, fry them. I hear great stories about people being on a chain gang for murdering someone, doing fifteen years on a chain gang in nineteen twenty-six. The guy rips off his clothes and runs into the river and escapes. For two years, he's on the lam up in Indianapolis, Indiana, bootlegging. A chick turns him in and he's back on the chain gang. Just fabulous stories. Jail's filled with interesting people.

BUCKS COUNTY PRISON
RAYMOND WARD BURNS, INMATE

Somebody get on your nerves or just push you the wrong way, might wind up hit him in the head with a pipe or something. That was me. I hit one guy with a bucket, hit another guy with a pipe, another guy with about a three-inch round span, broke his jaw in about seven places. The other guys—split his head all the way around with the bucket, other guy got a concussion from the pipe. It's either that or get hit yourself. Now, I learned a lot there. Used to be the fool that stood and got hit first. Not any more.

I've had one paranoid trip. I was walkin tiers one time. I usually wear a headband. And one time I was walkin down and I felt like somebody was grabbin it from behind. And I looked around and nobody was there. And every time I'd start to walk, felt like somebody jus kept grabbin it in the back. I'd turn around—pretty silly, you know. Then I jus started grinnin and said, "Boy, this stuff's out-a-sight, man, way out." So I walked down to the first tier—the tiers are on top of the other, you got a railin and can look over all the way down to the first tier. I'm up on the fourth tier, and I seen a couple a dudes talkin up there that I knew, so I started buggin em. And I bullshitted with em, and one of em looks down, "Sure is a long ways down, now."

I look at him and I says, "Yeah. I'll see you later." So I went over to my cell and turned on my radio and turned off the light and stood in there.

Anything can happen here, you know. You might borrow a box of cigarettes from one guy, tell him, "Well, I'll pay you back next week." Then if you won't pay him—it's a two-for-three thing, you know—borrow a box, you gotta give fifteen packs back. So the money don't come in or, "Mind if I pay you next week?"

He'll say, "Well, it's gonna be two boxes next week." And it could jack itself up like that. And by the time you know it, you're flyin over the tier or you're walkin around in the yard with a blade in your back or some maniac will come by, stick you in the back with a shive or somethin. One of my homeys, he was watchin TV, and some dude come up to him and hit him right in the chest with a blade. For nothin. He didn't even know him. He died about ten minutes later. Any number of things can happen.

You trade cigarettes at the canteen, providin they're good cigarettes and they came from the canteen—the same cigarettes that came from the canteen. You can trade the cigarettes back for your shampoo, your toothpaste. You're not actually legal to do that, but in cases if you don't have the book to buy it, they will do it. And sometimes a guy'll say, "Well, I'll take the cigarettes. I've got a fifteen-dollar book, and I'll take em, and I'll buy the cigarettes and buy you your stuff." So you swap and trade around. If a guy knows I got two jars of coffee that I bought from the canteen, he wants one of em, he'll give you six packs for one of em. That's equivalent to a dollar and a half. Coffee costs a dollar and a half, so you're not losin anything. You don't try to make a profit on it.

INDIANA STATE PRISON
EARL GRADY, INMATE

Oh well, ah, cigarettes is money. But other'n that it's not much. You know we got the same thing here as anywhere else, gamblin and the whole bit. They're raisin hell about a deck of cards. They don't want cards inside the walls because it might promote gamblin. And they have football games, you know, the whole bit. They'll gamble on two roaches, you know. But all guys who wants to gamble are gamblin anyway. You know what I mean. I wouldn't think it'd be any different here than it would be in any other joint.

BUCKS COUNTY PRISON
RAYMOND WARD BURNS, INMATE

There's gambling to get cigarettes. Some guys got thirty, forty, fifty cartons round the block, you know. You're only allowed three cartons in your cell—no, four cartons, scuse me. Anything over four cartons is considered contraband. But there're some guys in the penitentiary who have, they might have over a couple hundred cartons of cigarettes spread around to guys that don't gamble—they might be holding four of them or something like that. And they could use them, but put them back.

The guards don't say too much about it as long as there's no trouble. When there's trouble, trouble over a gambling debt, then they want to get involved and stop everyone from gambling and stop everyone from using cigarettes.

Somebody can't pay it, somebody wanna start a fight about it or something—I've seen a guy killed for two packs, stabbed over a hundred and fifty times for two packs of cigarettes. I've seen it. There was blood on the ground. It was in the yard. There was blood on the ground. It didn't come off for months. It rained, they put lime on it, and everything. You know, there were still stains there. For two packs.

Seen another guy get stabbed, thrown over a chair for a carton of cigarettes. They place a lot of value on cigarettes. This is their life, you know. That's their money.

### CALIFORNIA STATE PRISON AT FOLSOM
### GARCIA PEREZ, INMATE

I think they sell a quart of brew for five packs. That's the goin price. A guy takes a chance—gets the sugar and the other materials involved—and he makes a batch. Five gallons, okay, five boxes.

### FEDERAL DETENTION HEADQUARTERS
### GABRIEL POTTER, INMATE

There's a lotta brew being made here, you know, whisky. Well, it's not whisky, but it's brew. They sneak the stuff upstairs and make it. And sometimes it's pretty good. Well, I'm a Southerner, you know, and the Southerners are the best brew-makers. Yeah. Yeah, we make it in the tank I live in, pretty regular. Well, they smell it, see, but we put it in a place where they can't—they have to lock up the whole tank or not lock up anybody. That's the way it works. So, they don't lock up anybody. They just take it and dispose of it. Then you make a new batch.

Everything it takes to make it you can buy in the commissary, except for the yeast, and you can get the yeast from the kitchen. No other way to start it fermenting, you know. You just get somebody to steal you a little bread dough, and that's enough. You get a ferment, just anything to get it to go.

### BEDFORD HILLS CORRECTIONAL FACILITY
### MICHELE RIVERA, INMATE

We make hooch. (I hope none of the officers'll read this book.) You take dried fruit, you know—any kind of fruit, it doesn't have to be dried fruit, can be fresh fruit—and you take rice. I make gallon jugs, you know, so I measure it by the gallons. So I would break the jug up into sixes and put like a sixth of the jar would be rice, you know, then raisins, then apples, oranges, you know—they got acid in em, right—bout three oranges for four gallons. And I put sugar in it and bread, you know, and potatoes—you can put potatoes in cause they have starch and when the starch starts fermentin it turns into sugar, you know, into alcohol. Then you have to keep uncappin it, you know, like every other day so that it won't blow up, you know. But it smells. Then let it lay for about a month. By that time, it's crude alcohol, you know, so you can get sick, the chemical change doesn't work right. But that's the chance you have to take. You just let it sit. There's really nothin to it. You just have to taste it like every week to see if it needs sugar, because when the sugar starts droppin, it means that you need to put more to make more alcohol. Then you drink it. It tastes nasty. I made two jugs, and they taste like beer mixed with wine. Yeah, man, you get blasted, cause it's crude alcohol, you know, and in that state, you can get blind from that, I believe, you know, I'm not sure.

We try to be cool, you know, like the clique I be with, we try to be cool, so that we won't get busted. Every mornin I have to squeeze powder in my room and open a jar of perfume or burn perfume on paper, you know, so that the room'll get a scent of perfume, cause it smells really—you know the rotten fruit smell. And then when it blows its top, you know—like sometimes it's too much yeast in it or somethin—then it starts drippin out, and I have to clean my room and wax it three or four times a day, cause you know, it's sticky on the floor. Oh, man, it's a hassle, though. We do it for special occasions.

Anything to get a head. They sniff nail polish in here. Lady in the commissary, I think she gonna stop sellin nail polish, cause everybody keeps buyin, you know, even the bulls you know, that you see actin like men, be buyin nail polish. And they start thinkin that, you know, now the gay people are buyin nail polish, so they start to think that somethin's jumpin off. Everybody bought the whole supply of nail polish out of commissary. They do anything. They sniff glue in here. I don't get nothin from nail polish. Matter of fact, I was doin it last night. They kept tellin me, "Man, man," and I ain't feelin nothin, you know, cept from the fumes—they were too strong. I'm not accustom to doin it, you know, so. No airplane glue or somethin, rubber glue, you know, like that rubber cement glue. I got high offa that one time. But they be so many cans that you have to pick the right can, cause sometimes you steal the can of that glue and it's not the right kinda glue to get high offa.

DISTRICT OF COLUMBIA CORRECTIONAL COMPLEX
JOSEPH SAKALAUKAS, SERGEANT, CORRECTIONAL FORCE

We sniff. This is where we find shoots, the alcoholic drink they make. And that's the way we find that. That's one thing can't hide—the smell, cause once it starts working—see, they try to screen it with blankets and paper and things like this, cover it, but you can't get rid of that smell. It's there. Always sniffin.

There's always some found. This time of year, the holidays coming, we expect to find quite a bit more than we usually do. Spoil the party. We report it—how much was found—report it to the captain's office. They keep a log of it. And then we just dump it down

241.

the sewer. It goes out to the river. The fish—you ever catch a happy fish, you know where you got it.

Catch a guy acting strange, take him and let him piss in the bottle. And, ah, I slate him, lock him up, see, put in a report that the man is under the influence of something. And sometimes we catch em just ready to go. This is the time we like to get to em, you know, cause nobody likes a drunken inmate around. They're bad enough when they're sober. So. We do find it, quite a bit, and some of it's good stuff—smells good, I'll tell you. No, I never tasted any of it. They make it outta peaches and cherries, fruit cocktail, you know. We always lock him up, cause we consider that serious offense.

The adjustment board tries to treat each case depending on the man, what the offense was, and the circumstances surrounding it.

Some of these guys, you give em a cup of juice, you gotta watch em, they make something outta it. I don't know what they doing in here. They oughta be working for Budweiser or Schlitz or somebody. Some of em here, they're very good.

BUCKS COUNTY PRISON
RAYMOND WARD BURNS, INMATE

You can buy steaks or chops or anything from the cook to eat at night. Your cooks in the kitchen, which are all inmates, they steal the meats. They put just enough on the line, try'n chop it up, make a stew out of it, you get all the fat meat and the garbage. Now after the meal's over, maybe even before, you get steak sandwiches for cigarettes. Now if you don't have the cigarettes, you're going to constantly be hungry, you know.

Up Western, I get five fillets for three packs, cook em myself in the cell with toilet paper—roll it up in a bunch so the smoke goes straight up, and it just don't blow all outta the cell. You get the toilet paper, and you roll it around your hand. Then you roll it into a ball—you take the ends and you roll it in so it looks like a doughnut. And this holds the heat in, concentrates it in one spot. It holds the smoke into one spot. And the smoke don't spread out. It don't make a lot of smoke all over the cell or something.

In a way, it's like a small burner, like when you roll it up certain way and the flame just comes straight up, you know, stead of spreading out. You can roll it so there's not that much smoke, you know. It's like a grilled steak. And the steaks, most of the fillets that are sold

242.

are stolen from the warden's private stock. He'll receive like a private stock, you know.

ATTICA CORRECTIONAL FACILITY
MATTHEW BAKER, INMATE

Guys make what they call a dropper. It's putting two stainless steel plates together, then putting two matches in between the plates and wind it up with a string or cord. And you drop this in the glass jar of water, and it will heat the water once you plug it in, you know. And also make stoves, like getting a coil from an old iron, make their electric stove out of it.

FEDERAL DETENTION HEADQUARTERS
ANTHONY CORCIONE, CORRECTIONAL OFFICER

Mostly what we find is food—fellas bringing stuff up from the kitchen at night. Men that work in the kitchen allowed to eat all that they want—they could sit downstairs and eat all night. They cook down there, you know, whatever they do, because it's cleared with the food stewards and the warden doesn't mind as long as they keep it at a moderate rate.

But sometimes they'll make sandwiches or they'll cook something and try'n bring it upstairs and distribute it out on the floor. That's not allowed, for the main purpose that it breeds mice and roaches, you know. They'll just leave it laying around. So we don't have any food on the floor, other than the commissary, like fruit and candy and stuff that they sell. But as far as cooked food, like down from the main line, doesn't go upstairs. So that's mostly what you'll find: guys trying to sneak a sandwich or three or four sandwiches for their buddies, you know.

You just confiscate it, send it right back down to food service. Don't write him up, not usually, unless he does it every night. But if you catch a man just once, normally what you'll tell him is, just take it back downstairs. He'll just turn around and bring it back down. And you're not gonna check on him—he might eat it on the way down just as long as it's not on the floor. Or if it's for him, he might have a container of milk and a sandwich. So you send him back downstairs. He might just go down in the dining room, sit down, get himself a cup of coffee, and just eat it right there. Nobody minds him doing that. Just as long as he doesn't take it and try'n distribute it on the floor or eat it upstairs in the tank, cause you make bad sanitation after a while, you know. You got food up there and cooked stuff be just laying around up there, you get all kinds of stuff and mice, you know, rats and everything.

243.

INMATE EATING SANDWICH IN HIS CELL, CORRECTIONAL TRAINING FACILITY,
SOLEDAD, CALIFORNIA, 1970.

I just try to become involved in it as much as I can become involved in it, whether it's stealing an extra cup of coffee or whether it's becoming involved in a drug group or a newspaper staff—anything just to keep my mind occupied. Even if it's stealing a sandwich, it's stealing the keys. I'm not gonna escape, you know—I don't need the keys, but if necessary just to keep my mind occupied, I'll take the keys, throw them away—just so the guard won't have them. Anything.

The nature of Lorton is what they would call liberal. It's not liberal really. It's just sort of placating the people. Because of this sort of loose atmosphere here, the homosexuality is very obvious. They call homosexuals here sissies. The sissies are in full drag, walk around Lorton with their arm around their boyfriend.

Now if you put five men into a little small cubicle, five men, five grown men in a cell, assumin you're livin together for let's say three weeks, you can rest assured somethin gonna take place in that cell. I say against the law of nature, it's gonna happen. You can't stop it. One way you can stop it is if you have more security guards in the institution supervisin these guys while they're at their leisure moments. Yeah. So it's goin on. In fact, I don't know how much of it's goin on.

I hear wisecracks made by some of the inmates, and I know it's goin on. But we cannot catch em. It's that simple. It's impossible for you to catch a guy in the act, cause the guys are wise. They know when a guard come down the line. They know there're only four men specially in this jail, there're only four men on duty at night. And this is what happens when they know there're four guys here. We can't be all over the jail. You got a hundred seventy-four guys and only four guards. So actually you go around the block now and then every two hours. You can rest assured there's somethin goin on down'n that block. So I blame it on society. Society put the guys here and, they say like, forget about em. And they are subject to these, say, incidents.

But we could never catch a guy in the act. It's pretty hard. You'd have to really get enough people here to actually prevent it.

You can charge em, but again, it's rare. It's very rare. Since I been here, have yet to catch anyone yet. I know it's goin on, cause again, used to be secret, top secret. Then certain inmates make wisecracks about certain guys. You try to keep an eye on that guy. But I work eight hours and that's it. The next shift don't give a damn about the guy or you just can't watch everybody. Outta a hundred and seventy-four there might be twenty guys there. And one guy cannot watch twenty men. And the inmates, they know.

Like at night, we have a thing we call canteen. That takes one officer to operate that canteen outta four. You got one man in the control center pushin buttons, openin gates. There's two officers left to supervise a hundred and seventy-four men. And two men cannot be over the whole jail. Cause at the same time you might have a commitment, like a new inmate comin into the prison. Then that takes another officer to pat the guy down, take his personal property. That means you got one more officer left to do somethin—to be on the guard for stuff like that—homosexuality. And that one officer might be the kitchen officer. He has to secure his kitchen. So he's down'n the kitchen. So who's monitoring the tunnel? No one. So this is when your—the acts are takin place.

DISTRICT OF COLUMBIA CORRECTIONAL COMPLEX
CHARLES HARMAN, INMATE

In the back of my mind I have a sneakin suspicion that this lack of bein around—not necessarily physically bein involved in a sexual thing, but just bein separated from people of the opposite sex—has a tendency to do things to some of these people's minds.

In a dormitory where I was at, there was some men writin lovelorn type of situations for Ebony magazine. I think they got a correspondence list or somethin. And one man met a girl from down in the country through the mail. I forget if it was through the mail or through a friend of his buddy's girl friend. But anyway, he wrote her a couple of letters, and they were gettin along okay as far as correspondence went. So one day—the thing is money also—so he says, "Send me twenty dollars. I need it," Just point blank, cause I read the letter. "And if you'll do that, I'll do anything for you when I get out. I'll even lick on your pussy." This guy said this plain. This is a young guy. This is the reason another guy showed me this guy's letter.

He said, "Look at this, will you." We sorta laughed about it.

246.

And seriously, you sometimes wonder about some of these youngsters. Cause that woman sent him ten dollars. And that youngster sent it back to her, said, "I want twenty, not ten," and cussed her out in the letter.

INDIANA STATE PRISON
WILLIAM SIMMONS, INMATE

Well, when I came here, I had been at the reformatory, so I knew what the situation was and what would be coming at me. I mean, I wasn't like a brand new inmate that had never done time and didn't know the ropes. But it was still difficult because I didn't know anybody here. And I had a run-in with a colored inmate who had quite a name about the institution, but fortunately—he tried to force his ideas onto me. He was kind of a—well, no, he had a very tactful approach. I'll give him credit for that. His ultimate intentions were, ah, a homosexual relationship. The average approach, I imagine, would be to offer you commissary, you know. And if you take it, you're in debt, and once you get in debt, they just keep putting pressure on you. And it depends on the individual how much pressure he can take or if he sees an out, how far he'll be pushed or if he's mad enough to stand up to it.

At first it was nothing but conversation. Then as time went on, he started to get a little more verbal, a little more pushy. And first year I was here I carried a knife. I made up my mind in adjustments and orientation when I first came here that I would never back down, cause once you do that you'd be ran over. So you have to stand up. Fortunately I made a couple of friends right away that was from my home town. And he was getting pretty rough. I think I was a couple of days away from getting into the real bad action. But two days before I figured he was gonna crash in, these two friends lived in the honor cell house, and they talked to an individual and got me transferred to the honor cell house. And temporarily I was outta there—I was outta the problem.

ARKANSAS STATE PENITENTIARY
JAMES JESSE JONES, INMATE

Lots of little, young dudes come out here, their peoples don't send em any money, and they eats lots of stuff and loan, borrow stuff, you know, borrow money. And if you borrow a dollar you have to pay a dollar and a half back. So the dude maybe let em have ten dollars. And they can't pay the fifteen back, so they go down to be homosexual, doin somethin wrong or stealin or killin somebody or somethin, and they get it. And they parents don't write em, and you know, that's the way they end up.

### BUCKS COUNTY PRISON
### RAYMOND WARD BURNS, INMATE

There're certain things that younger prisoners see that they would never have even thought of—things that go on inside prisons. And most of the time, the administration condones this. They want these things to happen, such as homosexuality. They wanna keep the elder prisoner or the so-called troublemaker, they want to keep him out of trouble. And they actually tell him, "Look, settle down and get yourself a kid." And this causes a lot of friction, because the older prisoners, instead of picking the homosexuals who are actually in prison, they tend to pick on new, younger boys that come in. And I've seen a lot of this.

### BUCKS COUNTY PRISON
### PRESLEY MIDDLETON, CAPTAIN OF OPERATIONS AND
### SECURITY

We give the juveniles peanut butter and jelly sandwiches at night, try to keep em quiet. And yet, still, things might go on that we don't know about.

### DISTRICT OF COLUMBIA CORRECTIONAL COMPLEX
### LOWELL MILLER, INMATE

One interesting thing: I was rapping with a friend. He has a nickname, his name's Blue. He was telling me he was doing time here in fifty-three, and a friend of his had a method of keeping people away from him. I'm using this method myself now. Seems you always find in jail the kinda people who just annoy you, persist in bothering you. But if they think you're crazy, they'll leave you alone. So the other day, I started this method, which worked so well for this other guy. I started barking. Now catch this. I'll be sitting at my bed, and I sort of get into it as theater. I'm ripping them off. This is really amusing to me. I'll start barking, "Wrff, wrrff," and I'll stop, and I won't do it anymore the whole day. And you know, I'll catch outta the corner of my eye, like this fella who's a potential problem look at me like I'm crazy. Now this guy will not have anything ever again to do with me. And every once in a while, I'll bark. I've been doing this for the last couple of days, and I've been having fun doing it.

CALIFORNIA STATE PRISON AT SAN QUENTIN
LOUIS S. NELSON, WARDEN

Homosexuality has many forms here just as it does in the street. We have some homosexuals that never create any problem by virtue of the fact that they carry themselves as ladies, and just the same as ladies on the street, they're very seldom disturbed by any masher, because of their ladylike bearing. That sounds kind of ridiculous, but it's true. These guys, nobody touches them. The ones who do cause a problem are the homosexual who just becomes a sloppy, lousy, stinking prostitute, because they feel the need to augment whatever income they have or lack of income by selling their body. A streetwalker, so to speak.

INDIANA STATE PRISON
HENRY WALTERS, INMATE

Now, um, a lotta guys don't agree with me, but I think that homosexuality causes seventy per cent of all your violent acts in here. Maybe higher. A lotta times the officials never find out that it's homosexual activity. All they know is guy got a knife in his back or he's all cut up or beat up, but they don't know what caused it. Ah, it's unheard of for inmates in here to just walk in the room, say, "Yeah, the guy was tryin to fuck me." You don't do that. You've got to follow the rules of convict society or you're an outcast. You can't afford to be an outcast in here. You see, it's very dangerous to have the reputation of tellin on people. If you are labeled as a snitch, your life is in danger all the time. That's why it's not a very good idea. But some guys are weak, and they go thataways for favor from the officials.

Now I thought the officials were havin a system where the man is rewarded for tellin on other inmates, not for his conduct, but for tellin on other inmates. Because what it does, it fosters a situation where a man may be livin with another inmate as man and wife, but to protect that relationship, every time he sees somethin happenin he goes and tells the captain. Now what the captain does is he tells all the boys, he says, "Look, take care of that boy. Any time he wanna see me, let him in." And when he gets in trouble, "Ah, hell, we'll overlook that." Now what are you doin? He doesn't know it, but he's been placed in a position where he's sort of a guardian over a homosexual relationship. He's keepin it goin by protectin the inmate that, you know, that's usually the man in the affair.

I was over in the dormitory other night. I said, "Okay, men, in your bunks," you know.

And some clown in the back say, "Ha! I don't know what he thinks he is. Ladies, I mean, ah, men, did you hear?"

CALIFORNIA STATE PRISON AT SAN QUENTIN
PRESTON S. SYMTHE, INMATE

People have to be close to other people, even if it's another man. It doesn't have to be a homosexual friend. Like you'll walk up and put your arm around a guy, it's contact, it's physical human contact. You'll say, "This guy, he's the only person I've got. He's warm, he's alive, he's a human bein. He's somebody I can stand next to," you know. Hell, you get out on the street, whish, it's done, because your interests are altogether different once you get out on the street. But here you're all in the same bag, and it happens. And this happens in war, happens in prison, happens in any place like that where—I spose it happens among a woman society, too, cause you've got to have that physical warmth with another individual. If you don't, you become so stagnated and dead-headed, I think that's why people jump off tiers. As long as you've got somethin to anchor to windward, let us say, to be able to reach out and touch another human bein, and know, well, God damn, this guy is in the same pot I'm in, so. And if you like him, so much the better. But you need this. You've got to have somethin, cause there's nothin—everything outside's alien. I don't care if it's a letter, a sweetheart, whatever. It's alien to you, and it really doesn't touch you. All you got is each other. And all this garbage they put down and around here about people from the outside comin in, do this, do that, an all these nice do-gooders and all these other things make you feel like a pawn on a chessboard. And you are.

CALIFORNIA INSTITUTION FOR MEN
COMRADE SIMBA, INMATE

I remember the first time I forgot what it was like to fuck a woman. That day, man, was a helluva day. I lay there all night tryin to remember. I couldn't remember how it was like. And that was a year and a half ago; and that's a helluva experience, man—to forget. I relate to that as bein one of the basic things that makes a man a man, makes him hold his head up—basic things like air and water keeps him survivin, makes him a whole man. These are basic things a man suppose to have. Conjugal thing, that's definite positive, but not jus for any special group of people. This is a basic human desire, basic human need. Also a need of man to make him productive, creative, to make him happy. You're denied this. And like I said, it was cold to forget. I forgot. I can think about it. The main thing I know is—like some cats in one of the pads come back, and you sit down and ask them, "How was it?" It gassed me jus when he told me, "It was hot."

"Hot!"

"Yeah, it is, man."

You can't even imagine it.

DEATH ROW, OHIO STATE PENITENTIARY, COLUMBUS, 1947.

# NIGHT.

CALIFORNIA STATE PRISON AT SAN QUENTIN
RAFAEL HERNANDEZ, INMATE

At ten-thirty everybody's locked up. They ring a buzzer, call lockup. You either go to bed or stay up, maybe read a book or somethin like that. At ten-thirty that's, ah, count time again. And in the West Block, the block I'm in, as soon as the count's cleared, if you wanna come out watch TV until twelve o'clock, you can do so. But there ain't many that do. I go to sleep.

Sometimes I can't sleep, I go up and make a cup of coffee. I got a stinger in my cell. Stinger is somethin you heat water with. And since I have a plug-in, I can boil some water. They're contraband, but they don't usually say anything. They hardly say anything unless they're shakin down. Then might take it. Friend of mine gave it to me. He could see that I needed a stinger, so he brought me one. He probly got it from one of these shakedowns they had. He works in the custody office, and they usually bring all that stuff, all that contraband, they'll bring it in there and jus throw it in the trash can. And since he works late at night and no one's there, he can jus go in and rip one off.

I think about the outside. I think about the outside. I think about my family, wonderin how they are, if they're okay. Or I jus

253.

think about tomorrow. But you know, I usually think about the streets, how everybody is, wonderin if I'm gonna get a letter tomorrow or wonderin if I'm gonna survive, actually. That's what I usually think about.

CALIFORNIA STATE PRISON AT SAN QUENTIN
HAROLD W. BROWN, SERGEANT, CORRECTIONAL FORCE

After ten-thirty at night, in the main-line housing unit, where men are working, where the workers are sleeping, we try to keep it as quiet as possible to give those who are sleeping the opportunity to sleep. In the segregation unit, where men are not workers, where they're there for disciplinary purposes, they tend to act out a different role. And this is by being very noisy, very loud, sometimes quite nasty.

CALIFORNIA STATE PRISON AT SAN QUENTIN
JOEY WILLIAMS, INMATE

The first thing you do at night in the hole, you call, "Say, man, you wanna play some chess," or, "Whadda you read, whadda you have to read? Did you read this book?"

"Oh, man, I read this book. It was a hell of a book."

You know, cut up that book, you know. And maybe some fool might come in there to work in there. Say like, "Oh, we got that dog on tonight. We can't holler too loud," or somethin like that. "That dog" or "that pig," somethin like that, that's all we ever get em back, you know, cause you can't say anything derogatory to them.

At nighttime, that's when you hear a lotta different guys. Like some guys catch guys that sing well, you know, have a good voice. They might entertain the guys in there by singin, you know. And another dude might holler, "Shut up. I can sing better'n you."

Then the next dude holler, "You sing it then."

They get together, sing one, and everybody might crack jokes on one another or talk about one another, you know, different little gags on one another, talkin about. And everybody bein a big man and hollerin and screamin all night, you know, so they can sleep durin the daytime.

MANHATTAN HOUSE OF DETENTION FOR MEN
PETER BENNETT, INMATE

The question that I have on my mind late at night is: how many more times am I gonna do this? Was I born to be a dope addict? Am I ever gonna do anything meaningful in my life? Would it

254.

be better for me to be a revolutionist or die a revolutionist or to be what I am now? I'll be thinkin about how I been, how my people have been in prisons, and be tryin to find somethin to set the blame on, the situation that I'm in. I think about what's goin on inside me, because if I thought about the street it would drive me crazy. I don't associate myself with the street too much. The only time I do is when I read my mail. I save my letters til real late at night.

Dope is a twenty-four-hour thing. If I'm not shootin somethin, I just got through shootin somethin. Or I'm gettin the money to go shoot somethin or I'm goin to shoot somethin. And the dope is so bad now, where it would take me two bags, now it takes me six, seven bags.

So I have to make a major decision now—either I'm gonna do this and die a drug addict—and when I say do it, I mean go all the way, man, no more petty crime—either die tryin to get big money so I can do it the rest of my life, or leave it alone.

You never think of the bad parts of drugs. That's why we always go back. We never think about the times we were in the street and we were sick. We only think about the times when we had a whole lotta coke or we had a lotta money. We never think about the time when we was sleepin in the basement cause we didn't have no place to stay or we stood up on the roof cause we didn't have no place to stay. We think about the time we was in the hotel with carpet on the floor.

INDIANA STATE PRISON
HENRY WALTERS, INMATE

Well, you know, I think most guys will bullshit you when they say they go right to sleep and don't think about anything. I probably go to sleep as quick as anybody in the dormitory, and yet and still, between eleven o'clock and the time I go to sleep, it's possible, you know, that my whole life flashes through my mind, you know. Sometimes you can get hung up on how did it happen, how did I get here? I think it's worse for the guys, those of us who feel somehow that they're not really guilty, as far as the law is concerned, under the law they're not guilty. I think it's much easier on the man who has pulled a stickup or killed somebody and feels that he is really guilty. It's probably a great deal easier. And if a man's honest—and most of the guys have really reconciled themselves to the fact that they can't get out of here— they know they're guilty and they can't blame anybody but themselves, they do easy time. It's the guy that always blames everybody else for his trouble that you got a problem with.

Many guys cry many nights—not tales, you know, but inside. Wanna get out there. An a guy can lay in jail an make so many promises to himself, but when he get out there after lyin in here, it's beautiful to be on outside, but it ain't jus like he wish it is. It's a struggle out there.

It's a guy come back here other day. Get ninety cents. He made it a year probation. He'd been comin back an forth, an this is the third time he been here, so they knowed him. He was shopliftin, somethin like that. An I say, "Man, you come back to pick up ninety cents?" I say, "Put that money in the machine an get cigarettes an give a couple packs of cigarettes, give em to me. I know you come back some profit. I know you did."

He says, "It's hard out there. I come after ninety cents, an I wants to stay out there." He said, "It's hard out there, really hard out there," you know.

I work in R an D. I see em comin in. I see the same guys, same guys comin in fifty times within three months' period. The same faces. The same faces. I figure like this: anybody that's been comin through here for the last ten years'n has been in the street'n keep comin back, they're sick. Alcoholic, dope fiends, or not, if they keep comin back in here, they're sick.

You got guys up there will take a book an they'll cut pin-up pictures outta them. An you got guys up there, they'll take a book or somethin like Esquire magazine an they cut pictures of beautiful shoes, cause that's all they got in their mind, you know, to get these here things, you know. They never had these things. They have other guys' tuck. An they have guys up there probly would lie about how much money they made, how much they stold, how many times they got away, how many girls they got. You got guys up there—complexes—scared a talk to girls or talk to women or never have women. You got all kinds a different complex up there. Jus like I say, you got a hundred guys in here, you got a hundred different personalities.

Any time a bunch of men get locked up, the men in general an especially the life of underworld, mos the things they talk about is women, money, gettin drunk or gettin high, an good livin. The dreamers. You know what I mean. It's really dreamin. Everybody's a dreamer, you know. They live in a dream. They not facin reality. That's why I say ninety per cent of em is sick, because most of em is dreamin.

DISTRICT OF COLUMBIA CORRECTIONAL COMPLEX
CLYDE E. SETTLE, SERGEANT, CORRECTIONAL FORCE

A man in jail can be anything that his mouth lets him. There's not hardly a guy in here that drove a Ford or a Chevy in the street. Everybody in here drives a Cadillac. But you don't drive it behind Thirteen-Dormitory and drive it over to the kitchen in the mornin, you know. Everybody wears Petrocellas here, you know, but my uniform's blue denims. So you can be almost anything that your mouth will letcha be. You don't have to produce nothin except rap—conversation.

Some guy'll get busted for snatchin a pocketbook, and by the time he gets here, you know what he is? A bank robber. We only got four types of criminals here—that's bank robber, narcotics importers, pimps, and the springin'n—the Murphy men. That's it. The guy that robbed the Safeway, snatched a pocketbook or somethin, I don't know where they sent him. Sent him someplace else. Cause you talk with any guy here and he's bound to be a bank robber, you know, cause this is the thing to be. This shows you've got class.

DISTRICT OF COLUMBIA WOMEN'S DETENTION CENTER
JANE MASON, INMATE

At night, sometimes I think about my children, think about my charge, you know, my case, what's gonna happen in court, what am I gonna do with my furniture, what my children are doin, you know. Because I know they're not—the children are not used to bein away from me, you know, except like when I come to jail. Like when I did six years, I didn't have em, you know. And they're not really used to me bein away from em. And before when I was here, they came to see me every visitin day. They knew I was here. I don't have any secrets from em. My children know I used drugs, you know. Don't have no secrets.

They don't come now because they're in Junior Village—a place for children when their parents can't take care of em no more, you know. My husband, he's in Lorton. He got a second-degree murder charge. He got from seven to twenty-one years on it.

BUCKS COUNTY PRISON
RAYMOND WARD BURNS, INMATE

The loneliness. Loneliness, it's a drag. You could be in a crowd, still you're lonely. And this is nothing but a crowd—overcrowded conditions, you know. You're not with who you want to be with, and then you don't know who you want to be with. You know you

257.

don't wanna be with this crowd. You wanna be somewhere else. You wanna be out there, where there's a little bit of freedom—not that much now. There's not that much freedom out there, but I'd like to be out in it, you know. That's what I think about.

BEDFORD HILLS CORRECTIONAL FACILITY
BERTHA WATERS, INMATE

Sometimes you're afraid. Jail strips you of everything. You really don't even have your mind anymore. They strip you of that. Things that you would of done in the street, you're afraid to do here. Like a different person. You're not what you used to be. I forget how to spell my name sometimes. And it's not an alias, it's my real name. Sometime I'll be writin it, and I have to stop and then go on. I forgot how old I was. It dawned on me one night when I was layin in the bed—I thought I was goin to be twenty-eight and I counted the years back and instead it's twenty-nine. And that was a big shock, cause it's like I've lost a year. There's really nothin to help you to remember. This is like a different world. The people out there don't really care. If they cared, I don't think it would be as cold as it is in here. Not only do you feel the prison officials bein cold, but one inmate to another is cold.

CALIFORNIA STATE PRISON AT FOLSOM
GARCIA PEREZ, INMATE

On the outside I had a cleanin agency. I didn't do the actual work, but, ah, it was like a franchise, this Avon Cleaners and Dyers. I'd take the work in and the plant'll pick it up, truck driver, and then it's delivered. I had a pretty nice thing there. Lost everything.

You can make plans in here, but only up to a point. And that's when—for any reason, wife feels that—well, we do have one thing in common—the welfare of the kids, period, you know. I can understand her position. And I still like her, love her for that matter, but you have to be realistic, too. If she's able to maintain the home and keep up with the responsibility, fine. Whatever. But no matter what happens, she'll let me know the kids are okay. She's probably on welfare right now. Jobs are pretty tight right now.

I blew everything on this. I lost the business, which wasn't very big, just a job, actually that's all it was, but I still could have gotten a few dollars out of it—what I had invested into it. Had it for about twenty months. See, I was released from the federal joint in sixty-eight, and, ah, got into this agency about a month after I was released, and everything was goin good until, ah—just one of those things—one thing on top of the other. I mean, that was it.

INMATE WORKING PUZZLE, ELMIRA CORRECTIONAL FACILITY, NEW YORK, 1954.

It's on the record. They brought in an informer into the shop, and he worked on me for three days. This is straight. Now I'm guilty. I blew it. This is why I copped. I copped guilty. They wanted me to plead guilty. They made me a deal. Copped to possession.

"But if your wife will, too."

I said, "No." I'm not a hero, but you know, still this is my old lady.

They gave me the deal to plead guilty to possession, and she would plead guilty to possession for bein with me when they came to arrest me. And if I didn't plead guilty to that, and she didn't plead guilty, then I'd have to plead guilty to one count of dealin.

The so-called informer came in to me with his kid brother, who was a rookie out at police academy. He—well, he didn't twist my arm or anything, but he worked on me pretty nice, and I knew the guy from twenty years ago. He had a couple hundred dollars. He wanted couple a cubes, two cubes I had. And that's just what I did for him. My mistake was I went for the hokey-dokey. I hadda plead guilty. Period. Ordinarily it woulda been a five to life with a three-year minimum.

I'm tellin my friend here, "Hey, this is entrapment." Doesn't make any difference. Entrapment—they just laugh at that. And you know human nature's weak enough without adding temptation and generatin government crime like this. It just caught me off balance. But like I say, once you have a checkerboard past, you have no excuses. You can't successfully defend yourself in LA. And heaven help you if you're a chicano.

I dream sometimes. Oh, depends, I guess, on the mood, depends on associations and, ah, thoughts. Certain smells can trigger you off, you know. You start goin back to maybe a walk in the park maybe twenty years ago, certain smells. Certain maybe song on a radio, maybe say certain words from it, certain piano passage. These things will trigger you off.

The real wild dream, that's the one when you're awake. You wonder if you're gonna survive the sentence. You try to condition yourself to that. I don't know whether this is normal or abnormal. There's only so many years in a lifespan.

Then the sense of futility, emptiness, loneliness. These are things that people feel outside. They're amplified in here. People forget about you. Then they forget about you when you're outside, too. It's just that it's exaggerated in here. And then you compare the loneliness. Could be the loneliness is part of the punishment. Maybe this is what you're here for.

You find yourself here, you're directed daily, doin things. Maybe the people that are directin you need help, too, in certain things. I don't think they're vicious or anything like that. Cept it's just, they live in a certain way. Maybe they're treatin people the best way they can, although that might not be adequate maybe. They're part of the thing themselves. What are you gonna do? It's just a job, a lunch-bucket job, and you happen to be the merchandise. That's it.

The thing is, they're doin the best with what they've got, which isn't too much. It reminds me of, ah, some writin in an officers' washroom in Vietnam, where the same thing might apply, the thought content of what was written on the wall, that "This is a war of the unwillin led by the unqualified." In here, they're doin the best thing they can with what they've got, but basically it's a job. Why should they get involved, personally involved? Why? What for? They've got their family on their mind. Some lunch-basket thing. When the whistle blows, that's it. They go home, forget about this horrible place. What's in here? There's a lotta guys in here that project certain type of image that, ah, it's not a pretty picture.

CALIFORNIA STATE PRISON AT SAN QUENTIN
HAROLD W. BROWN, SERGEANT, CORRECTIONAL FORCE

Midnight, whatever keys I have checked out have to be checked back in, and I am free to leave. I usually go home. Sometimes I take home my wife a sandwich, cause she's in bed sleeping. I'll wake her up, give her a sandwich. It's a little thing we got going between us. Ah, this is the time of day I can have my glass of beer, my shot of booze if I'm gonna have it. And sometimes you really feel like you really want it, just to come back down to some kind of normal feeling again. This is the time of day that I get to check my mail over a little bit, check the kids and make sure they're all right, and all this. Sometimes wake them or don't get to talk to the kids. See them when they're asleep. And I have a bad habit of crawling in bed and putting on one of these talk programs so I can hear opinions and points of view throughout the Bay area here. And then, of course, going to and from work, I listen to a news-type CBS program, so I can pick up on what's going on around me. You can't become stagnant. You gotta keep up with what's going on.

Actually, like I tell everybody, "The job doesn't affect me at all in my home life. When I go home I line my kids up for head count and shake down their toy box." As much as I would like to not believe it, yes, I take my job home to a degree, various degrees—in looking at myself and trying to evaluate my actions and reactions of myself and my fellow officers. I think sometimes we tend to become a little bit more rigid and use a bit more discipline with our children. Maybe it's the subconscious fear of having them locked up someday that causes this. Sometimes you become a little bit more exacting. Sometimes I think that maybe I take a little chip home on my shoulder, which I try not to carry here, and my wife becomes an escape-goat. This I would assume happens.

ARKANSAS STATE PENITENTIARY
WAYNE E. MIFLIN, INMATE

I dream about all kinds a things. Mostly jus somethin round home. I dream every once in a while bout my wife. I dreamed I got executed here. Somethin I musta been readin bout the lectric chair. I dreamed they had us all—I was in a line of guys, they had us all stripped off. They would lead us out one at a time, execute us. There was a whole bunch of us. It was a real terrifyin dream. I dreamed once that there was another inmate, he and I were on parole. We got violated for some reason, we came back.

I dream all the time. Mostly home. I dream about home all the time, every night. I guess that's the best part, when you be dreamin that you're at home. Worst be when you wake up, find out you not. So that be another headache.

ARKANSAS STATE PENITENTIARY
JAMES JESSE JONES, INMATE

I remember one specific dream, but it might sound kinda ridiculous. It's about an entertainer that came into one of our groups. She was an entertainer. I had never met her, and we started rappin. And that night I dreamt that I had received a letter from her and her letter, it said that she may be comin down to visit me. So I woke up, and all durin the day it kept goin through my mind, you know. Afterwards, I never did pay attention to it. Bout three, four days later I received a letter from her tellin me she was comin down again to visit me. Jus one of those things, you might say, coincidence. It does happen.

CALIFORNIA STATE PRISON AT SAN QUENTIN
HAROLD W. BROWN, SERGEANT, CORRECTIONAL FORCE

I've had all kinds of bad experiences in dreams. Very few happy things in any dream that I've had of this place. I've had a lotta working dreams, where I've woke up and seem more tired than when I went to bed. But I think this is normal for any type of job. If I was working at a factory assembling TV sets, I'd probably dream about the wires.

One particular dream—it's kind of a silly dream, I spose, but it was one of those outstanding type that stays in your mind, you know. Dreamt one night that inmate come at me with a knife, and he swung it, and he caught me across the arm. I remember very distinctly that burning sensation of the blade going through the flesh. And I grabbed him in my dream. And I was holding him in a bear-hug-type deal, and for some reason I was able to hold him. And one of my fellow officers, which I'll call **BD**—that's his initials, I always refer to him as **BD**—was off to the side maybe fifty, sixty feet, and he had a gun. I was holding this guy, I called over to him, "For Chrissakes, **BD**, do something."

Well, for some reason he had a twenty-two rifle, which we don't have here, you know, and he raised the rifle, and he shot it, and he shot the inmate through the head, all the blood and gorey part being very real. At that moment I woke up.

Next day I come to work and I seen this officer, and I told **BD**, I says, "Thanks a million." And of course it threw the cools at him, you know. And later I told him what that was all about, and it was quite a joke then, you know, one of those hilarious things. But I don't know if this is inert fears, if this is triggered by what or who. I don't know. I'm not a psychologist. I don't know.

ARKANSAS STATE PENITENTIARY
SAMUEL LEXINGTON, INMATE GUARD

Oh, yeah, I've had some gruesome dreams since I been here. I've had guys tell me I was talkin in my sleep, nightmares and things. Seemed like I dream up this stuff that happened years ago that got me in here—shootin at the law. Jus come back to me and I dreamed it, only it don't work like they was doin it to me, only I was doin it to them. Like the good guys and the bad guys, see, only I had the upper hand over em, see. I don't know how you get a dream like that. One time I dreamed I was out in the freeworld, and I had this fine chick, having a party, livin the right life of Raleigh. Wake up here in the penitentiary.

CALIFORNIA INSTITUTION FOR MEN
MICHAEL COONEY, CHAPLAIN

Dreamed about my mother last night, for what reason—she's dead for many, many years.

263.

### BEDFORD HILLS CORRECTIONAL FACILITY
### MICHELE RIVERA, INMATE

I'm nasty, man. Everything is sex. That's all I be thinkin about at night. I had a dream the other night, a nightmare, that this ugly officer wanted to kiss me. She was ugly. She kept tryin to kiss me. I kept sayin, "Get away from me, get away from me." And I woke up, and I was glad I was dreamin. Ugly. She looked like a vampire.

### FEDERAL DETENTION HEADQUARTERS
### GABRIEL POTTER, INMATE

I guess the oddest one I've had—they have an engineer that works here, he's a young guy, he's twenty-four years old. I dreamt that he and a guy that I work with and myself robbed a bank, and we got caught leaving with the money, and we ended up leaving him holding the bag, cause he worked for the bureau of prisons. We made him escape, though, and we told the police that he was the one robbed the bank. So they took him away, and we took off with the money, left him going to prison.

And just like anything, if you stay away from sex long enough, you're gonna have wet dreams and dream about sex a lot, unless you masturbate. You have dreams about sex, and you can't help that. I guess every guy does in prison.

### CALIFORNIA STATE PRISON AT SAN QUENTIN
### RAFAEL HERNANDEZ, INMATE

One dream I was dreamin that I was in bed, and everything was in slow motion, it seemed, and my cell door—I seen somebody comin in through my cell door with a knife in his hand, and stickin me. He stick me about three times in my left shoulder. The only bad part about it was in slow motion, you know. He looked more ugly that way.

Sometimes somebody'll have their radio up too loud or somethin, but I'm usually a heavy sleeper. Or somebody out in some other cell'll sound like he's having a convulsion there, the way he's coughin. These are usually the old men, you know. Those are about the only things that wake me up. Or sometimes Man'll come by countin, one o'clock or four o'clock, and if he can't see you—you have to be showin a part of your body, you know, part of yourself—and if he can't see it, he'll stand there and keep shinin the light until you wake up. Nothin hardly ever wakes me up.

CALIFORNIA STATE PRISON AT SAN QUENTIN
HAROLD W. BROWN, SERGEANT, CORRECTIONAL FORCE

Making a count in the middle of the night, walking down a tier past the rows of cells with the people sleeping in them, the body odor or breaking of wind or what have you, the smells that you come up against—these things are disagreeable on a job. And these things are never talked about here—the type of people you come in contact with, the bad breath, all these things added together—the nasty, disagreeable aspects that you just really don't like, but you have to work at.

BUCKS COUNTY PRISON (EASTERN)
RAYMOND WARD BURNS, INMATE

I know one man that woke up one night about three o'clock in the morning, and a rat, large rat—was about almost two feet long, that's pretty big, one of the biggest ones I've seen—had chewed his toe off. And he was screaming, you can imagine. Chewed it off. He tried to shake it off and everything while he was screaming. It just kept chewing, kept gnawing on his toe until all the flesh was off his big toe. Another one woke up and his nose was half chewed fore he could get the rat off his face. That was in Eastern now. Now this don't happen all over. But rats will attack you, and some of the biggest ones I've seen were down in Eastern. I've seen them down there bigger'n cats.

CALIFORNIA INSTITUTION FOR MEN
COMRADE SIMBA, INMATE

I try to have what I call a people's dream. It's a beautiful thing to have a people's dream. I experience that a couple of times. It's not no mystical thing. It's jus a dream like thoughts. Like I use self-criticism in terms of dreams. I analyze them. Mos dreams people dream about themselves—they're experiencin somethin and they're gonna be affected by somethin. And I recognize that they be not a people's dream but a ego dream. But I have a few people's dreams where I was in the dream and I'm lookin at people, I'm checkin them out, I'm seein their changes and things.

People's dream would be—yes, I could think it's political, right. People's dream is social reality, you know, the reality of people livin—everybody has a different personality—learnin to understan those personalities and accept those personalities and accept em as bein people, recognizin the positive in their personalities and also the negative and helpin em to do somethin to the betterment of the positive.

A people's dream that I had recently was in the black community. I was in somebody's pad, some people's house, talkin to em. And the dream is that there's a hundred people in this family, like some regular family style of livin that some people don't have a father or some people don't have a mother, but the community, the people, is so close that it's like one big ole family. Everybody has a father and everybody has many fathers—the cat next door or down the street. And there's a certain kinda feelin, love in this environment, among these people. And this is where I was in. This is a people's dream. It's a common experience in the black community, you know. It's a reality where you have people, families, callin cousins or uncle or somethin. If a cat doesn't have em, a neighbor picks him up and relates to em, and he has a father and he has a mother—many mothers, many fathers, many kids. Parents have many kids. They have involvement with many kids. Then you have all these personalities—you have the kid that's on dope, you have the kid that's father drinks. But you understand it. You love em all. You can really survive in that condition because of that large family. That was the people's dream.

DISTRICT OF COLUMBIA CORRECTIONAL COMPLEX
JOSEPH SAKALAUKAS, SERGEANT, CORRECTIONAL FORCE

Overall, I think you got a bunch of happy inmates here—as happy as you can be in confinement somewhere. I mean, you couldn't find a better place than this, I think. Cause if I ever go to jail, I'm gonna ask to come here, if I'm gonna go into a jail.

266.

NASSAU COUNTY JAIL, LONG ISLAND, 1969.

This book has been set on the linotype in Antique #3. The display type is hand set wood type. The composition is by American Book–Stratford Press, New York. The printing and binding is by Halliday Lithograph Corporation, Plympton, Massachusetts.